DUST ON THE SEA

It is 1943, and Captain Mike Blackwood, Royal Marine Commando, is a survivor. Young, toughened, and tried in the hellish crucible of Burma, he labours, sometimes faltering, beneath the weight of tradition, the glorious heritage of his family, and the burden of his own self-doubt. For him, the horizon is not the lip of the trench seen by men of the Corps in the previous war, but the ramp of a landing craft smashing down into the sea, and the fire of the enemy on a Sicilian beach. Here, tradition is not enough, and Mike Blackwood must find within himself qualities of leadership which will inspire those Royal Marines who are once again the first to land, and among the first to die.

DUST ON THE SEA

Douglas Reeman

CHIVERS PRESS
BATH

First published 1999
by
William Heinemann
This Large Print edition published by
Chivers Press
by arrangement with
Random House UK Ltd
2000

ISBN 0 7540 1369 3

British Library Cataloguing in Publication Data available

Printed and bound in Great Britain by
REDWOOD BOOKS, Trowbridge, Wiltshire

For you, Kim, with my love.

'Done with the Compass—
Done with the Chart,
Your Orchid-boat contains my heart . . .'

Tradition by itself is not enough.

T.S. ELIOT

PROLOGUE

The assault landing craft, the L.C.A., was probably the ugliest and most uncomfortable vessel ever designed by man. Short, stubby and box-shaped, with a ramp for landing troops as a substitute for bows, the landing craft could be almost impossible to manage in anything but ideal conditions.

The wooden hulls were thinly protected by armour plating, a defence against shell splinters and automatic fire, and even that additional weight was a severe handicap in shallow water and at the moment of beaching. But, if properly employed, they were the best means of putting men ashore, men who despite all the discomforts and danger might be expected to fight immediately after jumping on to dry land.

Hard training, comradeship and pride, to say nothing of a sense of humour, made the small landing craft accepted as a weapon of war. Until the day when it was, for the first time, real and in deadly earnest. *Now.*

He was crouched down in the hull, one hand supporting himself while the deck swayed and shuddered below and around him. Behind him his men were still hidden in darkness, in groups of three, gripping their weapons, their helmets tilted against the spray which spattered over the sides like hail. The outer files of men took what advantage they could from the narrow steel side decks, while the ones in the centre suffered in silence, soaked by the spray and sickened by the stench of fuel and the hoarse rumble of engines.

Time had become meaningless, and even though his trained mind insisted that it was barely an hour since they had been cast off from their parent ship, it felt like an eternity. He had groped his way aft to speak with one of the L.C.A.'s crew, but he could not even remember how long ago that had been. On his way back to the forepart of the plunging, creaking hull he had gripped someone's damp shoulder to steady himself, or waited while the craft had yawed into a trough before continuing on his journey. Men with their weapons and equipment. Weighed down by it. Barely looking up as he had passed through them. The same men he had come to know, or thought he had. Now they were isolated even from one another. Men who had broken a last cigarette to share it with a special friend, who had always found time to explain the reasons for a stoppage in a Bren machine gun, or the secret of priming a live grenade, had, it seemed, become strangers.

He wanted to peer at his watch, but knew that somebody might see it as uncertainty, or anxiety, on his part. He tried to recall each face, but like the darkness they resisted him. He was their officer; that was all he could consider. Like him or hate him, trust him or doubt his ability, it was too late. Perhaps it was always like this.

A figure brushed past him, a sailor, strangely out of place amongst the weapons and steel helmets, his bare feet very white and delicate against the side of the tiny wheelhouse where the coxswain was fighting his own battle with sea and rudder.

Then it was nearly time. The movement was sharper, small, steep waves, so they must be close to the beach. To their objective.

2

He thought of the men behind him, a mingling of old sweats and the usual hard cases. But mostly they were youngsters who had not yet been blooded, or tasted the madness of battle. All that hard-won experience at the basic training centres, and the special combat courses where only the elite survived, and where they had learned to hate their instructors more than the enemy, and it could all end here. Today.

A muffled voice said, 'Final run, sir!' That was the coxswain, peering through the slit in his plated hutch, not unlike an armoured knight at Agincourt.

Something rattled against the hull, and he heard a man give a quick gasp of alarm.

A stone thrown up from the beach, a piece of flotsam? But they had learned about booby traps and underwater snares for the unwary . . .

He turned his face towards the ramp, and thought he saw water glistening on the dull metal for the first time. But the sky seemed as dark as ever. Would there really be sunshine again within hours? Would he live to see it?

A burly shape pushed down beside him; he knew who it was, just by the touch of him. A presence which somehow reassured him.

'Running in now, Sergeant.' He turned, but saw only the helmet. 'Everything all right back there?'

'They'll do, sir.' No heroics, no bluster. The true professional. 'The other L.C.A.s are on station.' The flash of a grin. 'I just had a dekko!'

Then he was gone. Maybe he had come to see for himself, to decide if his officer was up to it.

He tried to clear his mind of everything but the objective, and what might be waiting ahead. Maps, conferences and a few useless aerial pictures had been the only preparation; there had even been some private snapshots taken before the war, with a woman in one of them. He could recall her face, her smile. Where was she now, he wondered. What would she say if she knew her photograph had been passed around, and that a vital objective had been directly behind her?

He tightened his jaw and felt it click. He needed to yawn, but he knew he must not. Somehow the knowledge steadied him; it was something he recognised. *It was fear.*

'Stand by, sir!' The voice seemed loud, dangerously so. The engine vibrations were noisier too, the air clammy. He could feel his clothes sticking to his skin. *Fear.*

He sensed his men stirring now, and heard the mutter of a machine gun. It was never like the films, where you always knew when the gun was pointing directly at your favourite actor. This was real, distant and impersonal. He bunched his free hand into a fist to stop its trembling. It was like the sound of a woodpecker on one of those perfect, impossible days of peace, which they had taken so much for granted.

He heard the rattle of machinery and saw more seamen by the ramp. He felt his revolver in his wet fist, although he did not remember having drawn it from his holster.

He waited, counting seconds as the ramp began to come down like a drawbridge. How long would it last? But all he could hear was the bored voice of some instructor, as if from another world.

Never take a pistol out of the holster, sir, except to load or unload it. Or to use it.

'Now!'

The ramp was down, not exactly straight, and through the gloom he saw the sea boiling over it, while the engines thrust ahead to hold the craft in position.

He was on his feet. He did not look back at his men. He dared not.

Another voice, as though right here beside him. *They're looking to you. Don't let them down.*

He strode to the ramp; he could have been completely alone. But his voice was as steady as the one he had just heard.

'Royal Marines, advance!'

CHAPTER ONE

COMMANDO

Major-General Ralph Vaughan was a big man, in every sense of the word. He had served in the Royal Marines all his life and had a reputation for plain speaking, and a hot temper which had made him almost a legend in the Corps. Even on this bitter November day, with his impressive figure perched somewhat incongruously on a frail-looking shooting stick, his feet planted wide apart in the wet gorse and heather, he looked the part. 'A marine's marine', they said, something which never failed to please him. In his younger days he had been well known in the boxing ring, and had represented the Corps in many inter-service contests. A broken nose and a luminously ruddy complexion had won him great respect, and although he was generally admired by all ranks in the Corps, nobody with any sense ever took his famous intolerance over training and efficiency lightly.

Scotland in November. What a bloody awful place, he thought grimly. Only the high command would ever dream up such a location. Achnacarry, barely marked on any map and dominated by two big lochs, Arkaig and Lochy, was rugged terrain where marines could learn the skills and pitfalls of hard training under all conditions, harried by seemingly tireless instructors, and very aware of the additional danger of live ammunition.

A bloody awful place. But it worked. These were

no longer the old days of the peacetime Royal Navy, when the marines were called upon mainly for ceremonial and drill, with an occasional landing party to save the face of some unpopular British consul or to protect lives and property. These men had become professionals, and many of them had never served afloat except to be carried from one theatre of war to another. He frowned. And to cover retreats and setbacks on almost every front.

The year 1942 was drawing to a close, and perhaps for the first time in those three years of war there was a glimmer of hope that the balance might tip in favour of Britain and her allies. But a glimmer was all that it was, in the general's mind.

As a deputy chief of Special Operations, Vaughan made a point of dropping in on various units with little warning, or, like today, with none at all.

He turned his head to listen to some shots, muffled by mist and the occasional drizzle which had made his shoulders almost sodden. He wore no protective trench coat over his battledress, the left breast of which appeared to consist of a full rectangle of ribbons.

He considered the two matters which had brought him here by special flight from London. He was a blunt man, but not without emotion. It was a case of weighing priorities, even the smallest aspects of the overall pattern.

He heard his aide give a polite cough. 'The first section is coming in, sir.'

Vaughan replied, 'Taking their bloody time about it!'

The aide, a tired-eyed major of marines, sighed. It was not always easy to serve Major-General

Vaughan, D.S.O. and Bar, Croix de Guerre and all the rest. Equally, he knew he could serve no other. Life with Vaughan was usually hectic, but never dull.

Two of the instructors were climbing up the wet, sloping ground. Both stared with amazement at the senior officer perched on his shooting stick.

They saluted in unison, and one exclaimed, 'I should have been told, sir! I had no idea . . .'

Vaughan said, 'The first section is returning, right?'

The senior of the two, a lieutenant-colonel, nodded. 'Do you wish to inspect them, sir?'

Vaughan felt the drizzle on his collar, and touched the silver flask in his pocket. He shook his head.

'No. I want to see Captain Blackwood.'

The officer frowned. 'Lieutenant Blackwood, sir?'

Vaughan relaxed slightly. *'Captain.'*

The lieutenant-colonel sent the instructor away with a message, and waited uncertainly while Vaughan stood up and folded his stick before handing it to his aide.

'You will, of course, receive all the necessary bumf about it, but Captain Blackwood is required for Special Service. If he agrees, I shall try to hasten things along.'

The lieutenant-colonel's face cleared. 'He is an experienced officer, for one so young, sir.'

Vaughan listened to the tramp of feet on wet ground. Tired men. It was a sound which never failed to move him in some way, despite the passing of years. The Somme, Passchendaele, a million men marching into oblivion.

9

'It's a young man's war. We'd do well not to forget that!'

He turned to watch as a single file of khaki figures came into view. Too much pride could be dangerous, as Vaughan knew from bitter experience, but he could not contain it at times like these. Not marines who had joined up as boys and young men because of some ideal, or because there had been no other employment available, but another generation, errand boys and bus conductors and clerks, and those straight out of school. Because they wanted to do it; because they were so desperately needed, and took little heed of what lay ahead.

He recognised the young Blackwood immediately, although they had not met for years. He was very like his father.

Vaughan knew that all the men here today had been on their feet since five in the morning; he had made it his business to know; but the young officer in the mud-streaked battledress and camouflaged helmet, tilted to keep his eyes in shadow, was not even breathless. He was carrying a Sten gun loosely in one hand, a little too casually, some might think, but Vaughan's trained eye saw it very differently. This was a man who had seen action, a man who had been tested. A survivor.

Michael Blackwood was not quite twenty-five years old. Men younger than he were daily fighting in the skies over Britain, or flying long and perilous missions to Germany night after night. They were on the seas, too, and in the Western Desert, and that youth was mirrored here in this young officer. His was an intelligent face, and one which would interest any woman. And when he threw up his

10

hand in salute and his helmet tilted slightly, Vaughan saw the eyes. Green, as his mother's had been. What would she have said about her son following the Blackwood tradition? The Corps . . .

Vaughan held out his hand, and said abruptly, 'Sorry to drop in on you like this. But it's important.'

The file of marines, and a second party coming up the slope, the lieutenant-colonel and his instructors, could all have been invisible.

'I have to tell you that your father, Colonel Blackwood, died yesterday. He was my friend, the finest man I ever met. I thought I owed him this, at least.'

Blackwood asked quietly, 'How did it happen, sir?'

'Plymouth. An air raid. He was there when a stick of bombs fell. He was trying to help some people.' Vaughan shrugged. 'He was killed.' He touched his arm. 'Walk with me.'

They climbed the slope, their boots creaking in the wet heather.

Vaughan said, 'As you know, I served under him in Flanders. I was there when he was wounded.' He paused. *'Again.'*

They turned as if to some unspoken signal and faced one another.

Vaughan said, 'You would have been told today anyway. I needed to see you first. There's an appointment with Royal Marine Commando, Special Brigade. Others could do it, but I want you. For all kinds of reasons.'

Blackwood tried to accept it. It happened in war; it was happening all the time. Only yesterday he had sent a corporal home to Liverpool, where his

11

entire family had died in an air raid. His father had given everything to the Corps, even his health; he had never fully recovered from his wounds. He had been retired prematurely, but when war had erupted once more across Europe he had been determined to serve again. Any bitterness at having been rejected by the life he had loved had remained hidden; he had never offered anything but support and encouragement to his son. And now, characteristically helping others, he was gone.

Vaughan said, 'I can fix two weeks' leave for you. That's all. Arrange things ... I'm not doing this very well, am I?'

Blackwood looked across at the men with whom he had been working, recalling something he had once heard his father say. *It's what we are. What we do.*

'I think I knew, sir.' He faced him. 'We were always very close, even more so after my mother died.' He smiled, and afterwards Vaughan thought he had looked exactly like Jonathan Blackwood in those distant, terrible days.

Another appointment, then. Some dangerous mission at the end of it, like all those others. Men following the tradition, and the family name. It was a lot to carry.

'I hope I can live up to your faith, sir.' Vaughan had to turn away. He was not often moved, but Michael Blackwood had just unwittingly repeated that other young Blackwood's words, before the last great sacrifice on the Somme.

He said gruffly, 'My aide'll hack through the red tape. You can fly south with me. I can give you a couple of hours.'

Blackwood stared through the drizzle. The

marines were relaxing now, trying to light their cigarettes.

'I shall be ready, sir.'

So easily said. He saluted as the major-general strode away, followed by the lieutenant-colonel and his staff.

He peered at his watch, and saw the rain on his wrist. The skin was still tanned despite the months since he had returned from the smoke and flames of Rangoon, and the Japanese domination of Malaya and Burma.

He pushed the memories away and walked down to meet his sergeant.

What we are. What we do. It sounded like the perfect epitaph.

The sergeant's name was Tom Paget, and he had been with Blackwood when they had fired the oil storage tanks south of Rangoon to prevent their capture by the advancing Japanese. He had proved his worth time and time again, and should have got a medal for what he had done; perhaps they all should. He had been made up to sergeant, and looking at him now in the drizzle and biting air, it was hard to imagine him ever being anything else.

Blackwood said, 'You can fall them out now. I'll be leaving you in charge until a replacement arrives.' Then, 'They did well today.'

Paget watched him impassively. 'I hear you've been promoted, sir. Good show! I've told the lads.'

There was no point in asking how he knew. This was the Corps, the family. There was rarely such a thing as a secret for long.

'I have to go south. My father has just died. An air raid.' Short, dry sentences. It was as though his mind was still rejecting it. His father. Always

13

interested when he went on leave, even though he must have ached to be back in the service himself. He thought suddenly of the bluff, outspoken major-general. Vaughan had been a frequent visitor to the rambling house at Hawks Hill. Blackwood had been in awe of him at first, but had come to view the friendship between him and Jonathan Blackwood as something very special, something which, in a way, he was part of. And then the visits had grown less frequent, and he thought he could understand why. Vaughan had served under Jonathan Blackwood and was perhaps embarrassed, even ashamed, that on every return he seemed to have gained some better appointment, or yet another promotion.

Paget was saying, 'I'm very sorry, sir. I never knew him, of course, but they always spoke so well of him.' He hesitated, the old training acting like a warning. 'Afterwards, sir . . .'

Afterwards. It said it all. 'I shall be taking a new posting. I think the Royal Marine Commandos are making a big impression higher up!'

The sergeant fell into step beside him. 'I'd like to come along, if you need a good N.C.O., sir.' He smiled, for the first time. 'My old dad always said that an officer was only as good as his sergeant!'

They laughed, Blackwood rather surprised that he could.

All those years he had felt somehow guided, and secure. Perhaps that was why he had avoided the more usual seagoing appointments that fell to the Royals. In Burma he had stood alone, and had relied on his own skills and resources to survive, and to lead.

Afterwards. It would be a difficult two weeks, he

14

thought.

They shook hands, and Blackwood said, 'You'll be the first to know.' Then they saluted, formally. It was what made them different. At sea or in the desert, or even here, in the bleak Scottish Highlands, they were Royal Marines.

*   *   *

Michael Blackwood walked across the high-ceilinged room and gazed out of the window. The house was huge, too large by modem standards, but it was the only home he had ever known. The rain had stopped, and he saw the familiar line of trees, leafless now, and beckoning to the high copse like black spectres.

Hawks Hill had been originally a fortified Tudor farmhouse, complete with moat, which had been altered and enlarged over the years since it was bought by Major-General Samuel Blackwood. He was always described in the old diaries as 'the last soldier'. After him, for no reason that Blackwood had ever discovered, all had entered the Corps.

It was a house full of memories, fine paintings depicting battles ranging from The Saintes to Trafalgar, from the Crimea to Jutland. There were none portraying the Royal Marines at Gallipoli and Flanders. Like so many things in this house, he thought, too many painful reminders.

He could see the old moat in the distance, or what remained of it. Hawks Hill had been used as a hospital for officers in the Great War, and his mother, the daughter of a local doctor, had worked here, teaching young men who had been blinded to read with their fingers, and not to reject the world

15

they had once believed in.

The moat had all but collapsed, but it was still a haven for geese and ducks, gulls, too, at this time of year. Hawks Hill estate was only twenty miles north of Portsmouth, and some seven miles from Winchester. The local village was Alresford; he had glimpsed it when he had arrived, and had been surprised to see so many uniforms in the narrow lanes where he had played as a child.

He touched the long blackout curtains beside the window. Cold and dusty, they seemed so alien in this peaceful countryside. But even here they could see the fires in the sky when Portsmouth was attacked night after night, and there was an anti-aircraft battery in one of the fields.

Such a big house; it even sounded empty when he moved across to another window. Between the wars life had been difficult on the estate, so it seemed strange that things were picking up again.

With severe rationing of almost everything, even the country's smallest cabbage patches were playing their part. His father's enthusiasm for the estate, short of young men though it was, had made a real difference. The thought touched him like the tip of a bayonet. The funeral was tomorrow, in Alresford. After that it would be up to the lawyers, although there had already been some mention of the Ministry of Food, which was keen to expand the growth of local farms and smallholdings, backed up, apparently, by extra labour from Italian prisoners of war. It was almost unnerving to accept that he might be sent to kill Italians, while their relatives were working here at Hawks Hill.

He heard steps outside the room and turned as the girl entered, and stood looking at him in

16

silence. Perhaps she, too, needed to remember.

Diane Blackwood was twenty-one years old, with dark chestnut hair and eyes almost the same as his. Even a total stranger would know them to be brother and sister.

She wore a pair of jodhpurs and a thick sheepskin jacket. Despite the mud on her boots and her windblown hair she looked, as usual, in control. And beautiful. As their mother had looked, as she must have been when she had visited this house for the first time.

She walked over to him and touched his face. Her fingers were cold.

'Remembering, Mike?' She tossed the hair from her eyes, as he had seen her do a million times. 'It's so good to have you here. That you could come. Otherwise . . .'

'It always gets me. When I'm away I can't wait to see it . . .

'And now you're here, you can't wait to leave!' She smiled, but it only made her look sad. 'Dear Mike. I worried about how you'd take the news. We all did. Aunt May came at once—she's been a real brick.'

He said hesitantly, 'There'll be a few of his old chums there tomorrow.'

'I thought there would be. It's Armistice Day too, do you realise that? The war to end all wars.' She spread her hands as if to embrace him and the whole house. 'And here we are!'

He put his arm round her and felt her tremble. He had never thought of her like this, as an attractive, vulnerable woman, albeit a young one, who would soon have to cope alone. She was his sister, someone taken for granted. Like his father.

17

Like this house.

She said suddenly, 'You're not to worry. You're so precious to me ... I want you to be careful all the time. I heard about some of the things you had to do in Burma, covering the withdrawal.'

'Withdrawal? It was nearly a bloody rout, believe me!' Then he took her arm. 'Sorry. It gets to me sometimes. And coming back here like this ...' He could not go on.

'See? You're still the little rebel, despite the uniform!'

They laughed at one another, and for an instant life came back to the house.

*   *   *

Captain Mike Blackwood thrust his hands deeper into his greatcoat pockets and tried to settle more comfortably in one corner of the compartment. The train, with extra carriages attached, was packed, mostly with servicemen returning from leave, and others, noticeably noisier, about to begin theirs.

And it was slow, so slow. He half-listened to the wheels on the track, *clack-clack ... clack-clack*. It sounded like a walking pace. The compartment was illuminated by a faint blue light, only strong enough to reveal his breath in the cold air, and it was full, mostly with army officers who were either feigning sleep or genuinely too weary to talk to one another. One woman sat directly opposite him, a young W.A.A.F. officer, her legs pale in the darkness, her eyes shut, although she occasionally consulted her watch or glanced at the door. She probably needed to go to the toilet, but could not face clambering over the bodies squatting in the corridor or sitting on kit bags and suitcases. It might even be occupied when she got there: a small card game, going on in rare privacy.

It was too dark to see out of the window, even if there had been no netting glued across it. He had seen it when he had boarded the train, and the little printed notice explaining that the netting was there to protect passengers from flying glass in the event of an air attack, and apologising for any inconvenience.

Nevertheless, someone had cut away part of it with a knife, and had written neatly underneath, *Thank you for your information! But I can't see the fucking station!* Good handwriting, too. He half-smiled. But then, this was a First Class compartment, for officers only!

His head lolled against the damp headrest as he thought of his leave. Shorter than he had expected, and yet with moments, incidents standing out, as if he had been a spectator. Someone else.

Clack-clack . . . clack-clack.

The sounds changed, and he guessed they were dragging through yet another station.

Everything had seemed so different. Even when he had seen himself for the first time with his new rank, the three pips on either shoulder, it had been like a stranger's reflection. He could feel nothing, give nothing, only a numbness, an emptiness, which had made him seem even more like an onlooker.

Old Harry Payne had been there. Payne was his father's attendant, orderly and friend; he had been with Jonathan Blackwood throughout that other war, had been with him when he had been so grievously wounded, and had watched over him

19

ever since. He and his wife had a cottage on the estate. Odd job man, manager, like most marines he could do almost everything. Older now, but still straight-backed, as he had been that day in the church, his eyes far away as others had read and spoken of the man they had all known.

Blackwood recalled how his father had resisted the use of a walking stick for as long as he could; he had hated it. A constant reminder, a taunt. The wounds to his back and leg had weakened the muscles, but he had always squared his shoulders and smiled a greeting, even when his eyes bared the lie.

That was the cruel irony of it, he thought, after all he had given and done. Out of the blue, he had received an offer of a posting. *Out of the blue.* With his own rank, back in the life he had yearned for. It had not been much, an appointment to the Royal Marines Department of Recruiting. Not much ... but when Harry Payne had described it Blackwood could have been there with him. His father had been in Plymouth to accept the job. Fate had decided otherwise, in the form of a stick of bombs, a common enough occurrence in that battered naval port. There had been people trapped in a burning house and Colonel Jonathan, 'Jono', Blackwood had acted without hesitation. Then the building had collapsed. There had been nothing anyone could have done. They said.

He thought again of the funeral. Every pew in the small church filled, the vicar grave-faced in the presence of so many visitors, senior officers, and grey-haired veterans from another war. Listening, remembering. Sharing.

Vaughan had been there also, although no one

had seen him arrive or leave. It was his way of showing what their friendship had meant to him.

A lot of quiet condolences and firm handshakes . . . a few of the local women sobbing, if not for the man then for the name, the family which had been part of their lives for so long . . .

One old boy wearing a poppy above his medals had said, 'A hard path to follow, Captain Blackwood!'

Hard? It was impossible. Like the sermon, it was for the family, not the man. Two Victoria Crosses, and God knew how many other decorations. Africa, China, the North Sea and the Atlantic, wherever the world's greatest navy had shown its flag. *Impossible.*

Someone had reached the window and lowered it slightly, and the cold air was refreshing.

The anonymous shape muttered, 'Another bloody raid, by the look of it!'

Before he pulled at the strap again Blackwood saw the distant flashes in the sky, like tiny stars. Flak. Probably a solitary hit-and-run raider, without much chance of hitting anything.

The W.A.A.F. officer stood up suddenly, and then staggered as the train gathered speed again. She fell with one hand on Blackwood's knee, and he could smell her nearness, perhaps only soap, but in these dull, damp surroundings it was like perfume. She stammered something in apology and then he heard her dragging the corridor door open. There were a few sleepy remarks and nothing more, but she would know what they were thinking. For her sake, he hoped that the card school had broken up.

He tried to think clearly. London, then. Why not

21

Eastney Barracks, or Stonehouse at Plymouth? He wondered if the general public understood, the ordinary people who faced the rigours of rationing and shortages every day, and the unending dread of receiving one of those hated telegrams. *We regret to inform you that your husband, son, lover* . . . It never stopped, even in small places like Alresford. They clung to optimistic reports in the newspapers or on the cinema newsreels, grinning soldiers giving a thumbs-up to the camera, Spitfires performing a Victory Roll after another clash over southern England. Propaganda, part of the myth? It was all they had.

He considered the navy as it had been when he had joined his first ship, all the great names, as familiar to the public as to the men who served and later died in them. *Royal Oak* and *Courageous*, and the world's largest warship in her day, *Hood*, the nation's darling; *Repulse* and *Prince of Wales*, trusted symbols of power and invincibility. Now gone, wiped out as if they had never been. Even the aircraft carrier *Ark Royal*, the luckiest ship in the fleet, claimed as a prize so many times by the German propaganda machine, had finally been torpedoed and sunk by a U-Boat off Gibraltar. Her famous luck had, at last, run out.

Such awesome losses set against the smaller, little-known operations of the commandos and other special services, the 'cloak-and-dagger brigade', might have broken the morale of the nation. But it had not broken.

There were groans and protests as the door slid open again. It was the ticket inspector, a torch in one hand.

'Waterloo in 'alf an 'our, gents!'

22

Blackwood leaned back as the W.A.A.F. officer returned to her seat. She murmured, 'Thank you.' She sounded relieved, he thought.

The door banged shut again. He remembered leaning from this carriage window, and looked at it now. He had leaned out to touch his sister's face, and to kiss her. He had been aware of her anxiety, for him, not for herself. Some hurrying soldiers had whistled. *Lucky sod. Bloody officer—it's all right for some.* And so on.

The last running figures, the final good-byes; so much to say in so short a time, and no words to offer.

She had held him, staring up at him. 'I didn't want to worry you, Mike. Spoil things.'

There had been the shrill of a whistle. The train, this train, had given a jerk.

She had clung to him, keeping pace with the carriage. 'I passed my medical. My papers came through.'

'Medical? Papers?' He must have sounded stupid.

She had been dragged away from him, her eyes filling her face.

'I'm joining up, Mike!'

Even then, at the moment of separation, he had known its importance to her.

He had shouted, 'I love you, Diane! *We'll show them!*'

The rest had been lost in the din and the smoke from a passing goods train. Show whom? Did she really understand?

He had sat down, and had seen his fellow passengers avert their faces. Only the W.A.A.F. officer had looked at him, with what he thought

23

was a reminiscent pain in her eyes.

Maybe he was not feeling the full effect of it yet, like the funeral service, and the two Royal Marine buglers who had sounded the Last Post afterwards. Part of something else. Something he could never be.

*   *   *

It was exactly eight o'clock in the morning when Blackwood found himself at the appointed building. The air was still damp and cold, and the sky so dull it was barely possible to distinguish the buildings in and around Trafalgar Square; even the little admiral was lost from view on the top of his column.

He still could not believe he had done so much in so short a time since stumbling from the overloaded train at Waterloo Station. A petty officer with a Naval Patrol armlet had met him at the barrier and had guided him to a waiting car without hesitation, no easy thing amid the stampede of uniforms pushing through the gates, either to avoid losing their tickets, which might be used again if the collectors were too busy to notice, or to dodge the hard-faced line of redcaps and RAF police, the enemies of all servicemen anywhere.

Then a quick drive to a private room, where he had been given just a few moments to shave and change into a clean shirt and down a cup of awful tea before being whisked away by the same petty officer.

It had been too much after the lengthy, uncomfortable journey, and he felt like death. He

24

also knew the services well enough to accept that it was probably a complete waste of time. As Major-General Vaughan had said in Scotland, others could do it. They probably had.

The building was not what he had expected; it was more like an old shop, with sandbagged barriers and wire grills to protect the windows.

The petty officer watched him without curiosity. It was obviously better not to ponder on the fate of the officers he collected and ferried to this rendezvous.

He did say, almost apologetically, 'Used to be a big wine merchant's place, sir. So they tells me.' It was enough. He guided him through the doors and past two steel-helmeted policemen, either guarding the entrance or merely sheltering from the drizzle outside. Then there was a counter, and another petty officer standing behind it.

He glanced at Blackwood's identity card, and said, 'I'll take you down, sir.' He almost smiled, but not quite. 'They doesn't like to be kept waiting'!'

Blackwood turned to thank his driver, but he had gone without further word.

He was led to an ornate lift that looked like something from his schooldays; the gates were closed, the button pressed. The big lift gave a jerk and started to descend. For some reason, he had expected it to be going upwards.

It was unreal, going down, past another floor where he caught a glimpse of two civilians having a quick smoke, before the lift came to a shuddering halt and the gates opened automatically.

After the dull sky over London, and the dank air, it was another surprise: white walls and hard lighting, the clatter of teleprinters, and several telephones ringing. Wrens in shirts hurried past with their arms filled with signal folders and files; even the air was different, warm, but moving like some secret breeze.

A tall Wren greeted him. 'Good morning, Captain Blackwood.' She smiled. 'Traffic bad up top?'

He saw a clock on the wall. It was three minutes past the hour.

She seemed to sense his resentment, and added, 'I've been here in the Pit for so long I've almost forgotten what it's like up there!'

He forced a smile. Her casual question had jarred him, like a criticism. Greeting the new boy . . .

She said, 'I'll take you straight in. Commander Diamond is expecting you.'

They walked past several other rooms, she setting a brisk pace, and he noticed how solid the dividing walls were; they must have stored a few million bottles here in happier times. It was a good choice; London could fall on top of it, and you wouldn't feel a thing.

A new door, cheap plywood and painted grey. There was a small board which read, *Commander Roger Diamond, S.O.(O)*. The name rang a vague bell, but nothing more.

'Captain Blackwood, sir.'

It was like hearing a stranger being announced.

There were two men seated at a table. Neither of them moved as the door closed behind him. One he recognised as the harassed-looking major who had been with Vaughan at Achnacarry; it seemed like months ago, instead of weeks. The other man was big, heavy-jowled and formidable. His fingers

26

were resting, clasped, on a pile of papers, and the interwoven gold lace on his sleeves showed that he was a commander in the Royal Naval Reserve. The R.N.R. were mostly professional sailors who served in the merchant navy in peacetime, on the condition that they trained at intervals with the Royal Navy, and they had been a godsend to the overworked and expanding wartime fleet. Because of their experience they were usually navigating officers, or commanders of smaller vessels; Blackwood had never before encountered one on any naval staff.

Diamond nodded. 'Sit down. Glad you got here in one piece. Sorry about your father.' All in one breath, or so it seemed, like one of Vaughan's verbal telegrams. He had dark, deepset eyes and thick, greying eyebrows; the eyes were inscrutable. He glanced over Blackwood's uniform, perhaps noting the newly attached rank, or that he had shaved despite all the haste. If so, he gave nothing away.

Somewhere a telephone jangled, and then a small hatch slid back behind the table and a voice murmured, 'Chief of Staff, sir.'

Diamond did not turn. 'Wait.'

More murmurs. Blackwood took the opportunity to glance around. He heard the voice say, 'Ten minutes, sir.'

Diamond relaxed and waited for the hatch to close. 'Like a bloody confessional, isn't it?'

Then he looked at his companion. 'Major Porter can carry on.' He grinned; *bared his teeth* might be a better description. 'Tell him, Claud.'

Porter said, 'You were selected at Major-General Vaughan's suggestion, and your recent

27

experiences seem to have given foundation to his arguments.' He was neither cold nor severe, but matter-of-fact, professional. 'Since your return from Burma and your employment with the retraining programme in Scotland, a lot of thought and a great deal of work has gone into the preparation of another new force in Special Operations. Out of necessity, we have to work with the other services, and from time to time our army opposite numbers have thought fit to criticise the Corps for not being volunteers for this particular sort of work. For my part, I have read reports by our own people who have described the military participation, particularly in Malaya and in Burma, which you will know very well, as amateurish.' He gave a slight smile. 'I have pointed out to my superiors that this is not a contest between ourselves. Competition is always healthy, but not at the expense of results.'

He turned over some papers, but Blackwood thought it was to give him time, or to allow the formidable Diamond to form his own opinion.

'The retreat from Burma was deplorable. Good men lost, valuable ground thrown away. The stable-door mentality, like Hong Kong and Singapore. A close thing. Too close. Some say that the link between East and West will never recover.' He patted the papers with his neat fingers. 'We will cross *that* bridge when we come to it.'

Diamond was tapping out a massive pipe into the lid of a tobacco tin.

He said, 'You handled yourself well. You took charge of some old, clapped-out launches and local craft and helped get our troops across the Irrawaddy. It wasn't Dunkirk, and this time we could not have afforded to lose another army! Your commanding officer recommended you for a decoration.' He glared at his pipe and the ashes on the lid. 'Probably got bogged down somewhere.'

The major coughed politely. 'Things are moving in the Mediterranean, faster than we dared to hope. The Eighth Army stopped Rommel at El Alamein. It was not a fluke this time—the Germans are in retreat. We're getting results!'

It was the closest Blackwood had seen him to excitement.

Major Porter continued, 'The plan is to send a small force of commandos to North Africa. One hundred men, no more at this stage. You will have full co-operation from the navy, and the army can think what it likes. Anyway . . .' Again the small, private smile. 'The Prime Minister is behind us, so that can't be a bad thing. You would be second-in-command.' He frowned as the phone jangled again. 'Your last C.O. suggested that.'

Blackwood imagined he had missed something. Strain, fatigue; or was he just bomb-happy like all the others?

'Major Gaillard.'

The silence was complete, like going suddenly deaf.

The telephone rang again, and he heard himself say, 'I—I'm sorry, sir.' He saw them looking at him, and tried again. 'You see, I thought he was dead.' A voice insisted, *you know he is dead. You saw him fall.* 'On the Irrawaddy.'

Major Porter studied him calmly. 'He was wounded, but he is very much alive. His information was invaluable, and it seemed better to keep his recovery off the record.'

29

The hatch was open from the confessional, and Commander Diamond swivelled round in his chair with some difficulty.

'Yes? Speaking, sir. I have the documents ready for you.'

But his deepset eyes were on Blackwood, as Porter pressed, 'You agree, then? This is a Top Secret operation, but I don't have to spell it out for you.'

The telephone had gone and the hatch was shut again. Diamond beamed, and jammed his pipe in his pocket.

'Good to meet you, Blackwood.' He glanced at the door; the formalities were over. 'I shall expect you here tomorrow. Same time.' He heaved his heavy body from the chair. 'You got along all right with Gaillard, I hope?' The door opened, and the same Wren was waiting there with Diamond's cap. He did not wait for an answer.

Blackwood half-listened to the muted rumble of London's traffic far above this secret, bomb-proof place, the question still in his ears like an echo.

Porter said, 'I'll walk you to the lift.'

Gaillard was alive, and in command.

And I wanted him dead.

CHAPTER TWO

IT WAS NICE MEETING YOU

Captain Mike Blackwood climbed down from the taxi and glanced at the overcast sky. Yet another air raid siren was wailing dolefully, as if in pain.

'Is this it?'

The cabby watched him thoughtfully. A tall officer in a khaki greatcoat, with the Royal Marines badge, the Globe and Laurel, on his beret. What the hell would he be doing in a place like Putney? But he was an old hand. You didn't ask in wartime. You just had to wait.

He said, 'Small block of flats, guv. The river's just beyond.' He gestured with his mittened thumb. 'Putney bridge is down there. Least, it *was* still there this mornin'!'

Blackwood shivered. Anything was better than staying in the poxy billet in London, he thought. A stopover for officers like himself, a place so dingy it was a wonder it wasn't condemned. Even the taps didn't work properly.

It all seemed the continuation of a dream, like his visits to the underground headquarters, 'the Pit', as the Wren had called it. Nothing made sense, as if it was all happening to somebody else. From the old boy with the poppy and the heavy row of medals at the funeral, the grave faces and the staring passers-by, to this . . . this nightmare.

He had telephoned Hawks Hill to try and discover what had happened to his sister, but had only managed to speak with Harry Payne for a few moments before they were cut off. Payne had sounded delighted, full of it. Diane was in the W.R.N.S., or almost. He had exclaimed, 'And she's been put forward for our lot!' *Our lot.* He smiled. *Once a Royal Marine, always a Royal Marine.* Even after all these years and another war, Payne had never truly left the Corps in spirit.

Then the line had gone dead. Perhaps an operator had heard what she considered to be

31

careless talk.

He was pleased for Diane. She had just about run the estate single-handed, for their father's sake and for those who still depended on the place. Now she was free to do what she had always wanted. Like so many local girls: how would they ever settle down after the war?

He thrust his hand into his pocket. *If we ever win the bloody war . . .*

'How much is that?'

The cabby replied, 'I'm well over my limit, sir, an' I'm towin' this ruddy fire pump, so it's hard on petrol . . . .' He looked down as Blackwood put two notes in his hand, and grinned. 'You're a real toff, sir!' He drove away into the lengthening shadows, the little pump bumping along behind his taxi.

Blackwood stared at the flats, very square against the low sky. Right on the Thames. Must have cost a packet in peacetime.

He did not move, thinking of the London he had seen since his return from Scotland. People crowding the Underground platforms, not merely for a night, but every night, with their blankets and gas masks, thermos flasks, and maybe a sandwich to see them through. Trying to sleep until the first train ran in the morning; feeling the ground shiver to bombs, wondering if the house or the flat or a life would still be there when daylight came.

And trying to sleep in that awful billet. The walls were so thin that he guessed the hotel's enterprising owner had doubled the number of existing rooms with little more than sheets of plywood.

Each small room had only a single bed, but almost every night Blackwood had heard the man

32

in the next hutch entertaining a woman, not always the same one by the sound of it, a blow-by-blow encounter down to the last frantic gasp. So much for security . . .

But after he had received the telephone call, he had broken the monotony by banging on the wall with his fist and shouting, 'What have you got in there? A bloody tiger?'

He had heard the woman giggle, and then her companion had thumped the wall himself and shouted back, 'Don't make so much noise!'

But at least they had been quiet after that. For a while, anyway.

He walked towards the building now, his mind suddenly quite cold, contained. Almost as if he had known.

'That you, Mike? Good show! You can't get rid of me that easy.' Even on the phone, it was the same hard laugh. 'Just had the word. It's a go.' He had given the address, this address, and had added, 'Don't bother about getting back to that dump. You can pitch down here if you like.'

Blackwood glanced at the clouds and saw a searchlight make a wide practice swing beyond the river. Preparing for the real thing.

Suppose he had been wrong about Gaillard? Everything had been in a state of chaos, stampeding natives, upended vehicles and hurrying soldiers, wild-eyed in full retreat. There had been pockets of resistance and raw courage, too; there always were. But there had been too many mixed units, and often no overall command to minimise confusion. And the Japs had known it. They had even infiltrated past the last defenders, and their sniper fire had inflicted a terrible toll.

And, throughout, the marines with their ramshackle flotilla of local boats and launches had ferried exhausted soldiers and wounded civilians to the next place of safety, fighting a rearguard action all the way.

Several marines had been cut off while they were endeavouring to blow up a fuel dump in a sudden tropical downpour. Gaillard had ordered them to fall back, had even gone himself to speed up their return. An army sapper had been with them, but had been wounded by a single shot from a clump of trees; he had fallen into the river even as one of the launches had been backing away.

Paget had been there, too. Afterwards, he had said, 'The poor bloody sapper was calling out, pleading for someone to help an' not leave him alive for the Japs to get hold of.' They all knew what that would have meant. 'I heard a shot. The pongo either done for himself, or someone else did it for him.'

Shortly afterwards Blackwood saw Gaillard fall, holding his side, a revolver gripped in his hand. That was the last time he had seen him.

He found himself facing a door, and after the smallest hesitation he pressed the bell.

Gaillard had been reported missing, believed killed, although things had been and still were vague as to whether men were prisoners of war, dead, or truly missing. To the Japanese, the dissemination of information was not a priority.

But suppose I was wrong?

With a start, he realised that the door had opened. But it was a woman, and in the poor light she appeared to be wearing dark blue battledress, of the kind worn by air raid wardens or voluntary rescue workers. She was quite obviously neither.

She said, 'Well? Are you coming in, Captain Blackwood?'

He stepped into a hallway and she switched on the light. She did not offer her hand. 'I'll take your coat.'

She had a soft, educated voice, with an undernote of tension. As she turned to take his greatcoat he glanced at her quickly. Dark hair, quite short, shining in the light, hands small, well-shaped, and, he guessed, strong. About his own age, he thought, but with a maturity which defied him.

Most of his experience with women had been youthful, silly affairs, usually as the result of some big naval event, a fleet review or regatta. In the Mediterranean, under the spread awnings, to the music of the ship's bandsmen: light, simple and empty flirtations. Bare, tanned shoulders and roving eyes. But that was then.

She said, 'You will know me if we meet again, Captain.'

'Sorry. I was staring.'

'Yes. You were.' She did not respond to his smile. 'I'll take you in.'

Who was she, he wondered. Gaillard's wife, or mistress perhaps; he had never been slow where women were concerned. He followed her to another door. But even that might no longer be true of the man.

He stepped into the adjoining room and saw Gaillard standing by a fireplace, watching him, as if he had been poised for this moment. Tall, lean and hard, most people's idea of the complete fighting man. He had worn a moustache when they had last

35

been together, but he was now clean-shaven, his chin smooth but blue, as if it defied even the keenest blade.

It was Gaillard's eyes you always remembered. Very dark; what Diane would call 'button-eyes'. A man who rarely seemed to raise his voice, but one who could reduce an incompetent subordinate to a jelly without effort.

He was smiling now, holding out his hand.

'So here you are, Mike. Getting bloody fed up with all the delays and foul-ups, I'll be bound.' The eyes did not flicker or move; they never did. 'I've heard all about the training programme. Maybe now we can put it to good use.'

His handshake was dry and hard. Like the man.

'Drink, old boy?' He looked at the woman in blue as if he had never seen her before. 'You off, then? Good show.' He watched her walk to a cupboard and take out a decanter and two glasses.

She said in that same level voice, 'I'll not be long. There's some more Scotch in the kitchen.' She left them, and Blackwood heard her go out by the same door where he had waited, so full of doubts and misgivings about this moment.

Gaillard grinned. 'Yes, Scotch. I know what you're thinking. Well, why not, I say, you never know when the next chance will come, eh?' Again that short, hard laugh. It was no longer a dream.

Gaillard filled the glasses almost to the top and waved him to a chair; it felt new, unused. He glanced around the room: pictures dusted, but boring, a few ornaments. But it was not a home; it was just another place.

He realised that Gaillard was studying him, and said, 'That girl . . .' He got no further.

36

Gaillard shook his head. 'Hands off, old boy! Way out of your league!' He wagged the glass, so that some of the Scotch slopped over his tunic. 'Unless you've changed, eh?'

'I thought she seemed a bit on edge, that's all.'

Gaillard stared into his glass. 'We get all sorts in and out of HQ, you know.' He frowned. 'Gordon, that's her name. Joanna Gordon. One of Commander Diamond's little high fliers. A go-between, at the moment.'

Blackwood felt his muscles relax slightly. Gaillard was never vague about anything. Maybe he had made a pass at the girl and she had told him where to go.

Gaillard was saying, 'I can tell you now, Mike. We're off to North Africa in a matter of days. But keep it to yourself as much as you can. Walls have ears, too bloody many in London. Don't bother getting any special kit . . . that can all be fixed when we get there.' He flinched very slightly as the windows rattled to a far-off explosion, and muttered, 'Docks again, by the sound of it.'

It was something to say, Blackwood thought, to cover his mood.

He added, 'You'll meet all sorts. Special Boat Squadron, the schooner people, maybe even the S.A.S. They're all at it. It could spoil things, unless we act fast.' He studied him suddenly, his dark eyes shining in the lamplight like glass. 'You'll know all the details when we get there.'

Blackwood noticed that his own glass was empty, and yet he could not recall having drained it. He thought of a medical officer he had met in Burma. *Combat fatigue,* he had described it. 'You can drink a gallon of hooch and feel nothing. Then you go

37

out like a light. Oblivion!'

Gaillard stood up and walked to a window, and peered through a crack in the blackout shutter.

'I'll not be sorry to get back into it.' He spoke with unusual vehemence, and Blackwood saw him touch his side, where he had been wounded.

When he had gone into hiding. He allowed the thought to continue. When he had run away, and had left the wounded to their fate.

Gaillard swung away from the window, the mood apparently changed. 'We'll fly to Alexandria, via Gib of course, just in case the whole show's gone sour on us. Some of those duffers at the top don't realise what it's like—they're still fighting the Zulus, not an enemy which has been preparing and training for years, just for this! Take the Japs, for instance. Now they *know* how to fight, no messing about, and no white flag of surrender when the going gets rough and the other side forgets to play by the rules! God, what *soldiers*!'

Blackwood heard the front door open and felt a draught stirring beneath the chair.

She walked across the room and put some parcels on the table.

'Thought you might be hungry. Just needs grilling.' She looked at Blackwood directly for the first time. 'I've arranged a car for you.' She touched the front of her battledress blouse as if feeling for something. 'Tomorrow at eight. The usual place.' Then, for a second, her reserve seemed to falter. 'I hope everything goes well for you, Captain Blackwood.'

He stood. 'I'll get a cab for you. It's dark, and there's a raid going on.'

She smiled briefly. 'There usually is.' She shook

her head. 'There will be a car waiting for me.'

Gaillard said rudely, 'I'm going to pump the bilges.' He glanced at Blackwood and grimaced. 'Then we'll eat, eh?'

He followed her to the door, and out into the darkness. It was cold, but the air seemed somehow less damp.

She turned slightly, and he sensed that she was looking at him.

'I can manage on my own now, thank you.'

He heard a car start up, and wanted her to stay. He said, 'What exactly do you do in this outfit?' It sounded clumsy, and stupid.

'This and that. Nothing too dangerous.'

Was she laughing at him? Putting him on the same level as Gaillard, and probably all the others who made passes at her?

Then she said, 'I read about your father. He must have been a fine man.'

'Yes. We loved him very much.' It came out, just like that, and he could hardly believe he could have spoken so openly, so proudly. He felt her grip his wrist, her hand like ice.

'Remember him like that. Don't change just because of . . .' She twisted away, in control again as a large car drew up beside them.

Then she turned and looked up at the flats, or perhaps at him.

'Have a nice meal. I tried to find something you might like.'

He was still staring after her when the car had turned into the next street.

It was an uncomfortable meal, for all that. Gaillard seemed unusually restless, and left the table several times to make telephone calls, and to

39

switch on the nine o'clock news.

The girl had brought two healthy-looking steaks, and when Blackwood had commented on this in some surprise Gaillard had replied offhandedly, 'Rations? Not likely. You can get anything you want in London, if you're prepared to pay for it!'

He had tried to listen to the news bulletin, but it seemed like any other. The Eighth Army was still advancing in North Africa; a strategic withdrawal had been made somewhere else. The Royal Air Force had carried out a heavy raid over marshalling yards and U-Boat pens in France. *Thirty of our aircraft failed to return.* All in the same unemotional, well-modulated voice, as if it were a cricket score.

Gaillard had said suddenly, 'I have to go out. Don't wait up.' He had patted his pockets as if to reassure himself of something. 'Someone will be in to clean up after we've gone tomorrow.' He had gone, banging the front door behind him.

After a while Blackwood, too, went out, and climbed an internal ladder to the flat roof. He saw two figures huddled in a corner, wearing steel helmets: fire-watchers, staring at the sky over London. There was a bad blaze somewhere; he could see it reflected in the Thames, as if the river itself was on fire, and the tang of smoke and charred wood was apparent even here; occasionally he heard the distant clamour of bells, fire engines, ambulances, maybe even the cabby, with his little pump dragging behind his taxi. A city at war, the battle about which servicemen knew the least. Ordinary people doing extraordinary things. Fighting and surviving. Dying.

He thought of the girl, the way she had looked,

40

the feel of her cold fingers on his wrist. Where was she now, while all this was going on? If the raid came this way a single stick of bombs, like the one which had killed his father, and he, Gaillard and the girl might be no more. What, then, of the secret plans? Diamond had said clearly, *others could do it . . .*

He thought of all the faces he had known since the war had taken him from routine duties and made him what he was now. Young, eager, with little thought beyond the next day. After three years of it, there were not many left.

There was a loud explosion, and he saw a column of sparks rise into the sky like something solid. It must be miles away, and yet he imagined he felt the searing heat. He glanced at the fire-watchers, one wearing pyjama trousers beneath his duffle coat.

They were both drinking tea; neither was young, but Blackwood knew they would be ready to use their stirrup pumps and buckets of sand if incendiaries straddled this block of flats.

One of Diamond's little high fliers. He recalled the way she had looked back at him when he had caught himself staring at her. A defiance. But when she had spoken of his father she had seemed very different, or maybe she had been reminded of somebody.

He sighed, and the two muffled figures turned to peer at him.

It was stupid even to think of it. He would probably never see her again. In war, it was like that, and it was probably better so. In the same breath, he knew it was not.

He groped his way back to the ladder and one of

the fire-watchers called after him, 'Good luck! Take care of yourself!'

He paused and raised a hand to them. *And what about you,* he thought.

He let himself into the flat, and was thankful that Gaillard had not returned. It was ridiculous. *We shall be working together. Discipline, trust, determination.*

He looked around the room which was to be his refuge for the night. Clean sheets, and his greatcoat was on a hanger behind the door. She must have done that. The thought made him glance around with new eyes, although it was as plain and unimaginative as the others in the flat.

Then he sat on the bed, and imagined her here, beside him. Smiling, perhaps, at his clumsy uncertainty. But smiling . . .

He lay on his back and stared at the ceiling; he was still awake when the all-clear eventually sounded across London.

He got up, with effort, and looked at himself in a mirror. Maybe, like Gaillard, he was glad to be going back.

The face in the mirror regarded him impassively, and he was reminded of old Harry Payne at Hawks Hill.

Aloud, to the empty room, he said, 'You never left!'

He was ready.

*　　*　　*

They stood side by side in the bare, unheated waiting room, staring at the aircraft standing quite alone on the makeshift runway. A wartime airfield somewhere in Hampshire, at a guess, Blackwood thought, not all that far from Hawks Hill.

They had been driven down from London soon after dawn, with the same petty officer who had met him at Waterloo at the wheel. If the man remembered him, he gave no sign of recognition. Maybe all this cloak and dagger stuff was catching.

The aircraft was testing its engines, like a big, awkward bird, an intruder here, as incongruous as the small control tower, which looked as if it had been built overnight. There appeared to be no other planes around. It must be strange to serve in places like these where cows had once roamed, when life had been far simpler. They had already met the pilot, very young with a round, pink face, more like a choirboy than the captain of the camouflaged Dakota. He had greeted them cheerfully, as if he did not have a care in the world.

'Five hours with a following wind—should be all right. Reports seem fair enough.'

Just as well, Blackwood thought. The plane was unarmed.

He glanced at Gaillard. There was no hint of strain or doubt; he was as alert and watchful as ever. If anything, he seemed impatient.

He said sharply, 'God, these people take a month of Sundays to shift into gear! Wouldn't do for me!'

An aircraftman was peering in at them. 'All loaded, sir. You can board now.'

They walked together across the hard-packed ground and past an unmanned battery of Bofors guns. The sky was bright, and almost clear; their pilot would have that in mind while he was gaining height. Blackwood had already seen the filled-in

43

bomb craters near the perimeter fence; it was not always so quiet here.

Another officer, grinning, checked them against his list. 'Better watch your language, gentlemen. There's a woman in our midst!'

Gaillard remarked, 'Didn't I tell you? Your little friend's coming with us, part of the way.' He climbed up into the aircraft, effortlessly, as Blackwood had seen him scale cliffs at Flannel Alley, as it was nicknamed, in Cornwall. Where they had first met.

No, you didn't tell me.

Another airman was waiting for them. 'Up here, sir.'

There were several passengers, some already asleep despite the vibration of the twin engines. She was sitting by a window, and looked up briefly as he removed his greatcoat. She was wearing the same dark blue battledress, and her face seemed very pale against the curved side of the cabin.

She pulled herself to her feet, and as he protested she said, 'No. You sit here, Captain Blackwood. I don't like looking out when I'm flying.'

They changed round, and a light began to flicker to announce take-off. He sat quite still and upright in the much-used seat, very aware of her nearness, and the unreality of their meeting again like this.

What did she do for Diamond's team? Courier, somebody's secretary or aide? It must be something important; seats were like gold on these flights. Despite the ever-present danger, it was always a matter of priority. Everyone else either took the long haul around the Cape to Suez, where every troopship was a choice target for U-Boats and long-range Focke-Wulf bombers, or the shorter and even more hazardous route via Malta, when, at this stage of the war in the Mediterranean, an attack could be expected from any direction.

He looked out and saw men scampering away as dust and smoke fanned from beneath the engines. A couple of aircraftmen were waving; others were already walking unconcernedly towards the N.A.A.F.I., if only to show what old hands they were.

He could not see Gaillard, but he could feel him, imagined him watching them together, and enjoying it in some obscure way. He might even have arranged the seating; the R.A.F. transport people were always fairly strict in that respect, it was said so that they could identify the corpses strapped to their seats if a plane brewed up or crashed into the sea. What Sergeant Paget would call 'a right bunch of comedians!'

They were moving faster now, the fuselage swaying steeply on the crude runway. The control tower seemed so small from here, with an officer observing their progress through his binoculars.

Faster, faster, a cottage or two flashing past, a black dog jumping up and down, barking soundlessly.

He stiffened as he felt her hand on his arm.

She said, 'I'm *all right*. But I really don't like this part!'

He said nothing, afraid to break the spell, surprised that he could cling to something so frail. Like a thread which would soon be broken.

And suddenly they were off, and he saw their great shadow dashing across fields, and a khaki field ambulance in a narrow lane, the red crosses

45

very bright in the glare. Like blood.

He leaned towards her, and said, 'We're away. Nice take-off.' He felt her hand withdraw, and thought she winced as she settled deeper into her seat. 'Have you injured your back, Miss Gordon?'

She said, 'No.' It was almost sharp. Then, 'I'm all right now. *Really.*'

The thread was broken.

*   *   *

The Rock made an inspiring sight as the Dakota levelled off for the final approach. The bay appeared to be packed with shipping, many of them dull grey convoy escorts turning round for the next challenge. There were two fighters circling Gibraltar's craggy outline; no chances in this all-important base, the gateway to the Mediterranean and the desert war.

Throughout the flight she had scarcely spoken, except when one of the crew had appeared with coffee and sandwiches. The pilot had come aft to talk to Gaillard, and Blackwood had heard them laughing about something above the drone of the engines.

He saw that her hand was resting once more on his sleeve.

'This is where we part. Thank you for taking care of me.'

She was so serious that he was reminded of his sister when she had been about eight. It was exactly what she had been taught to say whenever she was taken out by friends of the family.

'I had hoped we might meet.' He hesitated, sensing the guard rising again. 'I don't even know where you're going, do I?'

She tensed as the wheels hit the runway, and he felt the fingers clench on his arm.

Then she said, 'But I do know where you're going, Captain Blackwood.' She would not look at him. 'So, please, be careful.'

The aircraft was already slowing down, ground crew and various machines converging on it like predators, but all he could think of was her utter sincerity.

Then Gaillard was beside them, grinning. 'Time to get off, Mike. I'm going to change into some brown trousers for the next bit of the trip!' He went away, pausing to slap another passenger on the shoulder in passing.

Blackwood smiled; he had forgotten how easily he was embarrassed.

'Sorry about that.'

She smiled faintly in return.

Then she looked at him with the same direct gaze, and said, 'It wouldn't work, I'm afraid.' She held out her hand. 'It was nice meeting you.'

She dragged out a small briefcase and turned towards the open door, and suddenly, ridiculously, he wanted to hold her, to explain. But the words would not form, and he could not move. The aircraft was suddenly empty, and more ground workers were hurrying in to unload some of the cargo.

The passengers had melted away, blurred, unreal, like spectres from some forgotten battlefield.

Someone appeared to guide him to yet another waiting room. This time, there was wine on the table.

47

Gaillard came through another doorway and stood looking at him in silence. Then he said, 'I've just been told. It's still on.' His dark eyes gave nothing away, any more than his voice. 'It's a raid. I'll fill you in while the plane's refuelling.' The grin again. 'I hope they've taken enough gas on board!' But the eyes were devoid of humour. 'We've got to get our hands on some bits of secret equipment. Urgent stuff.'

'When can we expect the rest of our company?'

'There are a couple of dozen already at Alex. It's enough. It has to be.' He looked at him calmly. 'No foul-ups, right?'

Blackwood said only, 'Right.' And she had known where this raid was planned to take place. How many others knew?

Gaillard watched a white-coated messman pouring the wine. The bottle was misted over, ice-cold.

He said casually, 'By the way, they're giving me a gong. I put you in for one, you know. Maybe next time.'

Not long afterwards, they were called to board the Dakota again. As they walked out into the hard sunlight, Blackwood glanced back at the huddled white buildings, wondering if she was there.

The same pilot was waiting for them, apparently untroubled by the prospect of the next leg of the flight. He merely remarked, 'Wizard show, chaps, bang on time!'

Blackwood looked once more over his shoulder.

It was nice meeting you.

He followed Gaillard to their seats and fastened his belt for take-off. No foul-ups, Gaillard had said.

He braced himself as the plane rolled forward,

knowing that Gibraltar offered one of the most hair-raising departures any passenger would ever experience. He could feel her hand on his sleeve.

They were airborne, the wingtip appearing only inches away from the Rock. Gibraltar, the only battle honour ever displayed on the Royals' cap badge.

*   *   *

It was nice meeting you.

From a window in the small, commandeered house, which had once belonged to a Spanish trader, she watched the Dakota lift hesitantly above the mass of anchored shipping, until the reflected glare made her move back into the shadow of a blind.

She would freshen up and change. She unbuttoned her blouse and allowed it to fall over her bare shoulder, then she looked at her reflection in a mirror and turned her shoulder to the light again, studying the ugly weals on her skin; some would turn into bruises before they healed. She touched the shoulder with her chin, remembering the marine's concern, and her own immediate caution. Always there; it was something still hard to learn, to take for granted.

And yet, for only a few moments, it had been easy to imagine herself with him.

She stared at the marks on her body. The instructors had told her that the impact of landing with a parachute was like jumping from a twelve-foot wall. The top of a house, more likely. They had not told her to expect these injuries left by the harness.

49

She buttoned her blouse again and crossed to the window. The sky was empty.

She thought suddenly of her brother; his name was Mike, too. Had been . . .

She tried to push it from her mind. And the man who had loved her. So brief, so desperate; it was hard to believe she was that same woman. They were both dead. Both pilots, they had been shot down within four months of one another. Bought it, their friends would have called it, not from indifference, or because they had become too hardened by war to care. They dared not speak otherwise of death . . . she had seen it in their faces often enough. As she had seen it in the marine officer's face. *Mike.*

She held out both hands and studied them. She had almost expected to see them shaking.

Surprisingly, she smiled. No fear, then. That would come. Again, she thought of the young captain called Blackwood. Doing what he must, out of a sense of duty, or because of tradition? She remembered the grey-green eyes, when she had spoken of his father. *We loved him very much.* So simply said.

She shook herself, angry, disturbed that she could be seeking escape, contemplating it, when there was so little time left, for either of them.

She watched as a fighter lifted away from the airstrip, the air cringing to its powerful engine. She followed it until her eyes watered in the glare.

'Mike.' The sound of her own voice startled her, because she did not know whom she meant.

CHAPTER THREE

OPERATION *LUCIFER*

In the relentless glare of early morning the protected waters of Alexandria harbour shone like blue steel. Like Gibraltar, the place was packed with warships and transports of every size and description, hard-worked destroyers and even some battered corvettes transferred from that other war in the Atlantic, as well as landing craft, cruisers, and behind the long line of floats which revealed the presence of anti-torpedo nets, two powerful battleships.

'Alex', as it was known, affectionately for the most part, by thousands of servicemen, had been resigned to falling to Rommel's invincible Afrika Korps. Only a little more than fifty miles away, a stone's throw in desert warfare, the Eighth Army, after so many retreats and setbacks, had made a final stand at a little-known place called El Alamein. If the Germans had broken through, they would have had Cairo, Suez and the whole of the Middle East at their mercy. The reappearance in Alexandria of so many ships and military personnel had been a great reassurance to the local people, although cynics still maintained that the patriotic portraits of Churchill and President Roosevelt displayed in most of the cafés and hotels carried those of Hitler and Mussolini on the reverse.

A little apart from the main cluster of moorings and naval stores was Mahroussa Jetty, the King of Egypt's own yacht base. Now, with sandbagged guard posts and a spotless White Ensign flying from its mast, the base had become H.M.S. *Mosquito*, and was used solely by the navy's light coastal forces, M.T.B.s and motor gunboats. But even here the forces were subdivided, and moored away from the others were two motor gunboats. They displayed no pendant numbers, and their lean, rakish hulls were disguised with garish dazzle paint, which at speed could confuse even the most experienced lookout or air-gunner.

They were small compared with the other vessels nearby, seventy feet long and low in the water, but they were powered by three-shaft Rolls-Royce petrol motors which could move them at almost forty knots when necessary. Their wooden hulls had been worked hard, and there were scars along the diagonal planking which even the paint could not conceal.

A force within a force. These two M.G.B.s were only a part of the Special Boat Squadron, which, in co-operation with the schooners and caiques of the other secret group, probed the enemy coastline in search of ready targets, or to seek information vital to the high command.

Both boats had just refuelled, and the stench of high-octane was still very evident.

They were designed to carry a company of twelve; even that made them crowded. But their new status had increased that complement to fifteen. Tolerance and a sense of humour were essential.

As well as machine guns in quadruple mountings, they carried a pair of twenty-millimetre Oerlikon cannon, to say nothing of the odds and ends they had picked up along the way, both

52

German and Italian.

In the wardroom of the leading M.G.B., her commanding officer, Lieutenant David Falconer, Distinguished Service Cross, Royal Naval Volunteer Reserve, sat at the small table, his briar pipe filled and ready to light once the last fumes had dispersed. His open-necked white shirt was fresh today, a luxury possible in Alex, but it was already getting grubby. Everything did in 'the boats'. He was twenty-six years old and had been on active service since the outbreak of war without respite, unless it was to attend some course or other. In destroyers on the Atlantic convoy runs, and then in light coastal forces, he had witnessed every sort of danger and the courage which inevitably stayed in company. His face and arms were burned by the sun, but refused to tan, and there were deep crow's-feet at his eyes: the look of an experienced sailor, much older than his years. He found it hard to remember his other life, when he had been a schoolmaster at a small and expensive boarding school in Sussex. To get away from it all he had joined the local R.N.V.R., and had been among the first to be ordered to the nearest naval base. He had never regretted it.

He glanced around the wardroom, and smiled. His own command. The wardroom was little more than a box, situated directly below the small open bridge and beside the W/T office. And close enough to the all-important galley to be able to make bets on the next meal.

He looked up as the M.G.B.'s first lieutenant peered in at him. Sub-Lieutenant John Balfour, wearing a single wavy stripe on his shoulder, was twenty, but in contrast to Falconer he looked extremely young. Before volunteering for the navy he had been at school, and by any other twist of fate could have been one of Falconer's pupils.

Unlike Falconer, he had tanned very easily in the short time since he had joined the squadron. He was pleasant, willing to learn, but a little over-eager to be popular, rather than respected. Falconer liked him, but still found himself glancing at the bunk on the opposite side, which served as a life-raft if required. It had also been the place where his last Number One had coughed out his life the day the Stuka had dropped out of the clouds near Crete, and had bombed and raked the boat with machine gun fire before climbing away like a triumphant hawk. He hoped Balfour would last longer than his predecessor.

Balfour said, 'Boat's clear, sir.' He was looking at the package of papers, which he had already seen brought aboard by a messenger from the base operations staff.

Falconer let him stew for a while as he lit his pipe with his usual care. The routine of smoking helped him in many ways, after a raid which had gone badly wrong, or an air attack like the one which had killed his Number One. More than once he had seen his fingers shaking when attempting to hold a light to this same pipe.

Finally he said, 'We've got a job, Number One. Up amongst the islands again.' He cursed himself inwardly; Balfour had not been with him then. 'Conference this afternoon. The brass will be thick on the ground, so I'd better not .. .' His eyes moved to the cupboard. *The bar.* 'Still, a gin won't hurt.'

As Balfour busied himself with the glasses and

Plymouth gin, he added, 'Royal Marine Commandos are involved.' He sighed. 'Bloody regulars, by the sound of it. That's all I need!' He held up the glass. 'Not *that* small, for God's sake!'

The orders were vague, but to Falconer they seemed to shout out loud. The commandos would be landed on an island. Intelligence had discovered a new detection device, a big advance on the enemy's radio direction finder, more like radar, which was never mentioned. The brass might have good reason to be worried.

Nobody had really believed that Monty's Eighth Army would be able to hold out against Rommel's giant Tiger tanks, but they had. Few had expected the attack to be turned into a retreat, but it was. The Germans were on the run, and showed no signs of standing and counter-attacking the Desert Rats. Falconer had become as sceptical as all the others, but as day followed day he had allowed himself to believe that the impossible was happening.

The Allies would have to take advantage of it without delay, and attack the enemy-held mainland. They would have enough choice: apart from Sweden, the whole of Europe and Scandinavia were under the German heel. Invasion would need landing craft, machines and men, above all *men*, and they would have to be transported by sea. It would be costly enough without the enemy putting some advanced detection device into the market-place. The other hush-hush boys, the schooner force, many of whom were based in Beirut, would also be taking part. Madmen, he thought. Sometimes forty knots seemed too slow; five or six must be suicide.

Balfour said quite seriously, 'I hope it won't interfere with Christmas, sir.'

Falconer stood up and seized his cap. 'If that's all you're worried about, John, it must be all right!'

Balfour stared after him. He had not heard him laugh like that since he had joined the boat. And he had called him by his first name.

He looked at the nude pin-up on the notice board, and grinned. Things could be a lot worse. He was accepted. Almost.

*   *   *

There was another pause while the vast wall map was replaced by another on a larger scale. Blackwood took the opportunity to glance around the operations room. A long, low-roofed building, full of scrubbed tables and hard chairs, it was more like a converted boatshed, which was exactly what it had been in the King of Egypt's day. A corrugated iron roof made the interior sweltering under normal conditions, and if there was rain, which was rare, the noise drowned out every word.

Unsuitable and certainly uncomfortable as these premises were, there was no doubting the easy efficiency of those men gathered here. Veterans, no matter what age they were.

They were a very mixed bunch, but he was used to that: a small group of naval officers from the motor gunboats which had been pointed out to him, a Met officer, two intelligence officers, and a Royal Navy commander in full uniform, the only one who looked completely untroubled by the lack of air and the drifting pall of tobacco smoke. Blackwood also found time to notice that the

56

commander's uniform was clean and perfectly pressed, as if he had just collected it from the wardroom stewards.

His name was Walter St John, and by his appearance he was a man who would take no nonsense from anybody. Aged about thirty, and a regular officer, he had a face which seemed to belong in another time; it reminded Blackwood of the paintings at Hawks Hill. A face which would not have been out of place at Trafalgar. St John was in charge of Special Operations in Alexandria, an extension of Commander Diamond and Major-General Vaughan in London.

Blackwood became aware of someone watching him, and saw another Royal Marine at one of the littered tables look away.

Lieutenant George Despard, who had been in Alexandria with the advance party of commandos, was an impressive character, tall, straight-backed and muscular; his arms, propped on their elbows, were almost covered with tattoos. He had a tough face, which could change completely if he smiled. Despard had come up the hard way, through the ranks; it was difficult to discover why or how he had ended up in the commandos. He was a Channel Islander, and that, too, marked him apart: the islands were the only part of Britain under German occupation.

Blackwood had first met him as a corporal, and their paths had crossed several times since. Despard was a man you would trust with your life, never short of ideas, or courage when he was in a tight spot. Equally, he was one you would never know in a thousand years. Not like Paget, not like anybody.

Commander St John eyed the new map, and waited for all the throats to be cleared, the feet to stop shuffling. Then he said, 'This is it. The island of Vasili.'

The lieutenant with the pointer touched the coloured map. St John continued, 'Just to the west of Rhodes, which, as you will know, gentlemen, lies at the approaches to the Aegean Sea.' He had a clipped manner of speaking, not unlike Gaillard, but there were a lot of broad grins at the dry comment, 'I would not wish you to be in total ignorance!'

Blackwood saw Gaillard himself sitting, legs crossed, at the commander's table. Those in the room would be watching him, measuring his chances, and their own by what they saw. The adjustment to Gaillard's battledress had already been made: a red medal ribbon with blue edges, the 'gong' he had mentioned, the Distinguished Service Order. He was surprised at his own anger and resentment; he was being stupid, unreasonable. It was the same highly prized decoration which had been awarded to his father. Gaillard had probably been ordered to display it now, to make the right impression, rather than await an official presentation at a more convenient time. It should not have mattered. But it did.

St John was saying, 'The secret equipment, referred to henceforth as *Lucifer*, is on this island for several reasons. It is a bad coastline, and should deter nosy people from getting too near. More to the point, it commands two or more local channels, so that the operators will be able to test and evaluate the accuracy of their device. It may be the work of cranks.' He looked around at their faces.

58

'But the human torpedo, the "chariot" as we now know it, was considered laughable when the Italians first produced it.' He raised one arm and pointed at the wall. 'And yet, only last year, around this time, Italian frogmen were able to cut through all our defences, right here in Alex, and place their charges under two battleships, the *Queen Elizabeth* and the *Valiant.* They were both knocked out of action, and would likely have been completely destroyed but for prompt action.' He gave a wry smile. 'And the presence of our Commander-in-Chief, Admiral Cunningham. That no doubt speeded things along!'

There was laughter, although it had not been funny at the time, with the Eighth Army in retreat, and heavy naval losses when every ship was priceless. The destruction of two battleships, a major force of the Mediterranean Fleet, could have ended it.

Even in Burma, Blackwood had heard about it. A Royal Marine band had paraded daily aboard the *Queen Elizabeth* for Colours and Sunset, as well as giving additional performances for her working parties. To the unwelcome observer ashore, or any enemy agent, the battleship had appeared as usual, and ready to put to sea. He had also heard that it would have been possible to have driven a bus through the great hole in her hull.

St John said, 'You will receive your orders tomorrow.' He looked in Gaillard's direction. 'You'll have all the assistance we can offer.'

They all got to their feet as St John and his senior intelligence officer left the room. Blackwood heard one of the motor gunboat officers remark, 'Rather them than me. It's a bloody awful place!'

59

He ran his fingers over the papers and the crude aerial photographs. A dicey one, then. He examined his feelings. They were always dicey. So what?

Another of the naval officers walked across, and offered his hand.

'I'm Falconer.' He smiled. 'David, if you prefer.'

'Right, David-if-you-prefer.' Blackwood liked what he saw. 'What do you make of this? You've done it before, I gather?'

'My boat's taking you most of the way.' He hesitated, seeing it in his mind. 'And picking you up, with Lucifer.' He nodded slowly. 'Piece of cake, if you keep your head down.' He looked at the others around them, ratings gathering up the papers, making sure that nothing was missing.

He remembered what he had said about *bloody regulars.* He had been wrong.

He said, 'Care for a gin? Come and meet the real sailors. The Survivors Club!'

Blackwood glanced round, but Gaillard had gone.

'I'd like that. Can I bring my lieutenant?'

Falconer nodded. 'Bring the gin too, if you like!'

It was settled.

*　　　*　　　*

Michael Blackwood opened his eyes and waited for his senses to awaken. His eyelids felt as if they had been glued together; it was even painful to swallow.

He lifted his wrist and peered at his watch in the darkness, the luminous dial bringing him back to reality.

Three days ago they had transferred from the

60

M.G.B. to one of the secret schooners, a small, dirty, two-masted vessel with a diesel engine so ancient that it had to be started with a blow-lamp.

He listened to it now, the steady *bonk bonk bonk* which said a lot for the mechanic who was in charge of it, a cheerful Cockney from the Mile End Road who had been working in a garage until he had decided to join up.

This was another kind of war, a war of stealth and cunning, venturing so close inshore sometimes that it had been possible to see people going about their ordinary lives. Islands too, blue and beautiful at a distance, but, close to, some were little better than rocks, and still men and women managed to scrape a living from them. Another world, a world of islands, and an endless procession of local shipping. Vessels like this one, shabby and hard-worked, caiques and rickety old steam boats.

He rested his head against somebody's pack and thought of the rendezvous they had made with two other schooners the previous day. One had been from the Levant Schooner Force, manned by the same mixture of men as this. The other had been Greek, the skipper of which had appeared very friendly, especially after the wine had been produced. And ouzo, that villainous drink beloved by Greeks. Blackwood wanted to groan aloud. He could still taste it, and feel it.

What made men volunteer for this kind of work, this isolation? The desert war seemed so far away, if not in miles then in spirit. The familiar names like Tobruk and Benghazi, and now El Alamein, were household words in England. Here, in this scruffy, overcrowded schooner, they meant very little. And to the north . . . he was forcing his mind

61

to calculate, to react, because he knew the dangers of lethargy ... how far? A thousand miles, maybe less, two vast armies, German and Russian, were locked in bloody combat. From the great frozen wastes to the murderous work of street-to-street, house-to-house, room-to-room fighting, men were dying every day in their thousands. With luck, it was quick. Otherwise you died slowly, freezing and forgotten.

He thought of this schooner's skipper, a young R.N.V.R. lieutenant, who, out of uniform, could have been only another wanderer or pirate.

One evening at sunset, he had joined him by the schooner's compass and they had talked. Each hanging on to something, for only a moment, before slipping away again to go their separate ways. His name was Terry Carson, and before the war he had been a student of archaeology, moving on to Athens to continue with his studies. 'It was one dig after another,' he had said. 'But I couldn't leave it alone. The past became real.' He had gestured towards the gunwale. 'Not like this.'

For him, this was a homecoming in some ways. The Greek islands; the dust on the sea, he had called them.

Blackwood sat up carefully, every bone and muscle protesting. The other marines were sprawled throughout the boat, making the best of it as only they could.

The skipper was kneeling beside him, a pale blur where there had been total darkness before.

He said, 'We'll be able to see the place soon. We'll go in first.' He waited for Blackwood to acknowledge it. 'The other two boats can stand off. There'll be lots of local craft about, Turkish ones too. We'll have to be careful.'

Blackwood recalled the words of an intelligence officer at Alex.

The Turks are neutral, with a very small 'n'. Think of them as Germany's friends. It'll be safer all round.

He thought of the two other schooners. The tough Channel Islander, Despard, was with one, and Major Gaillard was in the third: twenty-five Royal Marines altogether. Not exactly a large force, but anything bigger would have invited disaster; he knew that from hard experience. Except that this was the sea, not a jungle and that bloody river.

The skipper held out a mug. 'Best I can do.' His teeth gleamed in the darkness. 'It's tea. Not *ouzo* this time!'

Blackwood sipped it. Sergeant-major's brew; you could have stood a spoon upright in it, if there had been a spoon. But at this moment it was perfect.

'I'll get back to my lads.' The skipper touched his arm. 'These islands are guarded by Eye-Ties. They're pretty slack most of the time. But the locals don't want to spoil things. It would only bring the Krauts down on them—they're not quite so understanding. You get the occasional E-Boat, and the Stukas from Rhodes and Crete. Otherwise, they're kept too busy elsewhere.'

Blackwood could feel the other man's need to return to the deck. Dirty, clapped-out it might be, but the schooner was his command, until Special Operations dictated otherwise.

'The informant, you trust him?'

Carson shrugged. 'Up to a point.' Then he nodded. 'Yes, I do. He's never let me down in the past.'

He could almost hear Gaillard's last words, before they had separated. 'No bloody heroics. Just get the gear or blow the thing up and pull out, right?'

He thought of his men. Some he knew, most of them were strangers, but between them they had enough expertise and impatience to start a small war of their own.

He said, 'I'll check my people now.'

A quick grunt, and the other man was gone.

The marines were already on their feet, heads bowed beneath the low deck beams. They were hating it, the squalor and the crude conditions, the smell of sweat and engine oil. If the sea had got up, they might have been too sick to clamber ashore.

The sergeant he did know, from a long way back, but like Despard he was not easily forgotten. His name was Welland, and he had joined the Royals as a boy at the School of Music. He had been a drummer and his nickname, 'Sticks', still followed him.

Behind the smart façade of a Royal Marine musician, there was another Welland. In his spare time he played in a small jazz band, not beating the Retreat but having an audience watching in awe as he performed with rhythm brushes and snare-drum. One of his interests was physical fitness, and when he had played in the clubs he had received many admiring glances from women. It suited Welland. They were his other consuming interest.

He was watching Blackwood now. 'All checked, sir. Two marksmen with rifles. All loose gear, piling swivels an' the like taped down—you'll not get a squeak out of 'em.' He sounded alert and confident.

64

Blackwood touched his lips with his tongue; they were bone-dry again. He concentrated on the two marksmen. On a small raid, they could make all the difference. It was strange to think that one had joined straight from school, and the other had been a postman in Brighton. They were equipped with Canadian Ross rifles, a stiffer bolt action than the usual Lee-Enfield, but far more accurate.

He felt the engine reducing speed, the sudden roll of the deck, and said to Welland, 'I'll take a look.'

It was still very dark, but he could discern the strengthening profile of the land and hear the gentle backwash from the nearby rocks. He felt the sling of the Sten gun biting into his shoulder, checking it in his mind, even though he knew Welland would already have done so. A small, useful weapon, *like a piece of old gas pipe,* some wag had described it. But it was comforting to know that there were thirty-two rounds in the magazine. There was always the risk of stoppages, but if the enemy was that near, it would not make much difference.

Carson said, 'Make the signal.' Clipped and tense. It was probably always like this, from deathly quiet to the whole world exploding.

The seaman used a torch, not even an Aldis.

Blackwood heard Carson murmur, 'Come on. Come on, for Christ's sake!'

He gripped the gun more tightly. It felt damp, wet even, but he knew it was not spray.

Carson snapped, 'Once more.' He half-turned towards Blackwood. 'After that, I'll have to pull out. We're sitting ducks out here!'

Another voice hissed, 'Boat, sir! Port bow!'

Blackwood heard the gentle rasp of metal as one of the crew drew back a cocking handle.

And then the boat was right alongside, as if it had jumped the last few yards. It was very small, probably a fishing dory. There were only two men in it, apparently unarmed. One was climbing aboard, and Carson hurried to meet him.

Blackwood looked at the land. It seemed to tower over them, even though he knew it was only a tiny island. A speck of dust, dust on the sea.

Carson came back. 'It's off. He says that the Italians are being replaced tomorrow.' He sounded angry. 'The Krauts are taking over.' He glanced at the dark shape by the gunwale. 'Poor bastard's shit scared. Says we should have come sooner. I thought that, too. But they don't listen, do they?'

Blackwood's mind was working rapidly, when before all he had wanted to do was sleep.

'It has to be done, Terry. You know that.' He could see it like a film, as if it had already happened. Like the paintings at Hawks Hill, the sergeant of marines cradling the mortally wounded Nelson in his arms, the marines at Peking, the Crimea. They had probably said it even then, like the young lieutenant who had been so happy with his relics and his digs. *They don't listen, do they?*

'What shall I tell him?'

Blackwood watched a solitary firefly above the water, like a tiny star.

'To lead us to the place of safety. He must know that, otherwise he wouldn't have been here.' He turned away, sensing that 'Sticks' Welland was nearby. 'If he refuses . . .'

Carson was staring at him in the darkness. 'He won't.' They were suddenly strangers.

66

To Welland he said, 'Get them moving. First section into the boat, *now.*'

Carson said, 'I'll be back as arranged. I'll warn the other boats.'

He waited until the second section had slithered down into the boat. 'He's frightened for his family, that's all.'

Blackwood nodded, moved and disturbed by Carson's sincerity, when within a few hours they might all be dead.

He reached out and gripped his arm.

'Thanks for reminding me.'

Minutes later the boat was lurching over smooth rocks, and then as quickly they were paddling back to the schooner. Blackwood heard the sudden drumbeat of the old engine as she went astern to gain sea-room.

He found the man waiting for him; his companion had already disappeared. Then he turned and saw the marines moving away in separate sections, as they were trained to do. The schooner was gone; he could not even hear the engine any more, only the sea sighing amongst the rocks and inlets. Like breathing.

The man said quietly, 'Follow. Daylight very soon. A bad time, Capitano. *Bad!'*

He swung away and headed towards the cliff.

Blackwood unslung his Sten gun, and adjusted the commando dagger at his belt. Carson's words seemed to hang in the cold air.

They don't listen, do they?

*   *   *

Sergeant Welland called, 'Here comes the next

section, sir!'

Blackwood twisted on one elbow and lowered his binoculars. The sky was completely clear, and from their rocky vantage point he could see the village. Small, white-painted houses; there could not be more than a dozen or so. How did they manage to survive on this and the other islands?

He saw Lieutenant Despard crouching down to examine the 'place of safety', as it had been described by some comedian at H.Q. A low cave with two ways in and out. You'd still have to move quickly if somebody lobbed a grenade into it.

He tried to empty his mind of useless doubts. There was one large house above the village, where the new detection device had been stored and tested. The report stated that there were three men, civilians, probably Germans, working on it. The only military presence was a dozen or so Italian soldiers. A home from home to them, he thought. Far better than the desert, or fighting partisans somewhere.

He said, 'Everything okay?'

Despard slithered down beside him. He moved easily for such a powerful man.

'No trouble, sir.' He was tugging out his own binoculars, eyes moving from the village to the dark blue of the sea. There were several local craft about, just as Carson had described them, sailing vessels, some with colourful rigs which made them look like butterflies against the dark, heaving water. 'Our guide seems to think the Germans will arrive at noon or thereabouts. He'll be off like a bloody rabbit when that happens, I'll lay odds on it!'

Blackwood glanced at the strong profile. If

68

anybody dared to help the enemy, the Germans would show no mercy. There would be bloody reprisals, like some of the horrific cases he had heard about in Yugoslavia and in France. Despard had spoken without pity for the unknown guide. Was he thinking of his own home in the Channel Islands? Were there traitors and collaborators there also, ready to betray friends and neighbours merely to gain some advantage from the occupying power?

Despard had made no comment about the absence of the third section under Gaillard. Perhaps he was too well trained, hardened against the unexpected. The third schooner might have been too late for a stealthy approach; it could have broken down. Blackwood said, 'It's up to us.' He was ticking off the objectives as he spoke. 'Guard hut first—the wireless transmitter is supposed to be in there. Then the road from the village. Look, where those goats are.'

Despard steadied his glasses, his beret tugged forward to keep the light from his eyes.

'That's not too difficult.' He grinned. 'They'll have a fit when they see us!'

Blackwood smiled. Then he beckoned to their guide, wondering briefly how Carson had come to know him, and to trust him.

He was aware of the man's anxiety, as if he were only used to this kind of work by night. He was older than expected, with dark, liquid eyes: the face of a scholar, not of a fisherman or a labourer. Blackwood could smell his fear, and felt a sudden pity for him.

'I shall move forward in half an hour.'

The man nodded, barely able to swallow. 'The

Italian guards hoist their flag soon. They will all be there. Except the officer. He is in the house with the Germans.' He almost spat out the word. 'There are two other men down by the jetty. They watch the boats.' He stared at the sky until his eyes watered. 'Tonight is better.'

Blackwood saw Despard grimace.

'That is too late. For us.' He looked across the man's bent shoulders. 'Warn the others, George. We don't want to be caught with our pants down.' He turned back to the Greek, and did not see Despard's rare revelation of surprise, that he had called him by name. 'When we fall back . . .'

The guide patted his arm, nervously, fearfully. 'I will be ready to take you to the boats, Capitano.'

Blackwood raised himself on his haunches and watched a file of marines moving into a shallow gully. Not the sick, complaining men with whom he had shared the last few days. Loping along the uneven ground as if they knew it well, each man with his weapon held across his body, eyes moving from sector to sector. Ready for anything.

He said, 'You are a brave man. Try not to forget that!'

He stood up slowly and looked down the slope. Not a place, only another objective, but it seemed to challenge him. People lived here, as best they could, no matter what flag flew or which cult dictated the orders. They had so little to sustain them; why risk it because of someone else's war?

He sensed that the Greek was shivering. No one would care if men like him lived or died. No one would even hear of it. Perhaps, after all, theirs was the highest kind of courage.

Sergeant Welland was beside him again. 'Ready,

sir.'

Blackwood looked from right to left, but could see only two men, one already prone with his Ross rifle trained on the houses. He measured the distance to the low wall. There were no gates, only a barbed-wire barrier which had been pulled to one side. A goat was munching something by the entrance, but paused to stare with yellow eyes as if it had sensed the nearness of danger.

It was unreal, like a badly made film running in slow motion.

Blackwood was not sure what he had been expecting, possibly a bugle, like the sounding of Colours on board a cruiser or a battleship in those other, impossible days of peace . . . Instead, it was a shrill whistle, like that of a railway guard.

He heard the stamp of boots, and then saw the Italian green, white and red flag jerking to a spindly masthead outside the largest building. He leaped forward, the Sten gun level with his hip as he shouted, 'Now!'

An Italian N.C.O. was saluting, and a sentry was presenting arms to the flag as the marines burst in on them. If it had not been so vital it might have been comical, the expressions of utter incredulity and shock, Sergeant Welland pausing only to snatch the rifle from the guard as he yelled, '*Stand still!* Anybody who moves is a dead 'un!' It would have sounded the same in any language.

Weapons clattered down, and Blackwood ran past the confusion and kicked open the door, his finger tight on the trigger, his body stiffened, as if anticipating the crushing agony of a bullet.

One shot echoed across the yard, and he swung round in time to see a shadow drop past the

71

window; the marksmen must have seen somebody on the roof. On and on, feet pounding behind him, doors kicked open, grenades with pins drawn ready to silence anyone reckless or stupid enough to show resistance.

And all at once it was quiet. Just the faint hum of electricity, and someone groaning unhappily from the wireless room. Exactly as the plan of action had described.

Welland snapped, 'Somebody's in there, sir!'

Blackwood nodded, and levelled the Sten. Welland poised like a rugby forward converting a try and kicked the door with all his strength. It burst open and Blackwood raised the Sten, his mind excluding everything but the man who was sitting bolt upright in the bed. The officer, who never presented himself for the daily flag-raising. His uniform tunic hung on a chairback, and he seemed unable to speak as the marines dashed into the room and positioned themselves by another door and the shuttered window.

Welland rasped, *'Up!'* and stared as another face appeared over the crumpled blanket. A woman, and naked by the look of it. Not young, but 'Sticks' Welland licked his lips approvingly. Not to be sneezed at!

There was a battered wardrobe on one side of the room. Blackwood opened the door and poked at the hanging clothing with the Sten's short snout.

'Get dressed! Cover yourself!'

He swung round, his mind cringing to the shot, and saw the Italian officer falling slowly from the bed. In one hand was a heavy pistol, which he must have been pulling from beneath the pillow when Welland had seen it. The woman did not scream;

72

she was beyond it. She did not even attempt to hide her nakedness as someone dragged her from the bed and threw her a blanket.

Despard had appeared in the doorway, his eyes everywhere, his gun quite steady as he glanced from Blackwood to the dead officer, and then to the woman by the bed.

Then he stooped and tore the pistol from the dead man's hand.

He said, 'Useful.' He looked at Blackwood again. 'She'll have to find another companion, eh?'

It was there again. Blackwood tried to clear his racing thoughts. Despard remembering, perhaps. Or comparing . . .

A marine burst into the room, and skidded to a halt as he saw the small drama, Welland's gunsmoke still hanging in the unmoving air, the dead Italian's blood shimmering on the floor.

'A boat's bin sighted!'

Welland glared at him. 'A boat's bin sighted, sir! Where the hell do you think you are?'

He was so angry that Blackwood wanted to laugh, and knew if he did he would be unable to stop.

The man stammered, 'Large launch. Standing into the anchorage. Corporal Gilmour says it's a Kraut.' He winced at Welland's expression, and added, 'Sir!'

Blackwood said, 'We'll have to blow the place. Get what you can from the office, or safe if there is one. Put the Italians under guard.'

Despard laughed. 'They're too shit scared to breathe, let alone run away!'

Marines were hurrying around, as if it was only another training exercise, each man intent on his

73

part of it. Explosives, detonators, fuses. *No foul-ups*.

Blackwood paused to look at the secret equipment, silent now, with all the power switched off. There must be a generator somewhere; that had to be destroyed, too.

The Germans had arrived early. Maybe it was just as well. They would know this was a bona fide raid by the enemy, and there would be no excuse for reprisals among the civilians. Or would there?

'Eye-Ties are locked up, sir!' Blackwood smiled at the man, but could not recall his name.

Despard murmured, 'I could deal with them, if you like.'

Blackwood said, 'No. We've done enough. Let's get the hell out of here, while we still can.' He could have ordered it, or simply remained silent, and he knew that Despard would have acted upon his offer. And if he had been in command . . .

All at once it was over, and as they ran along the rough track he saw the guide waiting for them. Others would know the man's role in this lightning raid. Would he carry the blame, and pay the price for it? And the terrified woman, how would she explain her part in it when the Germans took charge here?

The air quivered to one and then to a second explosion, and when he stopped to look back he saw the smoke spreading across the sky like dirty stains.

He wanted to speak to the guide, but he had vanished.

And all they had were a few documents, not much to show for the risk and the danger.

It hit him then, not merely pride in this handful

74

of men who had performed so well, but elation. *They had not lost a single man.*

He watched the marines wading waist-deep in the water towards the waiting schooners, aware of the urgency, and yet somehow unable to move. Eventually it would reach the Pit, that strange underground headquarters off Trafalgar Square where they had once stored a million bottles of wine.

He checked that the Sten was at 'safe' and strode after the others.

It was the same dirty schooner. He knew it was the receding madness of action, but for some reason it mattered to him.

Like the girl, Joanna, who had known about this place. And had cared.

CHAPTER FOUR

NO TURNING BACK

The air temperature was high, in the seventies, unusual even for Alex at this time of the year. And in the long operations room which had once been a king's boatshed, it was like an oven.

Blackwood had positioned himself at a slight angle from one of the overhead revolving fans, but was barely aware of it. His shirt was like a wet rag, and he could feel his back sticking to the chair. It was all he could do to concentrate on the intelligence officer's leisurely summary of Operation *Lucifer*.

He was tired and he knew it was the aftermath of

the raid, and the seemingly endless passage in the schooner, some of which had been well within Turkish waters, until they had eventually sighted the moustache-like bow waves of three motor gunboats.

Not once had they seen an enemy aircraft, or any kind of pursuit; that was almost as unnerving as the actual raid. He had watched the schooners falling further and further astern, and wondered at their chances of survival. The M.G.B.s had tied up at H.M.S. *Mosquito* this morning, but there had been no time to rest, let alone write a letter or sleep.

He looked around at the others, only a small gathering this time. A few staff officers in white or khaki drill, their shirts and tunics blotched with sweat stains. At the head of the table Commander Walter St John was as neat and unruffled as before; even in his Number Fives he looked cool, untroubled by the oppressive heat. It was hard to believe that Christmas was only days away, that in Hampshire there would be frost on the hedges, and that old Harry Payne would be breaking the ice in the moat so that the ducks could use it. If someone had not stolen them for the pot.

Blackwood had had almost no chance to speak with Gaillard. As suspected, his schooner had broken down, and Gaillard had commented briefly, 'I knew you could handle it.' Then he had added, 'Any good officer should!'

He was sitting here now, arms folded, biting his lower lip as he listened to the end of the report. Strange that it did not sound like the raid Blackwood remembered at all; it might have been about some other group.

76

He tried again to stay alert. The report was not the reason they were here in any case; the full account would have reached London ages ago, and had probably been filed away. A thing of the past.

He studied the army officer seated beside St John. His name was Jocelyn Naismith, a newly appointed brigadier who had apparently made quite a reputation for himself in all aspects of Combined Operations. He had served in the Norwegian campaign and in Crete, in various capacities with the First and Eighth Armies. And now he was here.

Of him, Gaillard had remarked curtly, 'Naismith? Hopes to become the youngest general in the British army since Wolfe, God help us!'

He had a square, military face, with the neatly trimmed moustache affected by so many soldiers. Keen, grey-blue eyes, *steely,* a newspaper had described them, and a mouth so firmly held that it never seemed to relax.

There was a sudden silence.

St John did not get to his feet for so small an assembly. He merely said, '*Lucifer* was a complete success. Eventually the enemy will be forced to deploy more ships and men to oversee their occupied territory, even the smallest islands.' He gave Gaillard a thin smile. 'Well done.'

Then he turned towards the square-faced brigadier.

'Any comments, sir?'

Naismith gave what might have been a shrug. 'I think it was performed well enough. You will know my views on such isolated actions, the ever-present possibility that the cost will outweigh the result. It proved that combined operations *work*. Now it will

77

be worth seeing if the results here are equally gratifying.'

He looked suddenly at Blackwood.

'You were in charge, for reasons already stated. You took the Italian garrison by surprise and would doubtless have removed all or some of the secret equipment, had the German relief forces not arrived?'

St John said, 'I called for these officers to attend. It is their right, after what they have achieved. This is not an interrogation, sir.' He did not raise his voice, but his displeasure was clear enough.

Naismith lifted one hand and answered almost gently, 'It is also my right, Commander St John.' His eyes returned to Blackwood. 'Is that so?'

Blackwood was on his feet, although he did not remember standing up. He felt dirty and unkempt in front of the others, and angered by the implication.

'I would, sir. But it would have taken time, and that we did not have.'

'Quite. But there were some German technicians present. Could they not have been *persuaded* to speed up the process? You are a Royal Marine Commando. You will have to become accustomed to the realities of war.'

Blackwood thought of Despard, and of Welland's swift action, which had saved his life when he had turned his back on the Italian to search the wardrobe.

He said quietly, 'They were civilians, sir. It was not within my authority, nor was it my intention.'

'Because of the unexpectedly early arrival of the Germans?'

Blackwood found that he was quite calm, like

78

that moment when he had paused to look back at the island.

'No, sir. Because I *am* accustomed to the realities of war, and I see no point in inhumanity, for inhumanity's sake alone.'

Naismith had thin, ginger eyebrows. They rose sharply as he said, 'But you are of a famous family, I believe? Your father was not unknown, even in the army. What would he say, I wonder? Gallipoli, and Flanders—no place for the soft-hearted, I'd have thought.'

Gaillard cleared his throat and said sharply, 'The Royal Marines were at Gallipoli, and at the Somme, sir. I'm not much of a historian, but I seem to recall that it was because the army had made a hash of it!'

Surprisingly, the interruption seemed to please the brigadier. He smiled and nodded. 'Well spoken, Major Gaillard! A man of action. What I need. What we all need in the coming months!' Then he said abruptly, 'I think that will be all.' And to St John, 'No need for junior officers at this time, eh?'

Blackwood turned. There had been a movement behind him, and it was Despard, as he had known it would be. Big, straight-backed, expressionless.

He said, 'I was there, sir. Had Captain Blackwood fallen, I would have been in command.'

The brigadier pressed his fingertips together. 'Continue. I am interested in that. What might you have done?'

Despard looked at some point above Naismith's left shoulder. 'I am a Channel Islander, sir. I've been in the Corps since I was a boy—Stonehouse Barracks was more of a home to me than Jersey.'

Naismith said, 'I'm afraid I don't see the point of

this. Perhaps we might adjourn, Commander St John?'

Despard continued in the same unemotional tone, as if Naismith had said nothing; as if he was talking to someone else entirely.

'My mother and sister did not leave before the Germans invaded. Maybe they never intended to. It was their home, you see. One day, some German made a play for my sister. She laughed at him. Made him look a fool in front of his mates, I expect. She was a fine girl. Very pretty, too.' Then he looked directly into Naismith's eyes. 'For that, they arrested her. Later she was taken to mainland France. I heard she died in a concentration camp. An' for what?' He seemed to restrain some impulse to step forward. 'Yes, I'd probably have shot all of them dead that day, even if there had been no secret equipment, no nothing!' He lifted his arm and pointed to Blackwood, although he did not take his eyes from Naismith's. 'But for Captain Blackwood, I would probably have done all that, an' more.' His arm fell to his side. 'But then, I'd have been just like those bastards. I'll never forget what he did for me on that bloody island!'

St John rose to his feet. 'I think that says rather a lot, sir.'

The man who intended to be the youngest general since Wolfe picked up his cap and swagger stick and smiled. 'Time for a cool drink, I think.' A door was dragged open and, with St John beside him, he left the room.

Gaillard snorted. 'I can see we're all going to get along splendidly!'

Blackwood glanced at the intelligence officer, and did not understand the wink.

Gaillard said sharply, 'Something big is coming up. Brigadier Naismith will be in overall charge. Until our special company reaches here, we don't have the numbers for any operation of size.' He slapped his leg angrily. 'Of all the infernal luck!'

Blackwood looked back at Despard. There was no sign now of the intensity and the pain which had made him speak openly of something which must be a lingering nightmare.

'Coming for a drink?'

Despard shook his head. 'They've invited me to have a jar or two in the sergeants' mess. I sometimes think I never should have left it!'

Gaillard watched him go, and remarked, 'He'll get over it. Coming?'

Blackwood looked around at the folded maps and charts, the steel cabinets containing the aerial reconnaissance photographs. All tucked away, until the next time. *Something big.*

He said evenly, 'Why not, sir? We're all on the same side.'

*   *   *

Even as a very young subaltern in the cruiser *Rutland,* which had spent much of her commission in the Mediterranean Fleet, Blackwood had learned the ways and pitfalls of street bazaars, the souks of Egypt. To hesitate was the first sign of weakness; to bargain could end in disaster. You always had to remember that *they* were the experts, and you the victim.

But it was good to get away from the base, from the endless speculation, the occasional news of the war being fought everywhere else. He had

81

pondered over Brigadier Naismith's brief appearance, trying to fit a commando-style operation into any obvious pattern. The Eighth Army was still advancing, whereas on the other side of the map the newly established American and British forces were bogged down by appalling weather, torrential rain which had turned the desert into a quagmire.

He walked slowly beneath some overhanging blinds, ignoring the outthrust rolls of carpet and the offerings of large lampshades. Just what the average squaddie or sailor on a precious run ashore would need, he thought. There were bargains if you looked hard enough, but he had known some terrible brawls caused by sailors who had been sold ancient Egyptian relics, only to discover the *Made in Birmingham* stamp once they had returned on board.

The streets were a milling throng of khaki, with a sprinkling of sailors and even fewer marines. Australians, South Africans, Gurkhas, and soldiers from the Free Polish army. Nobody seemed to salute. It was just as well.

It would be Christmas in two days' time; he had seen some wilting paper decorations in the base wardroom. A brave link with that other life. There had been no mail, nor would there be until things settled down. He often wondered how his sister was progressing in her new life with the Wrens, a far cry, he thought, from the countryside and her bookkeeping for the estate. She would miss her riding . . .

He saw some soldiers pause by a line of stalls to watch something, grinning, and enjoying the spectacle.

A tall, robed figure in a fez was holding out a length of pale khaki material. It was common enough here for servicemen to have a lightweight rig run up in a few hours by street-side tailors. It was known unofficially as 'bazaar khaki drill', and was infinitely more comfortable than the regulation serge. Most of the officers and senior rates at the base wore it, and with the ever-growing diversity of uniforms in the Eighth Army, it hardly raised an eyebrow any more.

He stopped in his tracks as he heard a woman's voice exclaiming, '*No*. Please understand. It's *not* what I want.'

The grins on every side widened as the vendor solemnly continued with his patter while attempting to drape some of the cloth over the woman's shoulder.

No wonder the soldiers were enjoying themselves. It was rare to see a woman here, and a woman in uniform was like something from another planet.

The uniform was the blue-grey of the Royal Air Force, and Blackwood was instantly reminded of the W.A.A.F. officer in the train. It was impossible to accept that it was little more than a month ago. He should be used to it now, but he was not.

The soldiers had realised that he was amongst them, and they parted but did not disperse, unwilling to leave something so interesting.

The W.A.A.F. turned and saw him, her eyes moving to his face with something like disbelief. Shock.

Blackwood reached out and took her hand. It was not cold now.

'Joanna!' He raised the hand and examined her

83

cuff. Two stripes. But even that eluded him.

'I'm sorry . . .' He tried again; it was hopeless. She could not be here. 'Flight Officer Gordon. I don't believe it. I might never have known.'

She said, 'Captain Blackwood. I thought you'd gone. You see . . .' The khaki material was covering her shoulder now, the vendor unimpressed by their meeting. It was business.

She said, 'I was passing through.' Nothing was making sense. He had not released her hand.

'Seeing you like this, in uniform, I thought I was halfway round the bend!'

Then she laughed, her teeth very white against skin which was showing the first hint of a tan.

Blackwood looked at the man in the fez. 'How long?' and then, to her, 'Would you like it?' He felt her hand move in his as she nodded. He tapped his breast pocket. *The language* . . . 'Two hours. Then we come back, okay?'

Doubt flashed through the man's eyes. But this was an officer, and the woman was dressed like one. And anyway, he would make certain it would do for another if need be. He beamed. 'Very good, Colonel! Fine fit, you see!'

The watching soldiers had finally gone, and the throng in the street was moving again like an unblocked stream.

And they were walking together, their arms occasionally brushing, neither knowing how to begin.

She said, 'I thought of you a lot after you left Gib. Wondered how you got on.'

He said, 'I won't ask you how you knew, but I'm fine.' He wanted to stop and hold her, like any ordinary man. 'I had no idea you were in the

84

services.'

She glanced down at her tunic, and shrugged lightly. 'My brother was in the R.A.F. His name was Mike as well.'

Was. To most people it might mean little or nothing. To him, it said everything. Was . . .

She turned to look at a man with a performing monkey, and he watched her. The dark hair curling around the regulation cap with its crown and spread-winged albatross. The curve of her lip; even the tiny mole which had remained in his mind.

They walked on, and she remarked, 'How is your major? Still angry with everything?'

Something to say. She was recovering herself, looking for a way out.

He said abruptly, 'I want to see you again. Soon. I don't care how, but I'll manage it.' He was pleading, just as he knew she was listening.

'I'm not sure.' She hesitated, testing the sound. 'Mike.' Then she nodded. 'It suits you.' She smiled openly, without reserve. 'Mike.'

There was a chorus of shouted insults as an army despatch rider roared past in a cloud of dust and fumes. For an instant Blackwood saw her sudden alarm. Anxiety.

'It's all right,' he said.

She turned and glanced at him. She was quite slight, not as tall as Diane. She barely came up to his shoulder.

He said, 'I know a place where we can have some awful coffee. Then we'll come back and collect your K.D.' He almost held his breath, seeing the thoughts, the reservations in her face.

Then she said, 'Good idea. D'you think it really will fit me?'

They both laughed and some soldiers turned to stare. The same looks he had received when he had kissed his sister good-bye. *All right for some.* They walked on, past the brassware and the rugs, the vases and the garish robes.

She said, 'I'm awaiting passage. It's not a secret.' She did not look at him. 'Not to you, anyway. They put me in a house over in Rosetta, d'you know it?'

'I was there once, on my way to Cairo. I forget why.'

'Up to no good, I expect. The Chief of Staff's wife is staying there, officially. She's a nice old stick. It's taken over by the military now.'

They found a café; it was not much of a place, but it was almost empty. A grim-faced proprietor brought them small cups of thick black coffee.

They sat facing one another beneath the shadow of a faded blind. Each had one hand on the table, close but not touching; the other was kept moving back and forth like a fan. The flies in Alex were as persistent as the beggars.

The coffee was surprisingly good. When he looked up again he realised that she was gazing at him. Seeking something. Or maybe, like Despard, comparing.

He brushed a fly from her sleeve, but she did not flinch or draw away.

'Can we meet? It's not just a game, not to me. You see, I've never known anyone like you before . . .' He broke off. She must have heard that line so many times; it was as clumsy as *my wife doesn't understand me!*

He found her hand was resting on his, so lightly that it could have been an accident, although he knew it was not.

She said, 'I shall have to report to my superior this afternoon.'

'I'll come with you . . .'

She shook her head, then, after the smallest hesitation, removed her cap.

'No. I think that might be a mistake.' She did not explain.

Perhaps there was somebody else she knew here? No, it was not that. He waited, knowing that if he pursued it he would spoil everything.

She seemed to come to a decision, as if she had been having an argument with herself.

'You could come to the house.' Doubtfully. 'It's a long way.'

'I'll steal a Tiger tank if need be!'

She watched his eagerness, the impulsiveness which was the very young man again.

'Tomorrow, then?'

She looked down at their hands, the empty cups, with the flies moving eagerly around them. 'Christmas Eve!'

He stood up to call the proprietor and did not see her eyes fall to the webbing holster at his hip. Then she picked up her cap and looked at the dust on the badge. She would not turn back, not this time.

Blackwood examined his watch. 'Let's go and see how far your tailor has got.' He wanted to laugh aloud, to share this sudden, unexpected happiness.

She said suddenly, 'I did enjoy that.' She took his arm and guided him into another shadow.

She said, 'It will be crowded as soon as we move.' She lifted her chin. 'We must remember all officer-like qualities.' She sounded very tense. 'Kiss me. It'll be a secret.'

Their lips barely touched but he could feel her, taste her, and even though it could not possibly be happening, he knew he must not let her go. It was never wise to say or think such things in wartime. But in the noisy, crowded souk, the war was suddenly a long, long way away.

*   *   *

The khaki staff car stood outside the imposing house, the engine revving in time with the driver's foot.

'I'll be here at midnight, old son!' His eyes moved to the house; he did not bother to hide his curiosity. 'You be ready, or I'll probably turn into a pumpkin!'

Blackwood smiled. The paymaster lieutenant at the wheel was also the S.N.O.'s secretary at the base. He would know the Chief of Staff's wife was staying here. Perhaps she would refuse to let him in.

'I'll be waiting, don't worry.' The lieutenant was going to Cairo to collect some documents, or so he claimed. A good piss-up, more likely.

He watched the car roar away in a rolling bank of dust, and realised for the first time that there was a military police jeep parked a little way along the road. The sunlight reflected from the windscreen and he could not see the occupants, but somehow he knew they were observing him.

He walked up to the gates and looked at the house. Grand but shabby. Someone wealthy must have lived here once.

He was early; the paymaster lieutenant had driven like a maniac. He walked up to the door, his shoes loud on the loose stones. There had been flowers here, and a fountain, which was empty and covered with blown sand. Perhaps the owners had fled when Rommel's tanks had been reported making their final approach. It was said that a lot of people had made a run for it.

The door opened, and after the fierce sunlight it was like walking into a blacked-out room. And then he saw her. She was standing by another open door, watching him, one hand holding a towel to her hair. She wore a long bathrobe.

He was early.

She said, 'Come into the garden. I was just having a swim.' She laughed, he thought nervously. 'Salt water and none too clean, but it's sheer heaven for all that!' She waited for him to join her, but kept her distance. 'I'm so glad you could make it. I thought something might turn up and prevent you from coming.'

They stood side by side and looked at the swimming pool, where her footprints were already drying in the sun.

She said, 'It's like the *Marie Celeste* here. You keep expecting the real owners to walk in.'

He asked, 'The Chief of Staff's wife?'

'Lady Duncan?' She smiled. 'Tinker, as she likes to be called. She's in Cairo. Be back some time tomorrow. She's here on business, looking into the facilities at various hospitals, for the men coming back from the desert. She's at the Royal Military Hospital today, if anyone needs her.' She saw his face. 'What is it? Did I remind you of something?'

He took her arm and they walked across the tiled terrace. 'Strange coincidence, that's all. My father was there after Gallipoli, when he was

89

wounded.' He recalled with sudden clarity the only time he had seen his father's back, and the great star-shaped wounds running diagonally across it. He had never seen them again, as if his father had been ashamed of them. All he could remember was his own sense of awe, and his pride.

A white-coated servant had appeared from nowhere, and Blackwood heard them exchange a few words in French.

She faced him again. 'He's Tunisian. My French is better than his English.' She laughed, suddenly untroubled, happier than he had yet seen her. 'He'll bring some tea, or something stronger, if you like?' She looked at him in that characteristic, direct way. 'My grandmother was French, you know. We lived in Marseilles for a time. My father was a shipping agent then—we were always going back and forth.' The mood changed again, and afterwards Blackwood thought it had been like a cloud passing across moonlight. 'Poor Dad . . . he took it badly when Mike was killed. His heart's not good. And he worries a lot. Too much . . .'

'Your brother . . .' He hesitated.

'It's all right. I don't mind you asking about him.'

'Was he much older than you?'

She dropped the towel and combed her hair with her fingers.

'He was nineteen when he went down. My kid brother. I was already in the W.A.A.F. I sometimes wonder if it was because of me . . .' She did not go on.

He said, 'You mustn't even think it, Joanna.'

She glanced at him, startled perhaps by the easy use of her name.

'That was a nice thing to say.' She smiled. 'Mike.'

90

He heard the servant clattering crockery in the room they had just left.

He said, 'I saw some redcaps parked along the road just now.'

Her fingers paused in her hair. 'I must look a mess.' She seemed to recall what he had said. 'The M.P.s? Yes, they're always there, apparently.' Then, 'That uniform you bought for me—how much was it?'

'It's a present. For Christmas. I'd have got something a bit more exciting if I'd only known we'd meet again like that.'

She stood up almost abruptly. Against the coloured tiles her bare feet looked small, vulnerable.

'Would you like to see the house? Not as big as your place, I'll bet. Hawks Hill, that's what it's called, right?'

She slipped her hand through his arm and together they walked past a carefully laid table. He could sense her sudden tension. He did not realise it matched his own.

He said, 'I'll take you there one day. It's a bit of a shambles at the moment. Land girls and Italian prisoners of war, as far as I can make out.'

She did not look at him. 'I'd like that.'

They were at the top of a staircase. It was pure marble. Whoever they were, they must have been very rich.

She pointed along a passageway. 'That's where Lady Duncan abides.' She giggled. 'Tinker. A bit of a battle-axe, but she's quite sweet really, though she'd hate to admit it!' There was a long pause. 'Would you like to see the "bazaar K.D."? Was that what you called it?'

'I would.'

It was a large room, with slatted louvres at the windows which he sensed would overlook the garden and the pool, where two strangers had been standing together.

He saw the khaki drill jacket lying on a chair, her uniform cap on another.

She picked up the jacket, and said, 'What time is your car coming?'

'Midnight. But if you think Lady Duncan will be back before that, I can call the base . . .'

She turned towards him and said, 'Eight hours.' She put out her hand as he tried to hold her, to reassure her. 'It's not all that much.'

He said, 'It's a lifetime.'

She let her hand fall. 'Then make it a lifetime.' She held her face against his while he touched her neck and her damp hair. He felt her back stiffen as he found her spine and pulled her closer to him, until they were together. Then she freed herself and gripped his hand, as she had in the café.

She could not look into his eyes, but watched his hands on her robe.

Then she faced him again, her chin uplifted, her voice quite steady as the robe fell around her ankles.

'Take me, Mike. Love me. It's what you want, isn't it?'

She kissed him, even as he picked her up and laid her on the bed. She seemed so light, so supple that he ached for her.

He sat beside her, holding her, exploring her, until she drew him down and kissed him again. There was no hesitation, no lingering doubt or reserve. Their mouths were pressed together, open, their tongues driving away all caution.

He threw off his clothes, and she exclaimed, 'You're all brown! You have a beautiful body, Mike!'

Only once did the anxiety show itself. 'It's been so long. I want it to last.' She fell back, her eyes tightly closed as his shadow moved over her, then she arched her back to find him, to receive him. She cried out, the sound like an echo in the empty house, but the pain passed within a second, and she returned his passion with a fervour which broke down any remaining control.

Afterwards, she lay beneath him, her heart like a small, trapped hammer against his body. When he moved as though to leave her she gripped his shoulders until her nails broke the skin. 'No. Stay. I want to feel you like this . . . a part of me.'

Later, how long he did not know, she left him and walked across the room, her nakedness somehow natural and without artifice or hesitation. She returned with two glasses of wine. They had probably been chilled, but he would not have noticed. They kissed, and kissed again, and her hands aroused him in a way he would have thought impossible.

'I love you.' He scarcely recognised his own voice. He was so used to covering emotion, hiding his feelings and his fears, that to say it was like being freed from something.

She whispered, 'I couldn't wait. I needed you. Don't talk of love—just be glad we found it and took it while we could!'

Eventually they left the bed, and Blackwood put on his uniform.

The staff car arrived an hour early, but the

93

S.N.O.'s secretary did not come to the house. In his job, he probably knew all about discretion.

She walked with him to the big room, lit now by a solitary lamp. The untouched plates and cups had disappeared.

When she opened the door he felt her shiver. The night was much colder; this was a place of extremes and contrasts.

Blackwood saw the shaded lights of the car, and the jeep parked in the same place. Or maybe it was a different one.

She put her arms around his neck and raised herself on her bare toes.

'Touch me.' She gasped as he opened her robe and stroked her breasts, her hip.

'I shall see you soon, Joanna. I must.'

She smiled in the darkness, and then laid her fingers on his mouth.

'Don't hope for too much.'

And then he was moving down to the gates. Once he turned, thinking she had called after him, but the door was closed, black against the peeling white stucco.

The paymaster lieutenant was apologetic. 'Sorry, old son.' He had seen the girl's robe in the doorway. 'There's a bit of a flap on, I'm told. Nothing we can't handle.' He let in the clutch and pulled out on to the road.

Blackwood concentrated on the dim light given off by the shaded beams. He must remember every last detail. What she said. What they did. How she had given herself without shame or restraint. He could still feel her, like the moment he had entered her. And the scratches on his shoulders where she had clung to him. Her warmth when he had shown

94

concern for the fading bruises on her body. No wonder she hated flying.

A bit of a flap on. There usually was. And it was almost Christmas Day. But afterwards, he would see her again, as friends, as lovers. As one. He thought then of his father. How pleased he would have been.

*   *   *

The girl stood quite still in the same room, facing the wall mirror, testing each reaction; testing her strength.

She could hear the muffled murmur of voices from downstairs, the driver, and maybe one of the military policemen, the redcaps. She straightened her tie and ensured that the collar was properly attached and fastened. Then she put on her jacket, remembering his face in the crowd, raising her arm to look at the two stripes on the sleeve. Heard his voice again. *Flight Officer Gordon.* She fastened each button, slowly and deliberately, watching her reflection all the time. A stranger again.

She could see the bed behind her, where they had loved with such abandon, such need. In the past, it had been so different. He had been experienced, and often demanding, but even then she had known he was measuring each hour they had together.

But nothing like this. She had not merely submitted; she had returned his love in ways she had hardly dared to contemplate. Given herself again and again.

She glanced at the case and the paper parcel by the door. She had packed the khaki drill tunic and slacks last of all, holding on to the memory. She shook her head angrily. It was no use; memories would destroy her.

They had talked, too, lying side by side on that bed. About her brother who had been killed, and about his own doubts, of which she knew he had never spoken to anyone else. Of his admiration and pride in men like her brother, like so many of his young marines. They had volunteered because they had believed in it; because they cared.

She had watched him, his profile etched against the mosquito netting.

'I had no such moral commitment. It was my life, my career, whether I wanted it or not. Because I am a Blackwood and all that it means. I needed to see what drew such men to the Corps, to the real war. Not seen through a bomb sight at ten thousand feet, or the rangefinder of a cruiser's gun turret . . . or even through the periscope as it comes down, while the submarine is already diving, twisting away, when the torpedoes are still speeding towards their target.'

She had said, 'And have you seen it now?'

He had rolled over, and laid his head very gently between her breasts.

He did not need to answer her question.

She heard Lady Duncan's voice; she had arrived in the middle of the night. It was time.

The sealed envelope had been waiting for her; she had heard the motor-cycle sputtering away. The message was as brief as it was urgent.

Lastly she placed her cap on her dark hair, and stared at herself in the mirror. Then she picked up the case and the small parcel, and took one final look at the room. It was Christmas Day.

She opened the door, and heard the conversation stop instantly, like a radio being turned off.

It had been beautiful, the most wonderful thing which had ever happened to her. And, perhaps, to him.

She closed the door behind her. But it was just a dream.

'Ah, there you are, my dear. The car's here for you!'

Only a dream.

CHAPTER FIVE

'DON'T ASK. JUST DO IT!'

Captain Mike Blackwood lay on his back, his hands behind his head while he stared into the darkness. He was fully dressed and wide awake, his ears picking out the motor gunboat's internal sounds, the muted tremble of the big Rolls-Royce engines, the clatter of loose gear, or someone moving on deck above his bunk. Sounds which had become familiar in so short a time since they had climbed aboard, yet again under cover of darkness to maintain any vestige of secrecy in such a crowded harbour.

The M.G.B.'s small company were taking it well, he thought. Overcrowded at the best of times, it had been no easy thing to accommodate ten Royal Marines and two officers. They had all somehow found spaces to sit down, even sleep, once they had become used to the motion and the occasional bursts of speed, to avoid other vessels, to dodge enemy aircraft, or merely to make up distance: to the marines it could have been anything.

It was the same gunboat in which Blackwood had been carried to the schooners before *Lucifer*. Even the purpose behind that seemed hard to understand any more; it refused to fit into a pattern.

Like his men, Blackwood was fully trained, and probably more experienced than any of them except the characters like 'Sticks' Welland, and the withdrawn Despard, trained to assess any situation as he found it, and to react accordingly. Doubt and personal safety did not come into it. In his mind he could picture the chart as if he had just been studying it with Gaillard and the boat's skipper, Lieutenant David Falconer, the veteran who had once been a schoolmaster. At least his pupils would know the truth about this war, if he ever went back to teaching. If he lived that long. On the first night at sea in company with two other M.G.B.s, Falconer had touched on it only briefly. This little special squadron had consisted of eight boats when he had arrived in the Med. Now there were only three. He was not resigned, and not bitter. It was his war; the rest was somebody else's problem.

It had reminded Blackwood of his father, and one of those rare evenings at Hawks Hill when he had spoken about that other war, of the appalling waste and horrific casualty lists, because the general staff had been unable to adapt to a type of warfare which had outreached their experience and imagination.

He had said more than once, 'You should always remember. Individuals can win or lose a war. Not some unthinking mass of men, a flag on a map, or simply because it is something which needs doing. Remember the lonely men, the ones who are always on the prongs of an advance, or those left to cover a retreat. The *individuals*.'

Blackwood often recalled those words. He had thought of them at the hastily convened conference in the operations room after his whirlwind drive from Rosetta. As the S.N.O.'s secretary had commented, 'There's a bit of a flap on.'

Blackwood had imagined there had been a reverse in the desert war; even after all the Desert Rats' success, it could still happen. Or perhaps another convoy had been attacked, the one which would eventually bring the full marine detachment to Alex. Or that the Americans who had landed in North Africa in Operation Torch had been overwhelmed by the more experienced and hardened troops of the Afrika Korps. But again, that was another war, and despite all the efforts of war correspondents and broadcasters there was not much love for the Americans. In England there was a standard reply when asked what was wrong with the Yanks anyway? *Three things. They're overpaid, oversexed and over here!* In Devon, Blackwood had seen the same sentiment scrawled on the back of an army Bedford truck. *Don't cheer, girls. We're British!*

But the conference had nothing to do with allied friction. There had been various expressions of surprise and even annoyance when Commander St John had made his announcement. Admiral Darlan, the governor-general of French North Africa, was dead. Not killed in an accident, or murdered by terrorists as well he might have been, but shot by a haphazard assassin who had walked into his room and emptied a revolver into him without threat or explanation.

The ordinary squaddie in the line or Jolly Jack bargain-hunting in the souk might have been excused for saying, *So what? Who cares?* Darlan was, after all, a Nazi puppet, who had shown his bias by accepting high office from France's new German masters, rather than making any attempt to rouse resistance against the enemy.

In England, there was only bitterness that men like Darlan had chosen to collaborate and to betray. But to the confused and unhappy French inhabitants of North and West Africa, Darlan had represented a form of unity. Perhaps he had been biding his time, waiting to change sides yet again, now that the Allies were gaining ground despite all that the German army and the Luftwaffe could throw against them.

Blackwood had seen the reports of the fierce resistance encountered by the Americans landing at Oran and other strategic points, not from the Germans, but from the French army. It would not be forgotten by young American soldiers who had come so far to do so much, as they had believed, to help free the French nation.

But with Darlan alive and ready to keep peace amongst his own people and the allied invaders, to say nothing of his dealings with Berlin, there was some show of that elusive unity.

Individuals can win, or lose a war.

Blackwood stretched, but his movements were restrained by his webbing belt and ammunition pouches.

And now there was another contender, Admiral

Avice, one of Darlan's trusted commanders and a man known to favour closer ties with the Vichy government, and therefore with Germany.

Blackwood pictured the chart again. At this very moment the gunboat was lying almost stopped in the Strait of Sicily, that savagely contested channel between Sicily and Cape Bon in Tunisia. It was barely seventy miles across at the narrowest part, where the sea bed was littered with ships of every kind, and their crews with them. The hard-fought convoys to Malta, just to keep that island alive, even though enemy airfields were only a short flight away; submarines, minefields and dive-bombers; men against machines. Because of its position, the Strait had become vital to both sides. From Sicily and the Italian mainland stores and weapons were being forced through to the Afrika Korps, which was now in full retreat, at least from the Libyan desert. And at the other side of the campaign was the port of Bone, which had been seized after the landings of Torch. All the thousands of men, tanks, ammunition and supplies for the First Army and the Americans had to pass through Bone. Bombed around the clock and with too few R.A.F. or American planes to defend it, it was a lynchpin which could still swing either way.

But the navy continued to be resourceful. Most of the troops shuttled between Bone and Algiers were carried over the weeks by just four small ships. In peacetime they had been cross-Channel steamers, hardly designed for war. Despard had remarked as much, no doubt remembering them from his days in Jersey.

Intelligence had reported that the enemy was equally cunning. But where? These were not the

101

waters for heavy transport, no matter how well they were armed or protected by air cover. Even if they succeeded in landing their supplies, it was unlikely they would be allowed to make a return trip.

And so this hitherto unknown French admiral, Avice, had been put forward as the most likely culprit. He had refused to co-operate with the Allies; he had always staunchly supported Darlan, outwardly at least. It was not much for the Operational staff to work on, and at such short notice. *The King is dead* . . . And Avice was known for his unswerving views.

Blackwood touched the wooden side of the cabin. Probably not all that far from here. The Gulf of Hammamet, south of Tunis and not easy to observe by sea or from the air, was said to have suitable facilities for small craft. It was protected by a fortress which had once been a base of the French Foreign Legion. It was now Avice's headquarters.

Perhaps Darlan had been killed by his order. Patriot or terrorist, it only mattered which side you were on in the end.

He sighed and stood up, away from the bunk, to test the motion.

I'm getting as cynical as Gaillard.

He looked at his watch. Soon now, or not at all. He groped his way to the ladder and peered up towards the bridge. There were a few tiny stars, swaying from side to side. The air was foul with petrol and crowded humanity, and he could not shake that same feeling of unreality.

The small open bridge seemed crowded, and he was glad of the duffle coat he had thrown over his shoulders. The breeze across the screen was like a knife. Hard to believe it had been so warm during the day.

He knew Gaillard was hating it, and why. Because of Brigadier Naismith.

Just the job for your chaps, Major Gaillard, I'd have thought.

What about the 'something big'? Keeping it for himself, possibly. The next step up the ladder.

Falconer pushed between them, an unlit pipe jutting from his jaw like a tusk.

'No bloody E-Boats about, anyway. You can hear those buggers for miles!' Somebody stifled a yawn. No excitement, only routine, at least to them.

Gaillard said sharply, 'If anything shows up, we go straight in, right? No heroics, just do the job and fast out again!' He sounded strained, on edge, and Blackwood was reminded of her words only last week. *How is your major? Still angry with everything?*

They probably had Gaillards in the Raf, too.

Where was she now? On the ship she had been expecting? Passage back to England? Would she remember how it had been, what they had done together? The word seemed to speak aloud. *Together.*

He had been unable to contact her. Under orders. It was hard not to consider it, even if the smallest breach of security could put men's lives at risk.

Somebody asked hoarsely, *'What,* sir?' It was Balfour, the young first lieutenant. Blackwood had seen him writing a letter in the tiny wardroom, next to the W/T office with its stammer of morse. To his girl somewhere; he had had her photograph in a case lying open beside him.

He heard Falconer reply, 'It's them. Glad we

shut down, eh?' He sounded very calm, but his mind was busy. Trained for it, ready to move. The schoolmaster, like the archaeologist in his battered schooner. Individuals.

Blackwood turned his head, hearing it for the first time. A droning sound, more than one craft, moving fast. *In and out.* Or they might even lie up for a day under camouflage nets, as the little schooners did among the islands.

'Pass the word, and tell the Chief *now.*' The other two boats must be close by. The survivors. Blackwood heard the click of a magazine, or maybe a buckle as a gunner strapped himself into the twin Oerlikon mounting.

He saw faces light up as a flare burst somewhere over the starboard bow.

Gaillard muttered, 'Cheeky bastards! Must be sure of themselves!'

The muffled roar of engines was louder, as if they should be able to see something. But Falconer did not move, and Blackwood saw his hand tapping a slow tattoo on the flag locker.

He said, 'Let's hope they don't have any of that fancy detection gear.

He ducked down to peer at the compass. His first lieutenant had gone to his own station by the heavy machine guns below the bridge. The old precaution, Blackwood thought. So all the eggs weren't in one basket if the worst should happen.

Falconer had moved again, and was standing beside the coxswain at the wheel.

'Be ready, Swain. Steer nor'west, and full speed when I give the word!'

Blackwood recognised the excitement in the voice, the madness, the acceptance of the unacceptable.

He wanted to think of her, to hold on to the sweetness of memory. But he knew he could not, must not. It could be fatal.

Falconer yelled, 'There go the bastards! *Full ahead!'*

The rest was lost in a sudden roar of power which almost threw them off their feet.

Blackwood clung to a stanchion and turned to stare as the rising bow wave surged away from the hull to break and cascade across something solid. Land. They were that close. There was another flare, from a different bearing this time.

He heard someone shout, 'Too bloody late, chum!'

Then tracer. He made himself watch it, like balls of liquid fire, rising with such deceptive slowness, then passing their peak and flashing down, spitting smoke and spray as bullets or cannon shells clawed across the water.

They did not return the fire. Blackwood felt the steel fingers ease around his guts. *Weekend sailors,* they used to call them.

Now they were the true professionals.

*   *   *

Aboard the second of the three motor gunboats, they had already heard the fast-moving engines and seen the unexpected flare.

Lieutenant George Despard found himself wedged into one corner of the small, box-like bridge, his hip pressed painfully into some immovable fitting, his arm brushing occasionally against a rating at a mounted machine gun.

105

Despard had heard the boat's skipper, a young lieutenant, giving his Number One some stick just before they had gone to Action Stations. His subordinate had been more embarrassed than angry, probably because it had been in front of him. A Royal Marine, another passenger, and so a liability as far as they were concerned. He smiled grimly in the darkness. In front of a ranker. He could find some amusement in it now. It set him apart as something different, neither one thing nor the other.

They had joked about it in the sergeants' mess before Christmas. In many ways he was still one of them, but the barrier was there all the same. Some could take it for granted, like the lieutenant in the third gunboat, a willowy young man called Robyns, son of a lieutenant-general in the Corps. He was competent enough, and his men appeared to respect him, although one of the sergeants had described him as 'a toffee-nosed, patronising prat'. Despard had felt irritation, but had decided to ignore it.

He considered Michael Blackwood, how their paths had crossed repeatedly over the years. It must be quite a load to carry, as he had thought often enough. In the Corps you could never forget the Blackwood dynasty, even if you wanted to. At Stonehouse there was a Blackwood cup for marksmanship. He smiled again, glad of the dark. *For musketry*, it was still engraved. At Eastney there was a silver shield, an earlier Blackwood's contribution, in recognition of the best sailing team. There were a lot of Royal Marine families, father to son, it was what made them special, but for Despard there had been no such connection.

His father had been a bricklayer, a good one too; many of the houses around Jersey had been his work. Perhaps because of his skills, he had avoided serving in the Great War, although he was always one of the first to show his respect for the fallen on Armistice Days. Despard had seen his own future as a bricklayer, and, like his father, dropping in at the pub on his way home at the end of a long stint, until one day a destroyer from the Home Fleet had paid a courtesy visit to St Helier, and had been open to the public. Entertaining as only the navy could, as he himself had helped to do when he had joined his first ship, a light cruiser. Roundabouts made of capstan bars, ice cream and sticky buns, kids being allowed to peer down the barrel of a gun, and see the polished rifling glinting against the sky. The Royal Navy, *the sure shield,* as it had been then. Not the splinter-ridden ships he had seen go down protecting convoys, the survivors floundering, calling out for help when there was none to offer, because the others had obeyed the signal to hold their formation. *Don't stop. And don't look back.*

The destroyer had, of course, carried no marines, but somebody had given him a recruiting leaflet. And even now, after all he had gone through, and everything he had seen and been forced to do, he knew in his heart that if he ever met up with the man who had given him the leaflet, he would still have thanked him.

He had fitted in from the beginning. Drills, drills and more drills. Bellowing N.C.O.s, impatient officers, the mysteries of tradition and ceremony; he had done it. Corporal, and then the impossible: he had been made up to sergeant. That was it, and it would do very well. He had thought that if he survived the war he might even rate colour sergeant. Instead, there had been a signal, and an interview with his adjutant. 'Take it, Sar'nt! Join the Club!'

A good bloke, but even as he had shaken Despard's hand he must have known that the new officer would always be 'a ranker'.

He stiffened as the skipper's duffle coat appeared beside him.

'You know what to do? If those boats go in, and are carrying supplies for the enemy, we take them!'

Despard had learned a lot about officers, long before becoming one. It didn't matter what uniform they wore, you could always tell. Like this one, a man to whom he had barely spoken, but who had done this kind of operation in the past. In his case, too many times. *Do we know what to do?* It was an insult, or many would take it as such. This one was trying to convince himself, to be someone he was not, not any more.

Despard said, 'They're the enemy, as far as I'm concerned.' It stuck in his throat. 'Sir.'

'Not your show, is it?' Then he laughed and clapped him on the arm. 'Piece of cake, old boy!' The laugh was the worst part.

Despard reached down and poked a khaki shoulder. 'Ready, Corporal?'

The anonymous shape nodded. 'Both Brens, sir. Grenades too.'

'Good lad.'

Corporal Evans. A quiet enough man when he was sober, but drunk or in a fight and he was a different person entirely. And in action, at close quarters, he would change again. Evans had never learned 'the rules'. Despard felt the anger rising once more. Who cared what the French in North Africa thought about co-operation? They had given in to Germany, but they still wanted respect. Like their warships moored at Alex; it was said that their admiral never went ashore, and had no contact with the Royal Navy, with which he had worked before the war in these same waters. In the name of France he had refused to allow his ships to serve alongside the British and their allies, the very people who were fighting and dying every day to help free France and all the other occupied countries from a ruthless enemy. The Germans had sensibly torn up the rules long ago.

He squinted as another flare exploded, further away, drifting aimlessly to port.

And Blackwood was over there somewhere with Gaillard. The latter had a strong reputation in the Corps. A real fire-eater, they said. Maybe he and Blackwood were right for one another. His mind refused to consider it. But they seemed so different.

'Full ahead!'

The bridge seemed to rear like a surfboard as the engines bellowed into full revolutions. Spray dashed over the screen, stinging Despard's face like sleet.

The boat was weaving slightly, and he wondered how the machine gunners would manage if something unforeseen happened. He swallowed. Here was the tracer. Out of the darkness, like the displays after fleet regattas in peacetime, where he had seen his officers with pretty women, wandering beneath the taut awnings while the band had played.

He thought of 'Sticks' Welland, remembering

what he had heard about the ace drummer. Some of it was the usual bullshit, but Sticks did have a way with women.

The third boat was moving up now; Despard saw her bow wave rising in a white crest, the hull almost hidden by the churned water.

More tracer, much nearer this time, and from higher up. From the land.

He felt his Sten beneath the cover he had draped over it. A handy little weapon, and provided you stuck to single shots you were pretty safe. Give a Sten to some green recruit, and he always wanted to be James Cagney . . .

He tried to recall the chart and the diagram which Blackwood had shown them. Shallow water to port, and not too much anywhere else, either. A fortress by the first houses of the little town. He tensed; the boat was weaving again, more violently this time, and he saw the skipper up beside the coxswain, pointing into the darkness.

Somebody gave a nervous shout as the bridge quivered to a solitary crack. But nothing happened, and he heard a sailor call out to his mate on the opposite side.

It was a small shell, had to be. And it had gone right through the boat without exploding. Despard found that he could consider it with dispassion, like a problem at the training depot. An armour-piercing shell, probably an anti-tank gun, or even a tank.

It never left you. Observation, conclusion, method, *attack!*

He grinned, and it felt as if his jaws were glued together.

Not bad for a bloody ranker.

More shouts. The boat was slowing down, but

110

not much. There were more shots, and metal ricocheted from the paper-thin plating around the bridge.

'Target! Starboard bow!' The deck tilted over again. *'Open fire!'*

Flares were exploding over the water, but whose Despard did not know or care. They worked just as well for everyone.

He gripped his Sten and watched. He was quite calm; he was not afraid.

And there was the enemy.

*   *   *

Major Gaillard seized Blackwood's arm and shouted above the roar of engines, 'What's that bloody fool playing at? He knows he must hold his fire!'

Blackwood could feel the intensity of his anger, transmitted by the steel grip on his arm. The flickering lights in his eyes were the reflection of a sudden burst of tracer from the second M.G.B.

Falconer said, 'Probably saw something.' His tone suggested, *well, it's too bloody late now!*

A starshell exploded almost directly above the fast-moving hull, searing the eyes, and making the mind cringe as the water opened up on either beam like a stage. There were three boats right enough, big lighters, which had been used by both the Italians and the Germans in their constant efforts to supply their troops ashore, all the way across Libya to El Alamein, and now back again. There was the pier, too, a frail-looking construction in the glacier light, but enough for unloading supply boats under cover of darkness.

111

Falconer crouched against his coxswain and Blackwood felt the boat sag forward as the power was reduced, the bows swinging towards the lighter which was already lying against the pier.

'Ready, on deck!'

Blackwood felt Gaillard punch his arm. 'Get to it, Mike!' He grinned, so that in the glare he looked as if he was laughing. Enjoying it.

Blackwood left the bridge, feeling his men forming around him. Minds probably blank, treating it as another drill. It could be fatal to think beyond that. A tiny, unknown anchorage on the coast of Tunisia, protected by God alone knew how many Frenchmen who were only obeying orders, with little thought of the consequences. *Just like us.* And out there, inland, beyond this mark on the chart, was the real enemy. The whole coast would soon know of this raid.

He raised his Sten and saw the side of the lighter rising above the M.G.B.'s flared bow. Some seamen were already flinging grapnels over the rails, and although the light had almost died he knew the boat's guns were ready to fire. They must have done it often enough. Despard's section should be near the other end of the pier. Should be.

'Now!'

He flung himself at the rails and heard the water frothing angrily between the two hulls. One slip and you were done for.

At any second there would be resistance, gunfire; the lighter's crew must be fully aware of what was happening.

Bullets were whining overhead, some hitting either the M.G.B. or the moored supply vessel.

112

Blackwood was on the unfamiliar deck, his feet slipping on discarded mooring wires.

He stared around, his finger resisting all caution, and already too tight on the trigger.

A voice yelled, 'They've scarpered, sir! Two of 'em 'ave jumped in the drink!'

Then Sergeant Welland, in control, unruffled, as he had been when he had gunned down the Italian officer in his bed.

'No bloody wonder, sir! This boat is full of ammo!'

Blackwood ran past him. 'See to it! Set the charges!' The intelligence report had been correct: the enemy was running supplies through neutral territory. That should put the boot into the French admiral's chances, he thought.

It was suddenly very quiet, and he could imagine the French soldiers groping through the darkness, wondering how many attackers they were facing, and probably very aware of the floating bomb which was moored here.

More figures thudded along the pier and a solitary shot brought a sharp scream from somewhere, which ended abruptly. It was Despard, one arm pointing out positions to his section of marines. Some haphazard shots from the land brought an immediate burst of cannon fire from the gunboats.

Blackwood turned as a man called, 'The third boat's in trouble, sir!'

He jerked up his Sten, but lowered it again as the crouching figure below the lighter's small bridge was revealed as a flapping canvas dodger.

So hard to think, to remember. The faces in the third boat. The young lieutenant was called

113

Robyns. Very keen. All for it, as they said in the Corps. The boat must have stopped altogether, and there were staccato bursts of small arms fire, flashes on the water by the heavier bulk of another vessel. Not a lighter; too cumbersome. What then?

Despard strode past, his gun at his hip. 'They've got a bloody boom here, sir! Nobody said anything about that!'

In daylight they might have seen it, but maybe not. The third gunboat must have hit the boom even as some brave souls were trying to close it. *To keep us out? To trap us in?* They might never know.

He heard Gaillard's voice, clear and controlled, as if he were right beside him.

'Break off! Set the charges!'

Welland said harshly, 'Martin's caught one, sir. In the leg. Pretty bad, by the feel of it.'

Blackwood said, 'Get him aboard. We leave nobody!' The second M.G.B. was already thrashing astern from the pier. If they got out of this one, Falconer's boat would be standing room only. Blackwood wanted to laugh. Would anyone ever know about this, let alone care? Would she see a dusty report in one of her files and remember their only night together? He heard the wounded marine cry out in agony as he was hoisted on to another man's back. He reached out impetuously and gripped the dangling hand. It was sticky with blood. Pretty bad, Welland had said.

It was something like a shock when he felt his grip returned. Not much, but it was there. A link. And the man named Martin knew it.

Blackwood dashed his wrist across his face. A small thing, a fragment, some might say. *But it saved me.*

Faintly, he heard Falconer's voice through the commotion of scrambling figures.

'They'll try to get us as we pass the boom vessel, sir. I intend to use depth charges.'

Blackwood felt the hulls jar together, and then heard Despard ask with acid humour, 'You staying then, sir?'

He reached out, and felt a mooring line snake past his legs as hands hauled him on to the gunboat's deck like a sack of potatoes.

His mind grappled with it. Depth charges. Common enough when attacking small coastal craft. Minimum settings, maybe ten feet. But in this place they might easily all go up together.

Gaillard was beside him again. 'Well done. Time to go, I think.'

'What about the others, sir?'

'The second boat lost three. Killed outright, apparently. Not surprised after all the row he made coming in!'

Blackwood rubbed his eyes, feeling the ache, the grit, aware only of Gaillard's dismissal, a mild irritation, if that.

When he looked again, the moored lighter had been swallowed in darkness. A floating bomb. No wonder her people had all baled out.

The other gunboat was already in position, screws thrashing, a solitary machine gun raking back and forth over the boom vessel.

Gaillard snapped, 'I ordered them to pull out!'

Falconer replied quietly, 'I told the skipper to do what he could to get our lads off.' He turned away without further comment. 'Stand by, depth charges!'

There was a loud explosion, and Blackwood saw

115

fragments of wood and metal splashing down near the cluster of vessels by the invisible boom. He did not know who commanded the third boat, or even if he was still alive. If he was, he would be feeling it now, seeing his own command being destroyed to avoid capture.

The hull twisted violently and the bows lifted again, eager to be free and in open water. The crews of the two drifting lighters must have realised what was happening, and that they were next. Some would jump overboard as their comrades had done, and when the charges exploded they would be caught in the blast. Falconer would know that. He had served in the Atlantic, and would have seen men struggling for survival and caught in a pattern of depth charges flung into the air, human remnants, gutted like fish.

Somewhere, as though it were a thousand miles away, a bell tinkled and Blackwood heard the metallic clang of the charges being released. The bows were rising higher and higher, the engines so loud that it was impossible to think. But they heard the depth charges, and they felt the explosions rebound against the hull like sledgehammers.

Blackwood removed his beret and wiped his face with it. What had Falconer told him? Only three boats left, in their little squadron within a squadron?

Now there were only two. And a long way to go before they would be safe.

More explosions, but no fires or dazzling blasts of detonated ammunition. That would come later, probably when the local garrison ventured down to look at the damage.

Despard was so close that he could feel him

116

breathing. Dealing with it in his own, very private way. A man who would never break. The only time Blackwood had seen behind the shield was when he had spoken out about his sister.

Their faces, the wet deck and weapons were lit by two vivid flashes, and then came the explosion. On and on, like thunder over hills.

Falconer brushed by them, but paused to peer astern at the reflected glare of fires.

He patted the side of the bridge, his bridge. 'Made it! But she's a tough old bird, this one!' He moved away to attend to his duties.

Tough old bird? Two years, at the most. Blackwood listened to another muffled explosion. In Falconer's kind of work, that was old.

When dawn found them, they had the sea to themselves. Probably not for long, but they had done it. Blackwood swallowed a mug of something hot, tea, coffee, or that sickly, glutinous cocoa, ki, that sailors seemed to love so much. Whatever it was, he barely tasted it.

They were close enough to the other motor gunboat to see the rescued marines crouching in the first, cool sunlight. Robyns was with them, his face split in a grin. Full of it. There did not appear to be many of his section left.

Blackwood tried to think how he would have described it to his father, or perhaps to Joanna. But the only word that came was *expendable.*

It was probably better to be like Despard. *Don't ask. Just do it.*

'Aircraft, sir! Bearing Red four-five! Angle of sight four-five!'

Blackwood felt the mug snatched from his hand as the seamen swung their weapons on to the

117

bearing.

Someone gave a derisive cheer, and another exclaimed, 'Must be another foul-up, sir! It's one of ours!'

Blackwood saw Despard gazing at him. Comparing again.

He turned to watch the flashing shape against the clouds.

And there was another response. *Pride.*

CHAPTER SIX

FACES OF WAR

'Straight through there, sir. Hut seven.' The white-jacketed orderly waited while Blackwood brushed the sand and dust from his khaki shirt. 'They'll not give you very long, sir.'

Blackwood thanked him and entered a long covered way, part of yet another new wing of this military hospital. It had been completed so recently that he could still smell fresh paint.

There were wounded men everywhere, sitting in cane chairs in dressing-gowns, walking slowly and carefully with sticks or on crutches, encouraged by their friends or the staff. It was a place full of pain. And of hope.

He wondered if it had been like this for his father, or at Hawks Hill during its period as a convalescent hospital for wounded officers. His mother had sometimes spoken of her experiences then, helping men blinded in the trenches to learn Braille. It was still difficult for him to believe that

118

she was dead; it had come swiftly and with little warning. He had been at sea and had not been able to return home for the funeral. At least they were together again now. She must have been very like Diane as a girl ... that, too, would have been a constant reminder to his father.

He licked his lips, feeling the sand between his teeth. The car which had given him a lift had been an open Fiat, a smart little vehicle; the driver, a lieutenant, said it had belonged to an Italian officer who had beat a hasty retreat in the first heady days of the desert war.

The hut was in view now, and he thought again of the raid. One motor gunboat, twelve casualties. He bit his lip. Five of them had been killed outright, or had died soon afterwards. What had it proved?

Gaillard had remained non-committal, saying only that it was 'a step in the right direction, at last!'

'Can I help?'

He stared, momentarily taken aback by the sudden appearance of a nurse in the entrance lobby, very cool and clean in her uniform. It seemed so strange to find English nurses here, although to everyone else their presence was a matter of fact, was accepted.

'Captain Blackwood, Sister.'

She smiled gently. 'Staff nurse. Through that door. Don't be long—the P.M.O. will be round shortly.' She made him sound like God.

It was a long, plain room, like a giant packing-case. Beds on either side, highly polished linoleum down the centre.

Most of the beds were occupied: men sleeping or

trying to read, men with bandaged heads and plastered limbs, several with missing arms or legs. Soldiers, airmen, marines; it was hard to distinguish in this place of anonymous suffering. Some of them were watching him with expressions he recalled from other hospitals, where their eyes had asked, 'Why me, and not you?' It was impossible to cover it by saying someone was lucky just to be alive. Here, it was meaningless.

He saw two Royal Marines sitting stiffly on a wooden bench beside one of the beds. They both stood up, and Blackwood said, 'As you were. Relax.' But they remained standing. *Because I am their officer.*

Sergeant Welland was one of them, as he had expected it would be.

'How is he?'

They all looked at the face on the pillow, the marine named Martin, who had been wounded in the exchange of fire on the pier. Not a man he had found time to get to know, but he had done well during the raid. *And he saved me.* Just a handshake. A link. A bond.

Welland said, 'Doing fine, sir. He'll be up and about in no time.'

Blackwood took the marine's hand, and thought how hot and dry it felt. Even the face was changed, the skin tight across the bones. He watched the eyes open, and saw recognition in them.

He said quietly, 'Looking after you, Martin?'

The marine moved his head, and winced at the effort.

'Not too bad, sir.' He attempted to smile. 'Proper home from home!'

Welland glanced at the wire cage beneath the

120

scarlet blanket and murmured, 'Took off his leg, sir, the bloody bastards. Never give him a chance.'

Blackwood had rarely heard such anger, such bitterness, and certainly never from 'Sticks' Welland.

He felt the dry hand tremble in his and asked, 'Anything I can do?' Martin stared at him. Hanging on, remembering, it was impossible to tell.

'You could write, sir. I'm not much of a hand at it. It would help . . . coming from you, sir.'

Welland murmured, 'His mother, sir. Lives in Devonport.'

'I will.' He squeezed the hot hand, but it felt lifeless now. 'She'll be proud of you.' He stood. 'As I am.'

At the foot of the bed he paused and looked back. He must never forget.

Sergeant Welland said, 'I'll walk with you, sir.' The other marine, a friend of the wounded man, sat down again.

Welland glanced at the beds as they passed, falling into step with his officer.

'You did the right thing, sir. He'll remember that.'

'It was bloody awful, and you know it.'

Welland smiled. That was more like it.

'You know what they say, sir.'

'"You shouldn't have joined if you can't take a joke!" Yes, I know!'

The same nurse was still at her little desk, and looked up as they appeared.

'Here he is now, Lady Duncan!'

Blackwood turned, the girl's description of 'Tinker' Duncan as clear as if she had just spoken aloud.

121

She was not old, but definitely not young, with short grey hair.

A bit of a battle-axe. Now, dressed in a starched white coat, she looked all of that. He could not imagine anyone daring to call her by such a frivolous nickname.

'Captain Blackwood? I heard you were in the hospital.' She thrust out her hand. It was a very strong grip, especially when compared with the wounded marine's. 'I missed you at the house in Rosetta. Joanna told me about you.' She studied him calmly. 'Not married?' He said nothing. 'Thought not. Good.'

'I've been trying to make contact since we got back.'

'Yes.' She glanced at the ward. 'I heard something about your recent escapade. It was good of you to come.'

'He's one of my men.'

She shrugged. 'A lot wouldn't give a toss, believe me!' She walked to a window and stared at a passing ambulance. 'Never stops.' Then, without turning, 'You care, don't you?'

He knew she was watching his reflection in the dusty glass.

'About her?'

'Of course.'

'Yes.' He was surprised that it was so easy; he felt no resentment, not even a sense of intrusion. 'Very much. I know what they say about the risks in wartime . . .'

She faced him, and sniffed. 'A lot of people say stupid things about "wartime", my own husband for one!'

Sergeant Welland drew his heels together very

122

quietly.

'Beg pardon, sir . . .' He did not look at Lady Duncan. 'I'll be outside with the transport.' Then he saluted, with great formality; he could have been mounting guard at the palace.

She said, 'Another one of *your men,* I assume, Captain?'

He smiled. 'Yes. A forceful character.'

She took his arm and guided him to the opposite side of the lobby. The nurse had pulled up her apron to smooth out a wrinkle in her stocking, and he thought it was a pity that Welland had gone. He would have enjoyed that.

'She left under orders. There was no easy way she could have told you, even if she had wanted to.'

Don't hope for too much. The touch of her skin beneath the robe when the car had come for him, an hour early. And now she was gone.

Lady Duncan watched his face, his emotions. It was hard, sometimes impossible, to see such men as Blackwood in those other circumstances. Like the young marine who had lost his leg, like another, only an hour ago, who had wept in her arms when he had heard that he had been recommended for a medal. Then, like so many others here, he had died, without making a fuss.

She said, 'She told me you had given her courage.'

He turned it over in his mind. 'I don't understand.'

She put her hand on his sleeve. 'I think it was something dangerous. Say or do nothing which might harm her, or yourself. But I imagine you know all about risks, Captain Blackwood?'

Doors swung open and more white-coated

figures strode into the lobby: the P.M.O. doing his rounds, the gleam of a stethoscope, the faint smell of gin. Someone said sharply, 'What is that officer doing here?'

Blackwood walked to the window and watched the ambulances, the orderlies hurrying to them with stretchers, their faces like masks. *Something dangerous.* Why had he not seen it? Was he so blind, so full of his own uncertainties?

She had been warning him, preparing him. *Don't hope for too much.*

Lady Duncan, Tinker to her close friends, watched him walk out into the sunlight, past the ambulances with their glaring red crosses. A man who might turn any woman's head.

But a casualty, as much as all these others.

*   *   *

Commander Walter St John looked up from his desk only to wave Blackwood to a canvas-backed chair. A petty officer writer waited beside the desk, his features expressionless while he passed letters to be signed, signals to be initialled, or untidy clips of notes in a steady stream. Blackwood thought he would have made a good butler.

Nobody had spared him so much as a glance when he had entered this building, and yet he had the feeling that everyone knew exactly why he was here.

He gazed at the calendar on St John's desk. 1943. Was it possible? Another new year of war.

There had been no word from Joanna Gordon and he had given up trying to tell himself that it was because she wanted their relationship to go no further. Perhaps she had made that plain from the beginning, but he did not believe it.

He looked up from the calendar as the petty officer writer moved away with two armfuls of files and signal pads. Glided, would be a better description.

St John stretched and peered at his watch. 'Never stops, does it?'

Blackwood was reminded of the formidable Lady Duncan.

St John said, 'I have a job for you. Major Gaillard has no objection, and Brigadier Naismith put your name forward himself. I'll bet that surprises you.'

Blackwood attempted to relax, and waited.

'I must say that 1943 has begun a lot more promisingly than last year.' He glanced towards the wall map. 'The Eighth Army is still driving the Germans to the west—they'll be in Tripoli in no time at this rate. The German army was held at Stalingrad, and they're in full retreat there, too.' His eyes hardened slightly. 'We're established in North Africa, and when the weather gives us a break things should improve for the Americans, and the enemy will face defeat in Tunisia as well. Not bad. Not bad at all.' He displayed a second's irritation as one of the long-bladed fans overhead faltered and squeaked to a halt. 'We can hope for big things this year. I'm informed that the Prime Minister is adamant that Italy must be knocked out of the war as soon as possible. When that happens Germany will have her forces stretched to and, one hopes, beyond the limit. But to accelerate all this, we must help all those who are willing to stand up and fight against the enemy. Partisans, Resistance,

125

opportunists, call them what you like. The policy will be to back those people in every way we can, irrespective of the colour of their politics.' He was referring to the extreme divisions in occupied Yugoslavia. At the beginning it had been decided to drop military supplies to General Miliailovich's Chetniks, mainly because he was a royalist. It was soon discovered, however, that Marshal Tito's Communist partisans were fighting most effectively against the Germans, despite savage reprisals and executions, and the Chetniks had been co-operating with the occupying forces. So Tito was the one who would receive assistance.

St John frowned as the fan began to move again. 'Even amongst the islands, we can help. For the first time there is hope for these people.' He opened a clean file, and said, 'A cargo of battlefield clearance stores. B.C.S. as the boffins call them, is ready and waiting to be delivered to such a group. Italian weapons mostly, dropped by their army when they were surrendering in droves before Mister Rommel made an appearance, and changed the face of the desert war. Agents have carried out careful assessments, of course, but now it's a matter of putting our hardware where our mouths are!' He became more serious. 'The final part of it must be official, and seen to be so by the people in question. Not some half-baked promise which can conveniently be forgotten when the fighting is over. In short, they want an officer to complete the handover. It will be the first of its kind in this particular theatre. Not enough to start a war, but perhaps sufficient to help end one, right?'

Blackwood nodded, wondering why Gaillard had not told him first, or demanded to go himself.

126

'And if you're worrying about your duties with the new commando company, let me put your mind at rest. Your company will be in Suez in two weeks. They were delayed at Cape Town while they waited for additional escorts, but it gave them time to get their knees brown, and now they're on the last run in.'

Hard to believe that it had been such a short while ago, on that rain-sodden hillside when Major-General Vaughan had come to tell him about his father, and to ask him to take this appointment. That special, hard-trained company would be here very soon, and he would be with them when their true role was determined.

Of course, he might have been shot on the pier beside the marine called Martin, or been killed on the previous raid on the island of Vasili. But that was not to be considered, let alone voiced in words. It only happened to others. It was well to remember that.

St John had dragged open a drawer. 'Drink?' He did not wait for an answer, but took out a bottle and two glasses. It was Scotch, and marked *Duty-Free, H.M. Ships Only.*

St John was grinning. 'R.H.I.P.!'

Blackwood took a glass. *Rank Hath Its Privileges.* 'When will I be required to leave, sir?' He felt the neat Scotch burning his tongue.

'You'll go, then?' He sounded neither surprised nor relieved. Just another job.

A telephone buzzed in a case like a trapped hornet. St John ignored it.

He said, 'Tomorrow. Everything's taken care of. M.G.B. as before, rendezvous with one of our schooners.'

'As before.'

St John swirled the drink around his glass. There was not much of it left.

'You will be advised how to proceed. You'll be in good hands. My own choice, as a matter of fact. You've met him, by the way.'

The telephone buzzed again, and this time St John unfastened the case. 'I'll brief you before you leave.' He gave him a level stare. 'There was one other thing.' He spoke into the handset. 'Wait.'

'Sir?' Blackwood was on his feet.

St John covered the instrument with his hand. 'I heard you were making enquiries about a Flight Officer Gordon?'

'Yes, sir.' Somehow he had known it would be mentioned.

'It's out of my hands, of course. Commander Diamond in London is more in the picture

'Is she all right, sir?'

St John observed him with surprise, or the closest he would ever come to it. 'You know you're not permitted to ask about such matters. In everyone's interests.' He stopped abruptly, and then said, 'She's safe. It's all I can tell you. Nothing must jeopardise this mission. A lot of people will be depending on you, remember that! If I thought for one second—'

'Nothing will jeopardise it, sir.'

She was safe. From what, was still unknown. But she was safe.

'Good.' He stared at the telephone as if he hated it. 'You'll need one other officer. Simply as a precaution.'

'Lieutenant Despard, sir.'

'Thought it might be.' He watched the door

128

close, and spoke into the telephone.

'On his way now, sir. No, I didn't tell him.' He scowled. 'Well, she *is* safe, as far as we know!'

He replaced the bottle in the drawer and closed it, thinking of all the faces he had seen across this desk since he had taken command. And of all those who had gone.

He had been in command of a submarine at the outbreak of war, and had seen plenty of action. He glanced around his office. The filing cabinets, the signals In and Out, the chair where young men sat and listened, in too many cases for the last time.

There was no comparison. Commanding the submarine seemed like child's play.

*　　　*　　　*

Blackwood climbed the ladder to the schooner's deck, shivering. After the confined and crowded hull, the breeze from the sea seemed almost icy.

He saw the skipper, Lieutenant Terry Carson, squatting by the tiller peering at his compass. It was nearly dark, the division between the horizon and the sky revealed only by the remains of a fiery sunset, streaks of orange-red, with the vague outline of yet another small island fading abeam.

Carson tossed him a duffle coat. 'Come up for some air?'

Blackwood was glad it was the same schooner, with the one-time archaeologist still in command. Everything else seemed unfamiliar. Some of the crew had been replaced; even the motor mechanic from the Mile End Road had gone. Perhaps Special Operations insisted on change to keep the men on their toes, or to prevent them from becoming too close to one another.

He joined Carson by the bulwark, feeling the hull shake to the beat of the ancient diesel. His mouth felt stale with oil, dirt, sweat.

The schooner seemed heavier in the water, but he thought that was probably imagination. They were carrying two hundred Mannlicher-Carcano rifles, clean and ready to use, as well as ammunition and explosives. Not enough to start a war, St John had said, but in the right hands they would prove deadly. And in the wrong ones? Intimidation and crime, settling old scores for personal gain: it had happened elsewhere.

He knew Carson was uneasy about it. Bitter. 'Of course it will tie down more German troops who could be fighting where they're most needed. It sounds so simple on paper. Does nobody ever consider the aftermath of some ambush or botched raid? People shot, innocent or otherwise, interrogated and tortured when they know nothing. Not that it makes any difference. It's the "example" that always counts!'

He reminded Blackwood of Falconer, after the raid and the destruction of the lighters.

'If Intelligence was so certain, why didn't we hit the bastards before they reached the anchorage? We could have nailed them easily. As it is, we've lost a boat and some good men, just to prove that some bloody French admiral isn't playing by the rules!'

Blackwood said, 'This man we're meeting, do you know him?'

Carson answered sharply, 'No. Just a name. Achileas. I wonder what joker thought that one up!'

He reached out and touched Blackwood's arm. 'Sorry. It's not your fault. I have to let off steam sometimes. This business gets you on edge.' He grinned. 'Past it, probably!'

Blackwood considered it. In the Corps you were trained to deal with a situation in a recognised fashion. If things went wrong, you used that same training to hit back, and fight your way out of it. No wonder men like Carson and Falconer were pushed to the limit. In hours this schooner would enter a tiny harbour on the appointed island. They would actually tie up alongside a jetty or some other clapped-out schooner or fishing vessel, and get on with the unloading.

Maybe the enemy already knew of this rendezvous. There were always collaborators and traitors only too eager to win favour from the occupying forces.

Carson was only a vague shadow in the darkness. What made men like him take such risks?

He thought of the other passengers, both soldiers, introduced as members of the Long Range Desert Group, but looking more like brigands than officers. The L.R.D.G. had become legendary in the cloak and dagger war; they often worked many miles behind enemy lines, blowing up supply dumps and transport before vanishing like nomads into the desert. One was a major named Savill, the other a captain whose name had not been mentioned.

They kept to themselves, but, as Carson had remarked, 'It's their show. We're just the dressing!'

He wondered what Despard thought of the situation. He had seemed pleased that his name had been put forward for this mission, and, possibly, surprised that another such had been considered. Blackwood had seen him examining one of the Italian rifles. It had looked almost small in his hands.

'Good enough, when properly used,' was his only comment.

Out of the darkness, Carson said abruptly, 'You're not married, are you?'

Blackwood watched the last streak of colour sink out of sight.

'No.' An ordinary enough question, for men unwilling to speak of the hours which lay ahead. But it had touched him, perhaps unreasonably.

Love me. It's what you want, isn't it?

Carson twisted round to study the helmsman and said, 'I was, once. But she got bored.' He laughed softly. 'Can't say I blame her!'

Blackwood stared up at the faint stars. 'I'm glad you know where you're going, Terry!'

Carson pointed over the side. 'There's an island out there. I went there once. I found a lighthouse, six, maybe seven hundred years old. Can you imagine? When Henry III was king of England, maybe before that.'

Blackwood looked away. Angry, bitter and aware of all the risks, and yet Carson loved this sea, its secrets and its past.

Carson said with the same uncompromising directness, 'Do you like what you do?' Then he stood up sharply and walked to the engine hatch, neither waiting for nor expecting an answer.

It was better to be like St John. *Just another job.* It was stupid and dangerous to see beyond that.

He allowed his mind to explore the memories again. She was the only one in his life who had shared and understood his doubts.

He heard Despard climbing on deck, and was suddenly glad he was here.

Achileas. It was simply something that had to be done.

And it was today.

After the final, nerve-wrenching approach to the island, and the seemingly endless delays before their masked signals were acknowledged, the coming of daylight was almost an anticlimax, revealing only a tiny village huddled around an inlet, dwelling leaning upon dwelling, with schooners and caiques as scruffy and scarred as their own.

Although they were in a sea patrolled and guarded by the enemy there was no sense of menace or danger, and the local people, if not overtly enthusiastic, were not unfriendly. Theirs was a hard life, and their only means of survival lay in their own resources and in their boats. The enemy would be well aware of this. Unable to spare enough patrol vessels or men to cover this sector of the Aegean and the approaches to occupied Greece, they relied on an occasional show of strength, and the ruthless destruction of any vessel found out of its permitted area. Carson had spoken of the deadly Stuka dive-bombers which were often in evidence amongst the islands. Boats had been bombed and sunk regardless of what or whom they were carrying. As an example, as he had put it.

Blackwood stood now in the broad entrance of a long, much-repaired hut and observed the harbour and the unhurried movements in and around the village, goats roaming the narrow streets, the smoke of charcoal braziers teasing his nostrils. It was like being invisible. People passed and glanced at him, only to avert their eyes without apparent surprise or curiosity.

Despard crossed the worn floor, where the piles of Italian rifles and ammunition were being arranged by Carson's sailors. Two Royal Marines in the middle of nowhere, here to lend the occasion an air of authority. Unshaven and crumpled, but in their battledress and webbing belts, with the familiar Globe and Laurel badge on their berets, they stood out like a military band. Even Carson had unearthed his uniform cap in the same spirit, the badge so tarnished that the gold wire was almost green.

Despard was chewing on a piece of cold lamb, wedged with a sliced onion in a chunk of unleavened bread. Even he was finding it hard going.

He said between bites, 'A few crates of bully-beef would do them more good than this! No wonder they all look so mangy!'

But he persisted, perhaps because he knew what it had cost these islanders to share their food with strangers.

There had been wine, too, plenty of it, in great earthenware jugs. It had taken all of Carson's threats to prevent his men from overdoing it. It was rough and raw, and, Blackwood guessed, heavy on after-effects. But it was doing the trick, and he saw several of the seamen grinning and waving to a group of grave-faced children on the jetty.

Despard said softly, 'Here they come.' He straightened automatically. Major Savill and his companion from the Long Range Desert Group walked into the feeble sunlight, and waited for

Blackwood to join them.

The man codenamed 'Achileas' ran searching eyes over the two marines. Not what Blackwood had been expecting, for a partisan, a leader of the Resistance, or even a terrorist, he was a slightly built man in a scuffed leather coat, very composed and self-contained. Between thirty and forty, it was difficult to say. His eyes were memorable, very steady, and utterly devoid of emotion.

Beside him, Savill seemed large and ungainly. He was wearing an outsized jerkin over his other clothing, and Despard had already remarked on the deadly-looking German machine-pistol it concealed. He had a soldier's face, like Brigadier Naismith, with clear blue eyes like chips of glass.

Achileas handed a cup to Blackwood and watched while one of his men passed more wine to the others.

'This is a great day.' He spoke to all of them, but his eyes were on Blackwood. He even smiled briefly as he lifted his cup. *'Gia Su!'*

Savill grinned, but Blackwood thought he was on edge, eager to get on with it. Beyond the hut he could see some of the villagers, fishermen for the most part, by their clothing. What were they thinking? There would be some pride in what they had become a part of; there would be fear, too, for their families, for one another, if the worst should happen.

Achileas was extending his hand. 'For the record, Captain Blackwood!'

Despard muttered, 'God Almighty!' But nobody heard him.

It was a man with a camera, self-conscious in his ragged clothing, but very aware of the importance

135

of this moment.

Who would ever see the end result? Would anyone care?

They shook hands, while one of Achileas's men held up two rifles as a background.

Then they faced one another and saluted, Blackwood in the only manner he had ever known, Achileas with a clenched fist.

Then someone shouted from the jetty, and Savill snapped, 'Tell those men to take cover!' He was fumbling for his binoculars, also concealed beneath the flapping jerkin.

Carson had joined them again, eyes narrowed against the strengthening sun as he found and tracked the small, solitary aircraft.

He said, 'Fiesler 156, a Storch. First I've seen in this neck of the woods.' He could have been remarking on the weather.

The monoplane dipped slightly towards the inlet before turning in a leisurely arc.

A communications and reconnaissance aircraft which the Germans made use of in almost every theatre of war, and vulnerable to flak and ground fire, it was nevertheless invaluable for spotting. Blackwood licked his dry lips. *Like now.*

Savill commented, 'Short-range job, less than three hundred miles.' No one answered. 'But when that "stork" comes back, it won't be carrying a newborn baby!' He looked at his companion. 'Changes things, that's all. We'll leave at dusk.' He glanced at his watch. 'Hurry them up a bit!'

Carson said quietly, 'They should be safe enough. They'll lose themselves among the islands.' He gazed at his small schooner. 'We won't have that privilege, I'm afraid.'

Blackwood listened to the gentle drone of the solitary engine, and tried to imagine the scene from their cockpit. A village and a few boats. Nothing unusual. Could it be that simple?

Savill was saying, 'This is where we part, Captain Blackwood. You did well. We shall take it from here. Trust is a great incentive to these people, you know.'

Blackwood watched him walk down to the jetty, where the last of the rifles were being stowed.

'How far can we get, Terry?'

Carson seemed unwilling to look away, as if he were discovering something.

'There's a fair breeze at the moment. With that and the old banger, we should log a hundred miles before the balloon goes up.' He paused. 'But we're not waiting until dusk, right?'

Blackwood heard a child laugh, and turned to see one of Carson's seamen handing some chocolate, nutty, to one of the onlookers. Good old Jack; underneath it all, he at least never changed.

One hundred miles, Carson had estimated. He recalled Savill's casual parting.

When they left this place, trust was about all they would have.

Despard said, 'Shan't be sorry to get back to some proper soldiering, sir.'

Trust . . .

CHAPTER SEVEN

SHADOWS

Major-General, Ralph Vaughan could barely contain his anger until the door to his outer office was closed, and then he exploded.

'How long have we been in Scotland? Two, three days? Then I get back here to London and find this bloody cock-up waiting for me!'

His quietly spoken aide, Major Claud Porter, watched him striding around the office, his shadow leaning from wall to wall in the hard light like some wild animal trapped in a cage. He had seen Vaughan in all kinds of moods and felt the edge of his tongue in moments of anger from time to time, but rarely like this. On the face of it, it seemed a minor matter when viewed against the quickening pace of the war, although he knew well enough that it was not. Not to the Deputy Chief of Special Operations.

'I want an *immediate* signal made to Commander St John at Alex, requiring a full explanation . . .' He broke off and glared. 'Well, Claud, don't you agree?'

Porter thought about the dossier marked *Top Secret* which was lying on Vaughan's desk. The Prime Minister and Chiefs of Staff had gone to Casablanca, where, in due course, they would be meeting President Roosevelt and his senior advisers. It should prove an eventful conference, and would demonstrate to friends and enemies alike that the Allies were ready to plan the next vital moves both in the Mediterranean and, perhaps, into Europe. It would be a security nightmare, and he was thankful they had been in Scotland to inspect two new companies of Royal Marine Commandos, which would be joining the first company in Alexandria. It was a fine achievement, a fully trained battalion, ready for anything.

One small moment stood out. Vaughan had been inspecting a platoon of young marines who had just completed a gruelling assault course, knee-deep in snow and slush.

The fierce-looking major-general with the battered face had picked out one marine, only a few months in the Corps and pleased with himself for making the grade. A little too pleased, Vaughan had decided.

'Ready to go, are you, lad?'

'Not half, sir! We'll show the bastards!'

Vaughan had tapped his arm quite gently and had said, 'See that you do!' He had looked over at the others, their filthy denims and cradled weapons. 'But you've never killed a man, have you? Well, I have. It's not that easy, not the first time. And if you screw it up, there is no second time, of course.' Some of them had laughed, but the cheeky marine had not.

Porter said cautiously, 'It probably seemed a good idea at the time, sir. Captain Blackwood is an experienced officer. Perhaps it was some inter-service exercise.'

Vaughan stared unseeingly at a map.

'I'll lay odds that Brigadier Naismith was behind it.' His mood was quite calm again, like a departing gale. 'I'm surprised that Gaillard agreed to it,

139

though.' He sat in silence for a moment. 'But to send Blackwood off on some crack-brained scheme, dishing out B.C.S. to a bunch of trigger-happy bandits—anything might happen!'

Porter tried again. He knew this was personal, because of the past, a part of Vaughan somewhere back there in Flanders, when the badly wounded Jonathan Blackwood had given the battalion to him.

Vaughan sat on one corner of his desk and stared at the dried mud on his boots. It was probably still raining over London. Here, in this bomb-proof, air-conditioned bunker, it could be doing anything.

'When the Germans are out of North Africa, and out they will be, our commandos will be on the prongs of any major attack.' He almost smiled. 'We should be damned used to that, eh, Claud? But much of the military engaged will be new, untried, vulnerable. They'll need all the skilled leadership we can find. I went along with the *Lucifer* raid because it could have been vital. Even the second one might have been useful, but Darlan is dead and the French have accepted General Giraud in his place. Given time, we might get some support from the French warships at Alex, although I'd not dine out on it just yet.' He was on the move again. 'It's all dropping into place. The Germans agreed not to invade Vichy France, but they did. They promised to stay out of Toulon where the other French ships were based, but they broke that promise, too. So the French admiral at Toulon . . . he snapped his fingers and Porter murmured, 'De la Borde, sir,' . . . 'scuttled his fleet, so neither side gets the benefit. Yes, it's all dropping into place.'

In the outer office a telephone rang, and was instantly silenced. Porter had noticed that there had been no sound from that usually busy place, and imagined every man and woman listening intently to Vaughan's powerful voice.

Vaughan said suddenly, 'I met de la Borde a couple of times. Fine man. But he hated Darlan almost as much as the Germans. He'll be for the high jump now, poor fellow.'

Porter chose the moment with care. 'The other dossier, sir, concerning your proposed visit to Alexandria. The admiral seems very keen on it, and especially the Chiefs of Staff.' He hesitated. 'And of course the Prime Minister is taking such an interest in the present situation.'

Vaughan recognised the bait and accepted it.

'Arrange it, will you, Claud? Might be just what they need. A good boot up the backside!'

'If you agree, sir, I shall remain here at S.O.H.Q. It might be wise.'

'Don't know what I'd do without you, Claud, damned if I do.' His voice hardened. 'But no matter where I am, I want to know when Blackwood's back, with that company!'

He looked at the files on his desk.

'I'll go and see the admiral now.' He raised one hand. 'No, I'll walk. Do me good.'

He picked up his cap with its bright scarlet band and halted by the door.

'That girl—the W.A.A.F. officer.'

Their eyes met, and Porter was almost tempted to play him along. Almost.

'Flight Officer Gordon, sir.'

'Yes. That's the one.' He thought of his wife, at home in Hampshire. She had a lot to put up with.

He was usually here, or inspecting some special unit, as in 'that bloody awful place'. She had remarked only recently, 'When you were at sea, Ralph, I saw more of you than I do now.'

He said, 'She all right?' He hurried on, not wanting to involve his patient and uncomplaining subordinate. 'I was thinking, provided that the A.O.C. would agree . . .'

Porter was quite shocked to see him so uncertain, so out of his depth. It was like blundering into somebody's secret.

He answered carefully, 'She's still in sick quarters, sir.'

Vaughan looked at him directly. 'In that case . . .' He did not even ask how Porter knew, or why.

'I think you should take her with you, sir. It might be exactly what she needs.' He flinched under Vaughan's gaze; he could look straight through a man, and he thought with some sympathy of that cocky youngster in Scotland. He said, 'The Chief of Staff would approve. Give it the right touch.' He looked away. 'I'll deal with it, sir, if you like.'

'She might refuse. I think I would.' Vaughan gripped the door handle. 'No, I'll ask her myself.'

The door opened and a chorus of typewriters and telephones burst in like a flood, timed to the second.

Porter regarded the untouched files and sighed. Nothing could ever be quite the same again after today.

*   *   *

142

The girl walked across the room and stood by the window. Then she opened the heavy blackout curtains and looked down at the garden, the leafless trees, and some small outbuildings where she had seen workmen replacing a few of the tiles. They looked so bright against the older ones, she thought. The gardens must have been quite beautiful in their day. Now, out of necessity, there was only grass and empty beds.

She touched the glass, and knew it was raw cold outside. Everything was grey, the sky, the buildings, the puddles left by overnight rain. There was strong wire mesh across the windows here; to keep prowlers away, or to prevent the inmates from escaping?

She was wearing a loose hospital robe, and beneath it her whole body tingled from a hot shower. Nobody minded how many baths or showers you took. Maybe it was all part of the therapy. She allowed her mind to linger on the word. Something she had thought she would never be able to do.

She tied the curtains back, aware of the bandage on her left arm. At least she did not need a sling any more.

She looked at the outbuildings again. There was a gravel path which ran almost completely around the sick quarters. She could not recall how long she had been here before her first walk in the open air, using that same path, a nurse strolling behind her as if there by accident. The men had been working on the roof then, and she had heard the hammers stop when she passed and knew they were staring after her, with pity, curiosity, or simply relief that it was not one of them.

She turned to face the room. A bed, a cupboard without doors, a small table and one chair beside it, where the doctor usually sat when she visited. They probably thought it was better for a woman doctor to be in charge. They must have dealt with every kind of stress and breakdown in this place.

She stared at the neatly pressed uniform laid out on the bed. Skirt, tie, air force blue shirt. She bunched her hands into fists until the pain steadied her. Her stockings were there, too. Things were like that here. Beds were made, trays of food came and vanished, and the doctor would look in to check her progress.

Not like the first time. She had struggled with the doctor and one of the nurses, words pouring out of her, her mind reeling to the same torment, unable to accept or believe that it was over. Or was it?

At night it was worse, and she had awakened gasping time and time again, the nightmare refusing to release her.

She glanced at her wrist; she still did it despite the fact that her watch had gone when she had been arrested.

She sat down slowly in the chair and studied the uniform. The doctor had told her that the choice was hers. A few more weeks might make all the difference. She must be given time.

Suppose she was right? She might crack wide open at the first challenge. She thought of the brief visit from the major-general of marines. *I want you to come with me. Do you more good than this place, I shouldn't wonder.*

And yet, despite his bluff, angry manner, she had felt that he had cared about her, that she mattered.

144

As she had sat here, in this chair, she had seen his cap badge, and had forced herself to fight back the tears as the memory had returned. That deserted house, the swimming pool, its surface covered with a film of blown sand. Sheer heaven, she had told him.

Make it a lifetime. Did I really say that?

She folded her arms and leaned forward in the chair, and immediately felt the bandage dragging at her skin.

It would heal soon, they said. She might always have a scar, they said. But she would never forget. She must be able to confront it, and not try to hide in shadows of her own making.

It had all gone so smoothly at first, but it was unnerving to see German uniforms in the streets where she had lived with her parents, where she had spent part of her girlhood, at school, and later helping at the shipping agency. Marseilles, the Port of Seven Seas, they called it.

She had not been afraid; breathless would describe it better. She had met her guide as arranged, and they had waited separately for the bus with the usual collection of homeward-bound workers. She had watched the German soldiers from her window at the back of the bus. Some were very young, peering into shops, or standing on street corners. She had been aware of resentment among her fellow passengers. Defeat had been bad enough, but the Germans had broken their agreement and had occupied all of southern France, even Toulon. She had seen older troops also, the strained, tired faces of combat, probably enjoying this welcome change from Russia or Poland.

One passenger, a young man of about her own age, had attempted to initiate a conversation with her. She had known that this was dangerous, and she had seen her guide turn his head to observe them.

Then there had been an explosion, more like a dull thud than anything else, and the bus had been forced to a halt. She had heard someone speak of sabotage, and she had sensed the anger, and the fear. Her new companion swore quietly as two police officers had climbed into the bus, shining their torches and demanding to see papers of identity. They were not Germans but ordinary French police, doing their job, turning their backs on a world which was beyond their control, or maybe just filling in time until the traffic started to move again.

They were slow, but thorough. Torches flashed; nobody spoke. She had felt her heart pounding like a trip hammer.

One gendarme had been almost level with the slatted wooden seat when the young Frenchman had bounded against the emergency door, and had jumped into the street.

She had heard the startled cries, someone blowing a whistle, and the sudden crack of a pistol shot. The two gendarmes had seized her arm and dragged her to her feet. Hazy, broken pictures. She had never believed she would ever be able to relive it.

She had seen his body sprawled in the road, eyes wide and staring in the glare of flashlights, caught at the moment of impact. The moment of sudden death.

She remembered the faces of the other

passengers as she had been taken through the bus. Not even pity. It had been more like hatred.

At the police station, she was seen by an inspector who had ordered her into a bare-looking office, where she was told to sit and await further questioning. She even remembered the police station, from those early days; she had gone there once to report a missing tennis racquet.

Looking back, it seemed an eternity, although she now knew it was only a matter of hours. The other officer had arrived even as a further explosion had rattled the windows. She had heard powerful vehicles roaring along the street, and German voices shouting commands.

The police officer was a woman. She wore no uniform, but her heavy jacket and skirt could have been just that.

The rest was still very distorted. It was at that point that the nightmare began.

She could recall the room, the glaring lights, the padded walls, soundproofing. There was a solitary stool, and a long, bare table, and an electric fire. The woman ordered her to sit on the stool and then to open her mouth while she shone a torch into it, pushing her tongue aside until she seemed satisfied. She had heard since that she might have been looking for a cyanide capsule.

She could remember her smell, stale sweat, just as she still recalled her sense of excitement. In a man it would have been lust.

But now she was on her feet again, fighting it, facing it as she knew she must. She looked desperately at the neatly folded uniform. She must wear it again if she was to escape from here, from the nightmare.

147

When the doctor here had first examined her, she had felt not her hands but those of the woman in the soundproofed room.

She had stripped her, and those same hands had probed into her; there were threats that she would fetch male officers if Joanna resisted. She had been forced to stand, naked beneath the glaring lights, while she had watched her clothes being examined, each label and cleaner's mark checked for flaws. The woman had found nothing. Even when she had slashed open the lining of the small bag she had been carrying, she had not discovered some last-minute mistake. The people who had sent Joanna Gordon on the mission never made such obvious errors.

But it did not seem to surprise or disappoint her tormentor. She had never stopped speaking, although, looking back, it was hard to be certain if it was in French or English.

A gendarme had entered the room to collect the clothing, and when Joanna had attempted to cover herself the woman had shouted at her not to be shy, or to plead innocence.

She paced across the room, her feet soundless on the hardwood floor. *After that.* She clenched her fists and forced herself to try again. She had felt her arm in the woman's iron grip, heard her own screams, like the screams in the nightmare, and there had been the smell of burned flesh as her bare arm had been forced against the electric fire.

Her interrogator had actually been grinning, shaking her gently back and forth like a doll. Telling her to get dressed again, but that she would not need her stockings or underwear. She had telephoned the German commandant, and his men

148

were coming to interrogate her. Underclothes would only hamper things.

And then another explosion, as if it had been right there in the room, although she knew that was impossible. Other hands holding her, smothering her protests with meaningless words. She could vaguely remember the pad over her mouth and nose. Then oblivion.

She went to the bed, and after the smallest hesitation picked up the stockings.

Aloud, she said, 'I need them now!'

The doctor, who had been standing in the open doorway, gave a faint sigh. In this place you could never proclaim a victory, but she went to the girl and put her arms around her. She felt her stiffen, but only for a moment.

There was always that terrible hurdle. And she had confronted it.

*　　　*　　　*

Michael Blackwood lowered himself into the schooner's tiny cabin and found Despard sitting at the rough table, a Bren gun propped on its bipod, gleaming in the feeble light.

Despard glanced at him. 'I must say that for a bunch of roughnecks Lieutenant Carson's people certainly know how to look after their weapons!' He ran his fingers along the barrel, and down to the curved magazine. 'One of the best pieces they ever made, in my book. Some say the Bren's too accurate, but it'll do me.'

Blackwood thought of the pitch-dark sea and the crouching watchkeepers he had left on deck. There was the merest hint of grey light over the port quarter. It would soon be dawn.

Carson had seemed pleased with their progress so far. The island of Rhodes was to the north-east, other islands too, but it could have been a vast, empty ocean in this small schooner. Carson had set the sails, and with a favourable breeze and the faithful engine they were making 'seven or eight knots'. He made it sound like an M.T.B.

Three hundred miles to go; but they would sight friendly forces long before that.

Blackwood tried to relax, and wondered if Despard was always so confident.

'Did you find it hard to change from sergeant to lieutenant, George?'

Despard looked at him, perhaps surprised that he found it easy or necessary to discuss things; to confide.

He shrugged. 'As I told another would-be general, there's more to it than a change of uniform. Getting used to stewards in the mess watching you trying to steer the right knife and fork in the right direction, and raising their eyebrows when you drop an aitch in the wrong place!' It seemed to amuse him, now. 'But when you've got men relying on you, doing what they can for you, it makes up for a lot.' He paused, and his voice was very level. 'It was the proudest day of my life, as a matter of fact.'

'When we rejoin the company ...' He got no further.

There was an almighty crash, followed by an insane clatter of metal, while the whole hull shook as if it had collided with another vessel. Then there was silence, broken only by Carson's voice, distorted in the wind.

Despard said, 'The engine's stopped, sir.'

Blackwood tried not to think of the pathetic old launches they had commandeered on the Irrawaddy to help the retreating soldiers. Too hard-worked, not designed as machines of war. Like this schooner.

They stood up, heads bowed beneath the low deck beams, Despard with one hand still on the Bren's magazine.

He remarked, 'That's torn it.'

Blackwood glanced at him and smiled. 'We'll see.'

Impossible, but it seemed lighter on deck since he had gone below only minutes ago. There was steam fanning over the bulwark, and a strong stench of burning, but no sign of fire. Blackwood heard Despard behind him. That *would* have torn it. It was a long swim to Alex from here.

Carson strode past. In the half-light he appeared to be wearing gloves, but Blackwood knew that his hands were black with oil and grease.

He saw them and paused, but he was still watching his two mechanics.

'Crankshaft's fractured. A bloody write-off! Of all the bloody luck!'

Despard said mildly, 'Can't it be repaired?'

Carson laughed, a bitter, rather wild sound on the cool air. 'They stopped making engines like this one before you joined. Before most of us were born, probably!' Then he was calm again, in control. 'There'll be local craft about soon. We could keep with them, then head for Turkish waters.' He rubbed his chin. 'I had hoped we might log a few more miles. Our chaps will know what's happening. They'll come looking.' He turned away

151

as one of his men called to him. 'Fingers crossed all round, I'd say.'

Blackwood took out his binoculars and trained them across the port bow. He could see what the seaman had just reported. Bat-like sails, resembling feathers scattered on the hardening rim of the horizon. Who were they? How did they manage to survive?

Carson called, 'We'll close with them. Should be safe. Nobody sees anything in these waters!'

The tiller creaked over, and the big mainsail came noisily to life. Despard looked towards the other vessels.

'I wouldn't trust any of 'em!'

Blackwood dropped one hand to his webbing holster. They were hardly equipped for a fight.

Despard must have seen the movement.

'I brought some 36 grenades, sir. Just in case.'

Blackwood watched the brightening sky, and imagined he could feel warmth where there was none. He remembered his father speaking about the ill-fated Gallipoli campaign; 'an heroic failure', he had called it. Towards the end of the campaign, the rules of war had long since been discarded. In savage hand-to-hand battles, on wiring parties, and during raids on enemy positions, there had been no quarter asked or given.

He gripped a stay and felt the schooner rise and dip beneath his feet. Carson and his men, like all of this special group, knew that the same odds existed for them. If captured, the enemy would be merciless.

Carson was drinking from a large and none too clean mug, and speaking with his petty officer. He was the first to hear the unhurried drone of a solitary aircraft.

As it altered course towards the scattered vessels, the wing tilted and the cockpit perspex flashed in the sun which, on the sea, was not yet visible.

Despard said, 'It's that bloody Storch again.' He revealed neither surprise nor anxiety, as if he had known.

The petty officer looked at his skipper. 'Thought you said they couldn't fly this far, sir!' He could actually grin about it.

Carson clapped his shoulder. 'Just this once, I was wrong!'

The little spotter plane was already turning in a final arc. They had found what they had come looking for, and it was back to base now, with, maybe, a run ashore to some Greek hostelry.

Carson stooped to look at his compass.

'South-east by south. Steady as you go, Miller!' And to Blackwood, 'Nelson would have been proud of us!'

Then he swung away and stared at the morning sky. The enemy.

'Break out the weapons.'

He was still standing alone by the tiller, watching the array of patched but colourful sails take on shape and identity in the misty yellow light, and Blackwood wondered if he saw instead the high-prowed galleys and triremes of these waters which had been his life. Bright helmets and breastplates, great sweeps rising and falling to the beat of a drum.

Joanna would have laughed if he had told her his thoughts.

The lookout, who had shinned up the mainmast,

153

yelled, 'Fast-moving vessel on the port quarter, sir!'

But now there was no time.

Carson shouted, 'Get to your stations! The rest of you keep out of sight!' He saw Despard kneeling in the small companion hatch, the Bren cradled in his arms. 'Glad to have you aboard!'

Blackwood felt it, too. A creeping madness when there is no hope left, and no tomorrow. Like Burma, and the chilling screams of the Japanese soldiers as they had attacked, again and again, around the clock, heedless of casualties.

Despard checked the spare magazines. 'Leave it to the professionals!'

A sailor was sitting against the bulwark, apparently stitching a piece of canvas. Beneath some spare material, Blackwood could see the butt plate of a Thompson submachine gun. Not very accurate, but deadly while the ammunition lasted.

Blackwood removed his beret and jammed it inside his battledress. With great care he levelled his binoculars, very aware that the enemy might be watching them.

Then he saw the other vessel, low and sleek with a finely raked bow, painted pale grey, with the Italian ensign streaming from her tripod mast. He felt his heart beating faster, louder. Not a warship; even the paint and the gun-mounting on her foredeck could not disguise her elegant, expensive lines. Probably some millionaire's motor yacht until taken over or captured by the Italian navy. But not German. Why should that make any difference?

Somebody said, 'One of them schooners is puttin' a spurt on!' It sounded as if he were speaking through gritted teeth.

Blackwood tore his eyes from the oncoming
154

vessel and turned as one of the other craft, a schooner like this, filled her sails to the wind, while beneath her counter came a sudden froth from her screw.

Carson said sharply, 'Smuggler, gun-runner, could be anything.'

The grey hull had reduced speed and was weaving busily to avoid the other small boats which were attempting to move out of her way.

Blackwood said, 'But for the crankshaft, Terry.'

Carson stared at him, his eyes suddenly alight with understanding, and possibly hope.

'We would have been over there by now! They think it's us!'

They all froze as the Italian vessel opened fire. Just two cannon, like Oerlikons, probably, but even at extreme range their effect was devastating. Blackwood gripped the binoculars and pressed them into his eyes. The bright red tracer seemed to drift so slowly towards the schooner before ripping down, raking it from stern to bow, tearing the surrounding water into spurting fountains of spray and smoke.

Even through the haze and the careering shapes of scattering boats Blackwood could see tiny figures running about the deck, before being tossed like bloody bundles amongst the wreckage. The sails were all ablaze now, and the schooner was turning very slowly towards her executioner, the engine still going but the rudder jammed, the helmsman doubtless dead with his companions.

There was a dull explosion and she began to settle down by the stern. The Italian commander was still not satisfied; a machine gunner was spraying the burning hull and scattered flotsam.

155

Nothing could survive that.

He lowered the glasses to look at Carson. His face was like a mask. Another example . . .

The petty officer reached down for his gun. 'They'll start sniffing around here next!' He rubbed his face with the back of his hand. 'Bloody cowardly bastards!'

Blackwood said, 'Then why not let them find us?' They were all looking at him. *Another death-or-glory maniac.*

Carson took a couple of paces, but hesitated as they all heard a solitary shot. Some poor soul found alive amidst all that destruction.

Then he said, 'It might just work.'

Blackwood watched their strained, unshaven faces, and saw the faint gleam of hope there. Anger, too. Anger enough. It was all they had.

He turned towards Despard and saw him jerk his head.

The lookout called, 'She's turnin' this way, sir!' He sounded hushed, as if he were more afraid of interrupting than of fear itself.

Carson watched the enemy. 'Break out some of that wine. Not too much, Miller. We'll need the rest for later!'

Somebody laughed. The madness was complete.

Blackwood clung to a wire backstay and used the flapping mainsail for cover while he watched the approaching vessel. About a hundred feet long, with a roomy wheelhouse and a small flying bridge, which had probably been added after she had been taken into naval service. She was close enough for him to see the dents and scars along her once elegant side, bearing down on the schooner with little regard for speed or the wind across her

156

quarter. Carson had seen the danger, and two of his men were already lowering rope fenders over the bulwark to lessen the impact when the Italian vessel lurched alongside.

They must suspect nothing until they were lashed together for boarding. Otherwise, the Italian commander would open his throttles and stand away to use his twin cannon as he had done on the other schooner.

He could see the man quite easily, probably a lieutenant, a reservist like Carson who had found himself in command of a craft designed only for comfort and luxury.

There was no sign of suspicion as the two craft angled together, the Italian's raked bow rising above the schooner's side like a ram. Her commander had even taken time to light a cheroot and was fanning the smoke away from his eyes for the final approach, unmoved by the slaughter he had just carried out without hesitation or question.

He sensed Despard crouched on the companion ladder, the Bren already cocked and trained. He also realised that he himself was armed only with the heavy revolver at his hip. One bullet would stop a charging man dead in his tracks, it was claimed. If you could hit him. In his pocket he felt the grenade Despard had given him. It seemed unlikely that he would have a chance to use either.

He heard the other vessel's engines cough and go astern, the wash lifting the schooner's hull like a dinghy.

One of Carson's men was waving a bottle of wine towards the Italian sailors, and one of them was grinning.

Two grapnels thudded into the bulwark, and the

slack was taken in sharply until both hulls rose and fell in an ungainly embrace.

Blackwood felt his mouth go dry as he saw the Italian officer lean over the small bridge and point, jabbing the air with his hand to attract attention above the growl of engines.

One of the fenders had been dragged over the unused canvas where a seaman had been pretending to work. His Tommy gun lay exposed in the weak sunlight, and even as the man snatched it up the Italian machine gunner threw himself on his mounting.

Shots cracked out, and Blackwood felt a bullet slam into the deck by his feet.

It was too late. It was too late.

And then, as if responding to a shouted command, he was out on to the deck and sprinting for the grey hull which seemed to tower over him. He felt his fingers tearing on rusting wire, and heard shouts, and the sudden stammer of a machine gun. But he could not stop himself; he was clinging to the Italian's guardrail, and felt the sea dragging at his legs as the trapped water burst upwards between the two hulls.

Somehow his mind recorded the sound of Despard's Bren, unhurried, single shots, and as he ran across the slippery planking he realised that the boat's commander was hanging head down from his flying bridge, his blood running down the side like paint.

He saw the seaman with the Tommy gun clamber over the stern, only to fall kicking against a covered motor boat. Someone had fired from inside the boat; the sailor had no face but was still struggling, refusing to die.

The Italian crew had fled below. All they had to do was wait. They could prevent anybody from taking the wheelhouse and securing the boat's controls.

He heard Despard yelling, 'Take cover, sir! *Get down!'*

It seemed as if the explosion came from beneath his feet. He heard the shot, but not the sound of shattering glass. He was on his knees, his head lowered as the agony burned into his thigh like molten metal. His head was reeling and he knew the voice gasping out in senseless fury was his own.

And through it all filtered the logic of training and hard-won experience. The shot had come through a skylight. From below. *I should have known. Should have seen it.*

And the two hulls were still tethered together.

He tried to stand, but it was too much for him. There was so much blood. He had failed them.

And yet he was on his knees again, his mind suddenly frozen, compressed into small, agonising decisions.

The grenade was in his fist, and he heard the pin rattle on the deck although he did not recall pulling it. He felt the lever stir against his fingers. The voice of some forgotten instructor. 'Four seconds, sir. Three, once it leaves your hand!'

He opened his fingers and watched the lever fall into his blood. It was live.

It was like something in slow motion: another shot from below, a sudden chorus of shouts, followed instantly by a muffled explosion. He felt the remainder of the skylight's glass dropping around him, and heard one lingering scream, like an animal caught in a trap. And then nothing.

He tried to touch his wound, but to his surprise there were other hands already there. He heard Despard's voice. 'Give me a shell-dressing! Hold his leg!'

Men were hurrying about, and through a haze of pain he heard the strident roar of engines. They must have cast off from the little schooner. It was over. The grenade had done it. Contained by this elegant steel hull, it would have been devastating.

He tried to focus his eyes and gasped, 'What's this?'

Despard answered almost gently, 'Rum. I know officers aren't supposed to drink the stuff, but to hell with O.L.Q.S.!'

And here was Carson. 'I've got her, Mike! Have you home and dry in no time in this thoroughbred!'

Blackwood laid his head back on somebody's knee.

'We did it.' His voice seemed to come from far away, through a long tunnel.

Despard watched him grimly. 'You did it, you mean.' He glanced up and saw Carson framed against the sky, where the Italian commander had been standing. It was something else he would never forget. Carson was not looking ahead, or up at the tattered White Ensign which he had brought with him from somewhere. He was staring astern at the listing shape of the schooner which he had just scuttled.

He heard Blackwood ask, 'Is it bad, George? Tell me.'

Despard looked at the blood-soaked dressing, recalling the solitary figure on this deck, like someone driven, or possessed.

'Nothing vital, sir. You'll be fine. Really.'

160

He felt the scarred hand grope for his.

'You did bloody well, George!'

Despard laughed. Had he been anyone else, he might have wept.

'Not bad for a ranker, eh?' he said. That night, St John's patrols found them.

CHAPTER EIGHT

NEED

The bicycle was very old and heavy and Diane Blackwood had wondered more than once if she should have kept to the main road. The lane, which led directly from the village of Alresford, seemed much wider than she remembered, and she guessed it was because of the increased use both by farm vehicles and those army units in this part of Hampshire. She saw a farm gate and decided to dismount. The lane was certainly no less steep.

She looked across the fields and saw part of a rooftop above the next slope. Hawks Hill. She licked her lips, suddenly dry, and looked next around at the hedges and long grass. There would be early daffodils here soon. It was hard to believe so much had happened to her in so short a time. Impossible.

She straightened her skirt, quite used now to seeing herself in Wren's uniform. The old bike, which she had borrowed from the postmaster, was no respecter of women, and the crossbar had made her skirt ride up her thighs when she was not paying attention. It had brought immediate and appreciative whistles from passing soldiers, and a few moist glances from men she now knew to be Italian prisoners of war, with coloured patches stitched to their uniforms to make them easy to detect. One soldier had told her that they need not have bothered; the Eye-Ties were having such a cushy time over here that they would never escape even if they were politely asked. *Live better than we do,* the squaddie had remarked. It was probably true.

She had seen other looks down in the village. *The Blackwood girl is back. Surprised she's not an officer by now.* If only they knew.

She was based at Southsea, right next door to Portsmouth, another strange experience at first. Eastney Barracks had always seemed a part of her life, even though she had never been there before. Her father had mentioned it often enough, and Harry Payne had a thousand stories about it, as did most Royal Marines, she supposed. She was still not quite sure what she had been expecting when she had been accepted for the W.R.N.S. It had begun tamely. Drilling on the square, instructed and chased by sergeants who somehow managed to control their language. Most of the time.

She lived with other Wrens in a pleasant-looking house on the sea front at Southsea; it had a green roof and was called 'Pantiles', but once inside it was a part of the service. Iron bedsteads and not much space, girls who thought nothing of walking naked to or from the bathrooms, and others who remained too shy to say anything at first.

It was presided over by a grey-haired second officer, who, it was said, had once been a teacher at Roedean or another of the top schools. She

162

addressed her Wrens as 'chaps' and kept an eagle eye on every hour of leave from duty. A sleeping-out pass was unheard of under her command.

But she knew her job well. She was never slow to warn her 'chaps' about certain officers at the barracks, the older ones, especially the married variety. 'Gropers', as she described them.

'Just tell me if one of them tries it, and I'll have him on a skewer in front of the Colonel!' She meant it.

Diane removed her jaunty cap from her dark chestnut hair and held it in the watery sunlight. It was the biggest change so far. Instead of the H.M.S. cap tally with which she had first been issued, her cap now sported a brass Royal Marines badge, mounted upon a patch of scarlet cloth. Old Harry Payne would like that. She smiled, thinking of the way people looked at her, anywhere away from a place used to marines. She was that much of a rarity. There were so many foreign servicemen and women in England now, French, Poles, Danes, even Czechs, that one old lady in Winchester had asked her if she was a Norwegian, as she had once enjoyed 'such a happy holiday there'.

At Eastney they had put her to work in the records office, and she had been given a badge to stitch to her right sleeve, the letter W, a writer. Necessary without doubt, but not what she had hoped for, boats' crew, or Signals, working at a base alongside the ships and the danger. The Wrens were reputedly the most popular of the three women's services, and there was a waiting list to prove it. So a writer she would be.

That was until three days ago, when the adjutant had sent for her and told her that Mike had been wounded. He was not on the second officer's list of gropers; he was considerate in every way and had assured her that he would personally keep her informed. Mike was not in danger and the worst was over. His eyes had said, *until the next time,* but they all knew that. Then he had said, 'I'm told you can drive. I can use you, if that's true.'

She could remember exactly when her father had insisted that she take driving lessons, not as the pampered daughter of a country gentleman, but as a working woman. It was rarely a car she drove in any case, more often the old van from the farm, humping fodder for the horses, or carrying machinery in need of repair to the local blacksmith. No wonder the estate had almost gone bankrupt, she had thought often enough.

But driving was comparatively rare amongst young women, and the Royal Marines had no facilities for training them.

The grouchy second officer had pouted a bit, but Diane had thought she was secretly quite pleased. Another of her chaps was doing well.

'One thing, my girl—just keep out of the back seat. They're a randy lot!'

Once she would have blushed, as she had done at the language some of her companions used, and the details of their affairs, most of which she guessed were only in their minds. But she felt something else, something new. A comradeship, a loyalty, which went far deeper than the coarse jokes and the suggestive glances. She straightened her skirt again and tugged at the underwear beneath it. It would be worth it just to wear some of her own things. She smiled. Passion-killers, they called issue underwear. They had a good point.

She stared at the front tyre and exclaimed, *'Bloody hell!'* and then looked round quickly, ashamed at her easy profanity.

She replaced her cap and took the handlebars. It would be a long push, then.

When she returned to Southsea some of her new friends might regard her driving job as favouritism. *Just keep out of the back seat.* She wheeled the bicycle to one side as she heard a vehicle on the road behind her. Grinding gears, with a total disregard for service property. It had to be the army.

She braced herself. *Want a lift, Jenny? What's a nice girl like you doing out here?* She was used to it, or should be by now. But once or twice she had given some back. It had usually shocked them, perhaps because of what everyone called her posh accent. It worked, though.

'Need a helping hand? It's miles from anywhere.'

She faced the lane. It was a fifteen-hundredweight Chevrolet truck, with a divisional crest painted on one scratched wing. The man who had spoken was a passenger, a soldier with a Royal Engineers cap badge. A sapper; and as he leaned out of the window she saw a lieutenant's pips on his shoulder. He had an open face, one used to the outdoors. The driver, she noticed, was staring straight ahead, probably wondering what the hell they were doing here. It only needed a tractor to come from the opposite direction and there would be an interesting stalemate.

She said, 'I've got a puncture.' She hesitated. 'Sir.'

He grinned. 'I'll put it in the back.' He did not order his driver to do it, but climbed down himself.

165

He was quite tall. There was something both different and oddly familiar about him.

She took a grip on her imagination. 'Just up the road, then. Thank you.'

He waited for her to climb in, and then sat carefully beside her. 'Must be beautiful here in the good weather.' He laughed. 'If you ever get any!'

That was it. The accent was Australian. No. Not quite.

'You stationed around here, miss?'

She smiled. 'No.'

He nodded seriously. 'That's the ticket. Careless talk, and all that.'

She ventured, 'You're a New Zealander, sir?'

He turned as if surprised. 'Clever girl. Yes, Auckland. Seems a long way away.'

He leaned forward suddenly.

'*Stop!* Stop right here!'

She felt the slam of brakes and sensed the driver's resentment.

He said quietly, 'That must be it. It's got to be.' He looked at her. 'Sorry about this. It's only for a minute. I've always wanted to see it.'

She looked past him. It was only the old gamekeeper's tower, now a water storage tank, and beyond it the superb Tudor façade of the main building, unspoiled by time, by war, by all the missing faces.

'Hawks Hill,' she said.

'I wonder if I could walk down and have a closer look?' He seemed to realise something. 'Would you mind?'

She shook her head. 'It's where I was going, anyway.' She took his proffered hand and stepped down on to the wheel-torn verge.

166

She knew that the driver was revving his engine with his boot and peering meaningly at his watch, eager to leave. Just as she knew the importance of this moment, without understanding it.

He did not release her hand. 'Where you were going, did you say?'

She removed the hand, very gently. 'It's my home, when I'm not with the Royals.' Then, 'Bring the bike, would you, please?' She tried to smile, to toss it off lightly. 'Sir.' She walked to the top of the slope. 'I'll get you some transport back to wherever it is.'

He did not appear to be listening.

'You must be Colonel Blackwood's daughter! I must have been nuts not to realise!'

She nodded. 'I'll show you round, if you like.'

He watched the driver at last unloading the old bicycle, but seemed unable to contain some emotion.

He said, 'I'm Lieutenant Blackwood. My friends call me Steve.'

She took the handlebars and started to walk down the slope with him. She did not hear the truck drive away, nor did she care.

No wonder he had seemed vaguely familiar. His face was in several of the portraits, spanning a hundred years or more. Like Mike, and all those others.

A huge dog bounded across the path, barking fiercely and wagging its tail.

She said, 'He's pretty old. He won't hurt you.' She looked at him fully for the first time since she had stepped into the road. 'It's his way of saying "Welcome home"!'

Diane Blackwood turned back a dust sheet from

one of the chairs and sat down, watching him while he moved from one portrait to another. She noticed how carefully he took each step, very conscious of the beautiful floors, and of his army boots.

She said, 'They call this the Long Room.' It seemed wrong to intrude on his thoughts. 'I don't know why, except that it is long.'

He turned and looked at her. 'My father described it to me once. I think he said it was used for displaying trophies in old Colonel Eugene Blackwood's day.' He nodded, deep in thought. 'I can feel it. As if I'd always been here.' He moved to a window and she was reminded of Mike again, their last meeting in this house after the funeral. She had told this quiet New Zealander about it.

She said, 'Tell me about your father now.'

He stood, his face in shadow. 'He was the black sheep of the family. Major Ralf, your father's cousin, the only one to survive the war.' He shrugged, and even that seemed familiar. 'He never really made a go of things after he left the Corps. *Required to resign* is the accepted term, I believe.'

She waited, knowing he wanted to talk. That he needed to be here.

'I was born in England, but we went out to New Zealand soon afterwards. A fresh start. But my dad wasn't the type to settle down. He liked *life* too much. Their marriage collapsed, and he went off with another woman. He came back to England apparently, but nothing worked out. My mother took good care of me, but when she remarried she made sure that I remained a Blackwood. Women, gambling, drink—it reads like a bad novel, but it did for him in the end.' He took a step towards her,

168

and halted, his arms at his sides. 'But he was my dad, and I still miss the old bugger!'

He walked back to the window, and, without realising she had risen from the chair, she joined him there.

The old dog was sitting on the flagstones and staring up at Harry Payne, who was holding something that shone in the sunlight. Her cap badge. *Can't let you be seen with a rookie's badge, Miss Diane! I'll give it a proper buff-up!* But all the time his eyes had been on the visitor.

When she had gone to his cottage for some keys he had exclaimed, 'Spittin' image of his father, Miss Diane! I hope that's the only likeness!'

She said, 'So we're sort of cousins?'

He looked at her and grinned. 'Sort of. Does it matter?'

She pointed at the other wing of the main building. 'That's used by the local Home Guard as their battalion H.Q. They have their drills here two or three times a week. You've never seen so many medal ribbons!' She paused. 'No, it doesn't matter.'

They completed the tour in the old library.

'What did you do before you joined up?'

'Farm machinery, mostly. Where I come from, the sheep outnumber the people by twenty to one!'

'And now?' She could not stop.

'I'm on leave, but it's up tomorrow. I'll be going to a place in Portsmouth, explosives, that kind of thing.' He gazed at the books and the portraits. 'The closest I'll ever get to the Royal Marines!'

Portsmouth. She shied away from it. It was laughable. Because of a name, or because they were both alone. And she did not even know him. *My friends call me Steve.* Her second officer would

169

think she was naive. Asking for it.

She said, 'This is careless talk, but I'm at Eastney Barracks. Not that far.'

He turned as a car entered the gates. He had used the telephone to call his unit, and now he was leaving. It was better this way . . . And she knew it was not.

He hesitated.

'I'd like to see you again. I'm sure there's somebody else, but—'

She walked with him to the library door and heard his quick intake of breath as he saw the portrait of her mother, Alex. It could have been Diane herself, although she had always denied the resemblance.

She said, 'No. There's nobody.' She ignored the warnings bombarding her mind. There *had* been nobody, not in that way. It had been a near thing once or twice, at the local hunt ball or at one of the farmers' parties. But she was strong, and an elbow in the right place had sufficed. Until now.

Harry Payne was in the yard talking to the army driver. He held out the badge and said, 'Here, Miss Diane. You need me with you to keep an eye on things!'

She stared at the badge with its crimson flash, so smooth that the markings on the Globe had been polished away.

'It's your own badge, Harry. I can't take that!'

She could feel the New Zealander watching, listening, sharing this small but significant detail, like a piece of a jigsaw puzzle.

Payne shook his head.

'You can give it back when I've worked some spit an' polish into yours, right?'

170

'Right,' she said, knowing he would never take it from her, and moved by the knowledge.

The sapper lieutenant shook hands with both of them, strangely formal after so many shared thoughts.

Then he said, 'I wouldn't have missed this for anything. You have no idea what it means just to stand here.' He smiled awkwardly. 'With you. You've made it perfect.' He released her hand and, surprisingly, saluted.

Together, they watched the car until it had turned into the road.

Then she said quietly, 'Well, Harry, what did you think?'

He did not look at her. 'Well, Miss Diane, he's not in the regiment, but he's a Blackwood right enough. That'll have to do, for the moment.'

From Harry Payne that was praise indeed.

She felt droplets of rain on her face; the sun had gone without her noticing. But it had been a perfect day, after all.

*   *   *

Michael Blackwood opened his eyes, and waited for his new surroundings to discover him. He had slept well, without the need for drugs, and even the pain was at bay. When he had come out of the anaesthetic at the main hospital he had been almost too weak, and too fearful, to reach down to his thigh. A nurse had seen his feeble efforts, and had brought him an old-fashioned mirror.

'See? Good as new. We'll be able to move you soon.' Somewhere a man had cried out in agony or terror, it could have been either, and she glanced round, her ration of sympathy dispensed. 'We need the bed.'

And now he was in Alexandria again, still in pain, but without despair. Familiar faces had hovered above him; even St John, immaculate as ever, had come to wish him well. And 'Sticks' Welland, and several other Royals he hardly knew, and, of course, Despard.

He half-listened to the bark of an N.C.O.'s voice, and the responding stamp of boots.

'At th' halt, on the right, *foooorm—squad!*' And then, 'For God's sake 'old yer 'ead up, that man! You're like a nun in the family way!'

Familiar and somehow comforting, after the passage in the armed yacht. Despard had told him most, but not all, he guessed, about the scuttled schooner and Carson's obvious distress, and the few Italians taken alive. They had appeared grateful to have survived, to be out of the war. The force of the grenade had jammed the cabin door, where one Italian seaman had miraculously survived the blast. The rest, Carson's petty officer had told him cheerfully, 'looked like an upended butcher's cart!'

Major Gaillard had visited him only once. A strangely reserved Gaillard, who had told him about the arrival of the new company in Alexandria. 'I want you up and about as soon as you can hop! This is what we've been waiting for!'

Blackwood had answered, 'I'm supposed to have a final checkup tomorrow.' *That was today.* And all he could think of was Gaillard's stiff, detached demeanour.

As he had been about to leave, Gaillard had said, 'You did a good piece of work. I'll see that it

172

doesn't go unnoticed this time. If you or any of your party had been taken alive, it would have ended very differently.' And then he had smiled. 'Like Burma, remember? No prisoners.'

Blackwood was still thinking of it as the door opened a few inches and a sickberth attendant peered in at him.

'Time for walkies, Mr Blackwood!'

The others called the S.B.A. Nancy. He could understand why.

He lay quite still while the dressing was removed, revealing a deep, livid gash in his right thigh. How it had missed a bone or an artery was beyond him. Or, as Nancy had murmured confidentially, 'And your wedding-tackle is all safe and sound, sir!'

A white-jacketed doctor paused outside the door and nodded with approval as Blackwood took the weight on his feet. Playing it down, he thought, which was probably the best therapy. And they *did* need the beds. He had heard about a new offensive, and more advances. Neither would come cheaply.

'Easy does it!' Nancy hovered around him, but was careful not to assist. Blackwood took a few paces and saw himself in another mirror. The scar was a bad one. Despard had remarked, 'When you need to find the seam of your trousers with your thumbs out there on the square, you'll have that to make it easier for you!' And they had laughed about it.

'That's enough, sir. I'll just put on a fresh dressing and make it comfy.'

He was quick at his job, but not so fast that Blackwood did not see the fresh blood on the

173

dressing. It had been that close; and yet he felt neither elation nor surprise.

Nancy was saying, 'I'll fetch some tea, and you should have a nice rest.'

'I feel fine,' he said.

Nancy pursed his lips. 'That young lady will be here tomorrow. Must look our best, mustn't we?'

Blackwood stared at him.

'What did you say?'

The S.B.A. said, rather severely, 'Well, you weren't supposed to know. Even now . . .' Then he relented, but only slightly. 'An R.A.F. lady. Came every day when she was in Alex. Most concerned, she was.'

'Where is she now?'

'Gone off with one of your big-pots, a major-general no less.' He sniffed. 'I don't know what the service is coming to!'

Blackwood lay back and gazed at the slowly revolving fan. She had been here. Right here in Alex. Perhaps he would wake up a second time . . . But he could still hear the raucous commands of the drill-sergeant, and was glad that Nancy had gone for the tea.

The fan blurred and his eyes stung with sudden emotion.

She was safe. And she had cared enough.

*　　*　　*

Major Claud Porter leaned back stiffly in his chair, then glanced first at an almost empty cigarette packet and then at the wall clock. One-thirty. He wanted to yawn but his mouth tasted stale, and the air, even down in the privacy of the Pit, was like

174

battery acid at this hour of the morning.

His desk had been cleared, the signals and folders already taken away to their various destinations. At times like this he often felt a certain loneliness, and knew it was not merely because of Vaughan's absence, although it would be a relief to see him back again. *The driving force.*

Porter had never married, had never felt the need to. Between the wars he had served on several undemanding stations, mostly in cruisers. Mess life and ceremonial had been his mainstays. The war had changed that immediately. He had been in the right place at the right time, but at one-thirty it did not feel like it.

He stifled a yawn as someone tapped at the door. He was not the only one about, apparently.

It was a fellow major who worked in Intelligence, another of Vaughan's private army.

Porter rubbed his eyes. 'Still here, Jack? Haven't you got a home to go to?'

He slammed his fist on the desk, furious with himself. Fatigue was no excuse.

'I'm sorry, Jack. That was unforgivable.'

The other officer's young wife and daughter had been killed in a hit-and-run raid two weeks before. They had gone together to the scene. A neat suburban road, with a line of trees; there were a thousand such streets within twenty miles of London. There was one gap, like a missing tooth. The remainder of the houses were untouched.

The man he had called Jack said without expression, 'It's all right. I'm coming to terms.' He put down a thin folder. 'Thought you should see this at once, in view of the general's absence.'

They both studied the folder, the diversion like a

lifeline for both.

'Our people have been informed as a matter of policy. But if it goes higher, the Judge Advocate's department could become involved.'

Porter pulled some papers from the file. A rough map, a cracked photograph of a young Royal Marine grinning at the camera. Porter noted the helmet and uniform. Pre-war. Another world.

His friend was saying, 'It mainly concerns a marine named Gerald Finch. He was serving in the *Genoa* at the time of the Jap invasion of Burma, and was transferred to the land force covering the withdrawal.'

Porter was suddenly wide awake.

'As you see by the notes, Marine Finch was wounded in the arm and in the neck during the final stages on the Irrawaddy, and has been in a pretty bad way. But he's out of hospital now, and due for a medical discharge. There was also damage to his vision. He can only use one eye.'

Porter read rapidly through the typed notes and various scribbled initials and signatures. The marine must have been about twenty at the time. The other man moved away from the desk, and looked up at the wall map with its little paper flags.

'He played dead until some natives found him and took care of him. Otherwise he would not have survived.' He gave a dry laugh. 'And we wouldn't be stuck with a headache.' He paused. 'Marine Finch has stated that during the retreat he saw an officer shoot dead four soldiers and a wounded marine, who were unable to stand or move.'

Porter said slowly, 'Do we have a name?' It was like stepping on a trap. He already knew.

'Major Gaillard. He might be mistaken, of
176

course, or it could be his way of working off an old grudge. He has nothing to lose now.'

Porter reached for a cigarette. 'The Judge Advocate of the Fleet would see it differently. There would be an inquiry, perhaps a court martial. And if the allegations were true, it would certainly wreck the plans already in motion for our people in North Africa. Gaillard would be recalled, he'd have to be, and Captain Blackwood would also become involved. He was there, and he was the last one to see Gaillard before he was wounded, and thought to be missing.'

The warning voice seemed to murmur, *except a twenty-year-old marine called Gerald Finch.* Porter recalled Blackwood's genuine surprise when he had been told of Gaillard's survival, and the 'invaluable information' he had gleaned during his escape from the enemy. He could not even discuss it with the forthright Commander Diamond. Another mystery: Diamond had been temporarily replaced by another, without explanation. Porter was getting angry again. This was the part of the work he loathed. Courage and honour standing shoulder to shoulder with deceit and treachery.

But this was different. It concerned the Corps, and had nothing to do with the hotch-potch of staff officers who controlled Special Operations. Later, it might come to that, but now something far more important was at stake. He looked around the spartan office. A decision was necessary. *And it has to be mine.*

He crushed the cigarette, still unlit. 'I'll make a signal to the general right away, Jack. It will be scrambled. You'll be in the clear.'

The other man regarded him curiously. 'It's that

important?'

'Yes.' It would be, to Vaughan. It felt like disloyalty even to think it, but Porter had never liked Gaillard, although he was an officer with a flawless reputation, a man of action and initiative. He had proved it several times, and had been awarded the D.S.O. And there was Blackwood. Could only two officers make such a difference to the next operation? Thank God Vaughan was out there, he thought; he might be able to judge for himself.

The other major, Jack, smiled for the first time, and seemed a young man again.

'Rather you than me, Claud.' He picked up the folder and said bluntly, 'Could you shoot one of your own men to prevent his being captured, by the Japs for instance?' Then he shook his head. 'Unfair question. Sorry.'

Porter reached for his pen, thinking of the signal. *Passing the buck.*

'It's not unfair. I think I'd want somebody to do it for me, but I'm not sure.'

'I'll come back in half an hour, Claud. I know a little dive where we might have a couple of drinks.'

'At this hour?'

'Like the Windmill, it never closes!'

Major Claud Porter was alone again, the *Most Secret* lettering glaring up at him.

When his friend returned it was two-fifteen in the morning, and there was an air raid warning south of the Thames.

A quick drink at the 'little dive' was out of the question. But the signal had been despatched.

*   *   *

178

Joanna Gordon stood quite still, half in the shadow of navigation buoys which had been hoisted on to the jetty, her cap shading her eyes from the forenoon sun. She had noticed that one of the brightly painted buoys had been punched full of bullet holes. It was something you had to take for granted, like the patrol vessel which had entered Alexandria yesterday morning when she had been on her way to the sick quarters to speak with Mike for the first time. The patrol vessel had been expected, and there had been ambulances on the jetty to meet her. There were three corpses laid on her deck, covered with canvas, sharing a solitary flag. People had turned to look, but nobody had commented. Like the youth who had tried to be friendly on the bus, lying dead in the road, his eyes staring into the lights.

She watched while Major-General Vaughan completed his inspection of the newly arrived company of marines. He took his time, and had a few words for almost everyone. Unlike most senior officers or visiting celebrities, she thought, who usually spoke to every third man or woman, so that the previous ones would not overhear what was always the same question.

Vaughan appeared to be really enjoying it, and there were several laughs despite the rigid shoulders and blancoed webbing. She had seen people looking at her, also, but had become used to it, especially amidst the khaki and navy blue. She had intended to wear the light drill uniform Mike had ordered for her in the souk. Had that really been so short a time ago? But her arm was still painful, slow to heal, and short sleeves were forbidden. She had already had a quiet telling-off from one of the doctors.

He had tried to soften it by saying, 'Your R.A.F. people are doing fine work with burns. You might consider an operation when things heal a bit more.'

She could feel it now, a constant reminder, if she needed one. She had tried to confront each lurking memory as it prepared to take her off guard. The iron grip forcing her over the table under the glaring lights, so she could be shown the drawer underneath, the neat lines of shining instruments, as if in a doctor's surgery. But those had been for causing unspeakable pain, on and on until death brought an end to it. If you were lucky. The woman had enjoyed every moment. Telling her that the interrogators who were arriving shortly were experts; forcing her to look at the straps where they would hold her down.

And somehow, inside that madness, she had thought of the people who made those instruments somewhere. Had designed them, knowing for what purpose they would be used.

Most of all, the nightmares brought back the hate. The woman searching her body, probing into her. Like being raped. Something obscene . . .

The operation could wait. She had seen many of the young men who had been shot down. They all seemed to have the same face; and saw the same world, and felt invisible.

She moved slightly, and saw Mike standing a pace away from Major Gaillard. She did not want him to see her, and yet she needed him to know she was here. She thought he looked tense, but less strained than at the hospital; he must be feeling his wound. She shivered. *As I feel mine.*

It was almost over; the ranks were breaking up, the rigid lines becoming individuals again.

It was something quite new to her. She had been used to the brave, casual informality commonplace on most combat air stations. Young faces coming and going, no time to put a name, or remember a voice. Like her young brother, who had gone so quickly. A few weeks, a few months. It was painful to remember. Better to forget.

And the ones who lived day by day, while others disappeared. Like the pilot who had awakened her to passion, always demanding, but now, in retrospect, as vulnerable as the rest. He had known, recognised it, perhaps remembered her so briefly when his plane had spiralled down like a fiery star in the last moments of his life.

Vaughan was walking away now, Gaillard and some other officers with him. They would never know the man she had come to like and to trust so much. He never asked questions; he gave her work not merely to keep her busy but because she was efficient. He would have packed her off back to England if he had thought her incapable.

She watched the groups of marines breaking up, talking with their N.C.O.s and some of the officers. She had seen Despard, probably the oldest man here apart from the general, but like a rock. It warmed her to know that he would be with Mike.

She thought of the too short moments together at the hospital. The embraces, the hint of a kiss, while nurses and staff bustled around them as if they were not there.

He had been deeply concerned for her, with only an impatient shrug when she had mentioned his wound, and the secret mission which had almost cost his life. She was a part of it now, and it meant everything to her.

She saw one of the sergeants, a tall man with a tanned face, putting his hand on Mike's shoulder, with a genuine pleasure she had never witnessed before. As he turned he saw her across the sergeant's shoulder, and smiled at her. Others were pausing to speak to him, and the realisation came to her like something physical. This was not ordinary discipline, or doing your duty because you were so ordered. It was like the sergeant's grin; it was genuine, and touched her heart. *They needed him.* Injured or not, they needed him. Because of his name, because of those qualities of leadership at which she could only guess. All the things which troubled him and had been shared with her alone, on that one night at the house in Rosetta.

Someone coughed discreetly, and she turned to see a slightly built marine watching her; Mike had introduced them on the day he had returned to duty. He was Marine Percy Archer, his M.O.A., something else new to her. A marine officer's attendant was servant, orderly, guardian, all of these, and many more.

Archer was not old, but he had an old-fashioned face, pointed and quizzical, like a knowing fox. A Londoner, from the East End's Bethnal Green, which he pronounced *Befnal Green,* he had joined the Corps after several narrow shaves with the law, which was odd, as his father had been a policeman in 'Befnal Green'.

Archer seemed to run his eyes right over her without moving them. She thought she could guess. *My officer's popsie,* or something less flattering. But she knew he was right for the job. Archer himself

182

had qualified it by saying, 'I'm also the best shot in this bunch of cowboys!'

'Sorry, miss,' he said, 'but the General wants you. Don't want to keep *'im* waitin' now, do we?'

'Have you known the General long?'

Archer eyed her, liking what he saw. 'What, miss, old Boxer Vaughan? I knew 'im when he ran a jellied eel pitch in Dalston market!'

He watched her laugh; he had heard that she hadn't had too much to laugh about recently. Very dishy, he thought, even the uniform couldn't completely conceal the girl underneath. Old Blackie was a lucky bloke.

He stepped aside while she looked across at the figures by the old yacht station, and saw her put her fingers to her lips and then turn them towards one man.

Archer had served a lot of officers in the Corps. Good, all right, or plain bloody awful. But he had never envied one of them, until today.

CHAPTER NINE

UNDER COVER OF DARKNESS

The Chief of Staff stood up and walked directly to the wall map in the operations room and waited for the usual scraping chairs and shuffling feet to fall silent. He was a tall man, a full four-ringer captain who was directly responsible to the Commander-in-Chief, Mediterranean. His face was severe and his hair almost grey, but one lock of it hung loosely above his eyebrow, and Blackwood found it

183

possible, even easy, to see the ambitious young lieutenant who had once served in destroyers, and at some time married a lady called 'Tinker'.

As his eyes travelled across the assembled officers they paused only momentarily on Blackwood. Had Tinker told him about his visit to the deserted house? Somehow, he knew that she had not.

He concentrated on the map and its coloured markers. The Eighth Army was still advancing, while in the west the Americans and the British First Army were holding their own. Due to faulty intelligence and the foul weather, there had been several setbacks on the Tunisian front and the Americans had suffered heavy casualties, and had been forced to give ground to the enemy. A certain amount of bad feeling between the allies had resulted; some said that the Americans had talked big, but when it had come to a real fight they had been too green to recover their positions.

As Vaughan had said at their one brief meeting, 'We were all green when this lot started! Let's not forget it!'

Now there it was, the last stretch of coastline under German control, with Cape Bon pointing towards Sicily, the last line of defence. At any other time it would have been unthinkable. The armed forces had become too used to foul-ups, 'strategic withdrawals', as retreats were euphemistically described. To the west, the port of Bone was fully operational, and the main point for landing thousands of tons of supplies, despite the relentless air raids which had put many ships on the bottom. And on the eastern side of the peninsula, Sousse had been taken. Although the enemy had attempted to destroy the port's facilities before abandoning it, it was already being used by the light coastal forces and minesweeping flotillas.

The Chief of Staff was saying, 'It has to be soon, and it has to be effective. The Germans will have to pull out of North Africa.' His sunburned hand touched the cluster of markers. 'Cape Bon is the gateway, and the enemy is well aware of our determination that no attempt at evacuation will go unopposed.' He waited, as murmurs of approval broke the silence. 'Recent progress by our inshore patrols have been severely hampered, even at night. One M.T.B. was lost, and two destroyers badly damaged by shellfire, almost always under cover of darkness.' He let the words sink in and added, 'A new detection device at this crucial stage would make things serious for us. Plans are already being completed for an attack on Sicily, but if it were to be further delayed, even for another year, almost anything could be thrown at us. Intelligence has already reported German progress on rockets which can be fired from aircraft, and homed on to surface vessels which might be carrying troops for such an invasion. I don't have to spell it out for you. And if a new radio direction finder is available to match our own advanced radar, we could be facing even more losses and delays.' He looked suddenly at Major Gaillard, who was sitting with Commander St John. 'We already knew they had something in the testing stage. Operation *Lucifer* and the information brought back from that raid was a godsend to the boffins at H.Q.' His hand rested on the map again. 'And now we've found it, right here on Cape Bon. Aerial reconnaissance has been almost impossible, and we've lost some fine

185

pilots in the process. But we're as certain as we can ever be.' He glanced around at their faces, and finally his eyes rested on Blackwood. 'We simply cannot afford any delays or setbacks. That site is the target. It is vital. I only wish I were free to tell you how vital!'

Blackwood took a moment to look at his companions. Six lieutenants including Despard and the languid Robyns. Two second lieutenants, and Gaillard. He thought of all the others, like Sergeant Paget who had greeted him like a long-lost brother when the Royals had broken ranks after Vaughan's inspection. And the brief moment alone with Vaughan, when he had mentioned Joanna for the first time.

'She's back on duty now, that's all I can say.'

It was the only time he had ever seen him waver. He had always hated favouritism, but there was no other word for it.

Then Vaughan had said, almost roughly, 'She was *used* by the intelligence people. The fact that she agreed to it cuts no ice with me. I would have stopped it right there. She was a courier. Sounds simple when you say it quickly. But if she had been captured she would have suffered for it, even though she knew nothing they wouldn't already have known or guessed.'

Blackwood had heard himself persist, 'But she's all right?' How ineffectual it seemed now. He had wanted to shout it, even though he knew it would have helped neither of them.

Vaughan had said only, 'She'll tell you when she feels like it. If not—'

There had been some interruption then, and he had sensed Vaughan's relief.

186

He realised that Gaillard had taken the floor. One hand on his hip, the other on the map.

'The first company of Royal Marines is now ready, and fully prepared.' He did not pause as a door opened and closed softly, but he must have seen that the latecomer was Brigadier Jocelyn Naismith. 'Eventually we will be at full battalion strength in this Commando, but until that time we shall act with determination and tenacity. I will accept nothing less.' Then he smiled, but in the hard lighting it made him look angry, wild. 'There have been those in the past who have thought fit to criticise the standards we take for granted in the Corps. But, gentlemen, there is a vast difference between rivalry and envy!'

He turned away from the map as the door opened and closed again, just as quietly. Naismith had taken the hint.

'Top security from now on, no leave, not even locally. I shall expect you to impress on your N.C.O.s and marines the utmost need for secrecy. Anybody who fails to observe this order, and I mean of any rank, will be placed under close arrest immediately. When you dismiss, go to your sections and tell them as little as they need to know.'

The Chief of Staff was on his feet again.

'That sums it up very well, Major Gaillard. It will be within the next two or three days.' He looked at Gaillard impassively. 'Or not at all.'

Gaillard brought his heels together.

'I shall be ready, sir.'

Blackwood felt the pain of his wound lance up his thigh like a warning. But why? If Gaillard was untroubled, why should he still cling to what was

187

now and must remain a blurred memory, left behind in the blood and stench of Burma?

Gaillard had spoken of the battalion. If it came about, a lieutenant-colonel would be required in command. It did not require a crystal ball to know who would be chosen.

I shall be ready, sir. He had spoken for all of them. They were committed.

He thought of the island where they had blown up what must have been an experimental detection station. So it had not been a waste of time, 'a crack-brained scheme', as he had heard Gaillard describe it. And he had not even been there.

A quiet setting for such instant violence. The Italian officer shot dead in the act of drawing a pistol. It could all have ended right there ... He remembered asking Carson, just before they had carried him to the waiting ambulance.

'What ever happened to those people, Terry?'

Carson had walked beside the stretcher, one hand resting lightly on his shoulder.

'The Germans rounded up most of the men and shot them. My informant disappeared, probably to another island. A brave chap, for such a mild character.'

'And that woman?'

Carson had stepped away while they had raised the stretcher. 'Oh, she was his wife. Didn't I mention that?'

Gaillard had joined him. 'Went well, I thought. Think you're up to it?'

'I wouldn't miss it, sir.'

Gaillard shook his head. 'You're an odd bird, Mike. Let's have a drink while we can, eh?'

Blackwood watched him wave to one of the staff
188

officers. Which was the real Gaillard?

He saw Despard observing them, keeping his distance. His way was the best. Just do it.

*   *   *

Even up to the last hours before they had disembarked from the destroyer which had carried Gaillard's raiding force at full speed westward from Alexandria, it seemed likely that the operation would be aborted. Sleep had been out of the question, and Blackwood had spent much of the time in the destroyer's W/T office, or wedged into the chartroom with the ship's captain and navigator.

Gaillard had been like a man possessed, and had scoured every item in the intelligence pack for more information. Aerial reconnaissance, at the cost of several lives, had confirmed that there was an abandoned observatory which had been built by a French millionaire several years before the war. It was a good position, and well able to monitor ship movements in the vital Strait of Sicily.

Gaillard had been satisfied that it was the only possible location. There were several sprawling refugee camps in the vicinity, people driven from their homes in Tunis and Bizerta to exist as best they could, hiding from a war they might never understand.

At dusk they had anchored off Sousse and transferred to a business-like F-lighter, which had been captured from the Germans during one of the recent inshore operations. The F-lighters were strange vessels, not unlike landing craft in size and appearance. But they were heavily armed, and well

189

able to defend themselves against the lightly built M.T.B.s and motor gunboats, with a draught so shallow that even a torpedo running at minimum depth could pass harmlessly beneath the hull. They were the main means of supply for Rommel's army, a convoy and escort rolled into one.

The marines had transferred with a swiftness and efficiency born of rigorous training. At the last moment Gaillard had decided to take only one troop, and leave the other in reserve in case things went wrong. When Blackwood had suggested that Despard should be left in charge of 'B' Troop, Gaillard had dismissed it without hesitation.

'No, we need every experienced body on this one.'

Blackwood had understood then what Gaillard had really meant. If this operation failed, there would be no second attempt.

The other thing which had struck him was the instant reaction of those marines being left behind. No sign of thankfulness or relief; even in that wreck-littered harbour he had sensed the disappointment and disbelief, like something physical.

He had listened to the parting shots from the reserve troop, to show they did not care. Only a fool volunteered anyway, they said. Idiots, who'd misunderstood the question in the first place.

Blackwood had shared it with them, and had known what it really meant.

'Don't get yer feet wet, Jack!'

'Hope you've got your brown underpants on!'

'Old Jerry will laugh fit to bust when he sees you lot!'

The shouted replies were no less colourful.

190

Despard joined him by the armoured wheelhouse, and remarked, 'I wonder what their folks at home would say if they could see them right now.'

He could have been speaking for all of them, Blackwood thought.

The skipper, a young R.N.V.R. lieutenant, explained his part of the operation. To avoid the headland where the detection site was positioned, they would make for a small cove which he had used several times for landing agents. He did not mention whether he had ever picked up any for a return passage.

Together, Blackwood and Gaillard studied the chart. The skipper, apparently taking their silence for doubt, said cheerfully, 'Don't worry, I'll keep well clear of the minefields—theirs *and* ours. I'll get you there in one piece!'

Gaillard shrugged. 'After that . . .' He closed his little notebook with a snap. He did not have to add that the landing party would have to march fifteen miles to reach their objective under cover of darkness, over country which was unknown to them but for the scantiest information, and to all intents hostile every yard of the way.

In itself, it was not a challenge. Some of them had done it before; all had been trained for it.

Gaillard said, 'Weapons check, Mike. Make sure they take enough water. Might be a long walk.' He was thinking aloud. 'Groundsheet and entrenching tools, no unnecessary extra gear.' He glanced at the skipper. 'Three hours?'

'About that. Have your people ready an hour beforehand. Just in case.'

'We're always *ready,* thank you!'

Gaillard strode from the wheelhouse, and the skipper murmured, 'Rather you than me, chum!' Then he leaned over the voicepipes. 'Full ahead together, Bob! Chop-bloody-chop!'

Blackwood found Archer waiting for him, an anonymous shape against the mounting wash from the blunt bows.

'Got yer sandwiches, sir. Coffee, too. Not that canteen muck, neither.'

His accent reminded Blackwood of Carson's motor mechanic from the Mile End Road. Another world. When he had mentioned Mile End to Archer, he had scoffed, 'Don't go *there,* sir. You need a bleedin' passport to get past the synagogue!'

He wondered if Archer was ever serious about anything for long. He had seen him making Joanna laugh after the parade. What she needed. He half-smiled. *Me too.*

Archer must have sensed his mood, and said, 'I'll check the old dressin' before we hit the beach, sir. Don't want to 'old up the show, does we?'

Later, Blackwood moved among the marines. They had finished checking their weapons and magazines, their bayonets and the explosives. There was no outward fuss or uncertainty; friends kept together, others had done all they could, and wanted only to get on with it.

Gaillard had ordered that each man should wear his helmet, although most marines preferred to rely on their berets. A touch of the old pride and swagger, as the drill-pigs would call it on the barracks square.

Sergeant Paget had put it more simply. 'If you're due to have your head blown off, a bit of tin won't help much!' He knew better than most of them.

Occasionally he felt someone touch his arm as he moved past, and there was a quick word or a grin, about all that was visible with their blackened faces.

He found Gaillard sitting on a life raft, a cigarette cupped in his hand; a man who seemed to need no contact, no link with the men he would lead. He said without looking up, 'Compass working all right?'

'Sir.'

Gaillard ground out the glowing cigarette and said, 'Might have to use the stars. You could wander about like a blind beggar once you leave the sea. God, how I hate this place!'

He stood up very lightly, and Blackwood saw his M.O.A. reach out to check his holster and ammunition. But Gaillard brushed him aside and snapped, 'Muster "A" Troop, or we'll be on the beach before anybody thinks fit to tell us!'

Blackwood stepped down and waited for the marines to file past him, soundlessly, like ghosts, men without faces, only the helmets offering an identity. Not so very different from the men his father had described, at Gallipoli and in Flanders. *Where no birds sing . . .*

He allowed his mind to explore it. Suppose it ended on this day. Something that should never be considered, never asked . . .

He thought of the old paintings at Hawks Hill, the brave faces and streaming flags. What would they show for him? An ex-German F-lighter in some godforsaken North African cove of which nobody had ever heard? One thing was certain: they would never portray the Desperados and the Percy Archers, the Pagets, or men like 'Sticks'

Welland, who could reprimand a marine for failing to show respect to his officer while the Italian he had just killed lay on the floor between them.

The big engines were slowing down, and against the first stars he could see the heavy machine guns training round as if to sniff out the enemy.

He felt men move aside to allow him to pass, and sensed that the other lieutenant, Robyns, was already waiting by the ramp, quiet now, nothing to say, no bravado. He touched his elbow and felt him start with alarm.

Blackwood could feel the sweat running down his back, when seconds earlier he could have sworn his skin was cool and dry. Like the moment when she had held him, taken him, loved him . . .

The screws were thrashing astern now, and he felt the deck shiver as the lighter thrust ashore. The noise was deafening, enough to rouse the whole coast.

But it was all in the mind. He raised his Sten carefully; Archer had even seen to that. Sling taped securely so as not to rattle or impede the cocking handle. He licked his lips and thought he could still taste the coffee. *Not that canteen muck.*

He felt spray on his face, and knew it was now.

Water surging around his legs and filling his webbing gaiters and boots, a young marine striding beside him, his breathing so loud that he sounded like a pensioner. Sergeant Paget hurrying to the point, his section fanning out behind him, as if they visited here every day . . .

Solid beach now, loose and treacherous for the unwary, but no one fell or even stumbled.

'A' Troop, four officers and some fifty N.C.O.s and marines, had landed.

194

He heard Gaillard's voice for the first time. 'Incline *right*, Sergeant! Bring up the Brens!'

Then he did catch his foot in something, and instantly some unknown hand seized his arm and he saw the white grin. 'You can't get out of it that way, sir!' And somebody else gave a barely suppressed laugh.

He thought he heard the rumble of engines as the F-lighter went astern to free herself from the land. The ground was sloping more steeply, and he forced himself to recall the maps and the sketches.

Once, he glanced back. The sea had gone.

Always the worst moment. He felt his lips crack into a smile. Even for a marine.

He could feel Archer's fresh bandage around his thigh. There was no pain. He thought of the girl, with her injured arm. Or had she been deliberately tortured; was that what Vaughan had been trying to tell him?

He quickened his pace. Fifteen miles to go before first light.

They had all done it; they would not let anybody down.

But it did not help. All he could feel was hate.

*   *   *

'All in position, sir.' Blackwood propped himself on his elbows and stared past the darker shadows of the men around him. They had accomplished it without incident, and his eyes had become so accustomed to the gloom and unfamiliar surroundings that it seemed like early morning. He was not even breathless, but his mouth was bone dry and his stomach muscles felt like iron against

195

the rough ground. The usual signs; you never got used to them.

He could hear some of the marines cursing quietly, moaning, as all servicemen did in the presence of danger. The long ridge would provide good cover when daylight found them, even from low-flying aircraft, but comfortable it was not, and it was covered with tangles of rough scrub with thorns as big as knitting needles, or so they felt to the unwary.

And beyond them was the sea, whereas before it had been at their backs. The Sicilian Strait, dark, shark-blue, still black where night lingered. Flat, calm and deadly.

He pulled out his binoculars and adjusted them carefully. Soon the sun would show itself over his shoulder; even the smallest reflection from the lenses would warn a sentry, and leave them naked on this ridge.

He held his breath, and heard Gaillard murmur something. He had seen it, too, very pale against the sea's backdrop. It looked alien here, like a folly. Who had decided to build an observatory in this wilderness?

Gaillard said, 'Pickets in place?' He did not wait for confirmation. 'Let's hope they keep their eyes open.' Then, 'So that's the bloody thing. Can't see any vehicles so far. Not too well guarded, maybe.'

Blackwood thought of the night sky as they had marched in single file, section by section, the first tension giving way to curiosity as the sounds of battle had reached them. Artillery like distant thunder, on and on, war at a distance. It was unlikely that the Germans could spare fighting soldiers to guard something so remote, so outwardly harmless.

The two lieutenants dropped down beside them, Robyns more his usual self. Despard lay on his back and stared at the sky, but one hand still held his Sten gun.

Gaillard said, 'We shall have to stick it out here until we get the lie of the land. According to my notes, there's another ridge to our left, and some derelict houses. The refugee camps are further along the coast, but we take nothing for granted, right?'

Robyns said, 'I could pick some men and get closer to the target, sir.'

Gaillard ignored him. 'There will be guards— how many is anybody's guess. The Brens can cover us when we move in. The right side of the building is a ruin. My guess is that the equipment is in the other part.' He nodded, as if to confirm it. 'Makes sense.'

Blackwood said, 'We'll get a better idea soon, sir. I'll take a look with these.'

Gaillard lay on his side. 'Suit yourself. I'm going to try and get some rest. Make sure the pickets are changed, one hour per man. They'll all be asleep otherwise!'

Despard rolled over. 'It's too quiet, sir.'

Blackwood glanced at Gaillard's shadow, half concealed by the treacherous thorns. 'You feel it, too? Tell me.'

Despard hesitated.

'Something missing.' He might have smiled. 'I'm not sure what I mean.'

Blackwood heard Robyns opening his water flask. He would regret it when the sun was up.

He saw his own hand resting on the binoculars:

he could even see the faint scars from the exploding skylight, before he had dropped the grenade and fallen in his blood. He watched the sun creeping across the tangled undergrowth. Brown, like the land; was nothing ever green in this place?

It was like seeing a film develop, murky and slow at first, and then with surprising haste. Texture and colour, even warmth across his neck. And the sea was alive again. Dark blue, unmoving, like something solid.

He trained his glasses again and winced as a thorn pierced his elbow. The landscape and the ruined building hardened into shape. There was a kind of tower still standing; maybe they had mounted a telescope there.

There were a few sea-birds, but nothing else moved. Far away, like a dirty smear across the brightening sky, he saw smoke. But not from guns. They were cooking fires, hundreds of them. Refugees.

The place was dead. They had been told that even the refugees had abandoned it. Another foul-up . . . He shifted his glasses again.

There were some wrecked vehicles, rusty or burned out, it was hard to tell. Victims of air attacks or discarded, they added to the sense of decay. He adjusted the range, and saw a small notice-board beside a carelessly erected barrier of barbed wire. The red paint had been blistered away by the sun, but there was no mistaking the skull and crossbones. He could not read it, but it would have displayed the grim warning *Achtung! Minen!* for the foolish or the unwary. He tensed as he saw what appeared to be some rags dangling from part of the barrier. Rags now, but once a human being who had failed to heed the death's head by the wire.

Despard muttered, *'He* won't be on church parade this Sunday!'

Robyns was crawling over to them, his eyes full of questions. 'There's nothing here, is there? After all we've done . . .'

He gasped as Blackwood seized him by the collar of his battledress and slammed him down on the ground.

'Shut up, and *listen!'*

It seemed a metallic hum at first, and then with a throaty roar the morning air quivered to the beat of engines.

Despard ducked down. 'Christ! Tanks!'

Blackwood released the lieutenant and pushed himself through the thorns. His hands and cheek were bleeding, but everything else was unimportant. He raised the binoculars and waited for his grip to steady again.

There it was, basking in the pale sunlight like something from a horror film. A solitary tank. He felt the sudden anger and despair. It was more than enough. It might have been waiting just for them.

He sensed Gaillard lying just below his legs, his barely suppressed disbelief.

It was a medium-sized tank, not one of Rommel's famous Tigers; he could even see the Afrika Korps insignia, palm tree and swastika displayed on the side of the turret. Its long gun was pointing almost directly at him.

'What are they doing?'

Blackwood watched the haze of fumes above the tank's armoured flanks. If they broke cover, its machine guns would cut them down without effort.

If they remained in hiding in the thorns, they would be squashed to pulp.

He swallowed hard as a hatch opened and a soldier stood upright, and after a glance around, gave a huge stretch and yawn to match. Then he climbed down and walked purposefully towards the next ridge. He was carrying a spade.

Despard murmured, 'Nice and tidy, like the Desert Rats. Going for the morning crap!'

Gaillard was on his knees. 'What the *hell* are you talking about?' He raised his own glasses, his habitual self-control suddenly gone.

Blackwood moved his binoculars again. The marines must be told, otherwise someone might break cover.

He said, 'That tank hasn't moved for ages. Look at the ground around it.' He saw the turret move slightly, so that another man could climb up through the command hatch itself. No cap, jacket undone; any soldier anywhere in a safe area. Away from those reflected bombardments, and the din of war.

He listened to his own voice, so level, so able to conceal the madness.

'I think it's because it *can't* move.' Gaillard was saying something, his tone angry, contemptuous; he found he could ignore it. He saw the second soldier's head and shoulders spring to life in the powerful lens. Sun-tanned. *About my age.* He seemed to be looking directly towards him.

He made himself explore the scene still further. Not like the Japs in Burma; this face looked ordinary. It was sometimes better not to see the enemy.

'Got it!' The others were staring at him, and he

knew that Archer had risen to his knees, his thumb already on the safety catch of his Lee-Enfield. He lowered himself to them, surprised that his limbs were not trembling. He had thought he was shivering, like that night aboard Carson's schooner.

'There's a cable, sir. Remember Vasili?' Of course, Gaillard had not been there to see it. Welland with his smoking rifle, the dead Italian officer, the naked woman . . . He smiled, and knew they would think he was round the bend. *And the generator.* 'The tank provides the power for the spotting gear, sir. Right there, on that ridge.' He could feel the maniac laughter dangerously close to the surface. 'Where the Kraut just headed off to answer the call of nature!'

Despard said, 'We would have attacked the wrong place. Been caught in the open. Disabled or not, that bloody thing could take us apart, no trouble at all.'

Gaillard said, 'Pass the word to the others.' He was breathing sharply. 'I agree. We'll move before dusk. I might have guessed the mines weren't there just to scare off a few local looters!'

Archer remarked, 'Old Jerry's comin' back, sir. Feels a lot better, I'll bet!'

The safety valve, exactly when it was needed.

When he looked again, the tank was exactly as before. As if nobody had ever been near it, or, like the tattered remains on the barbed wire, it was just a reminder of something past.

He looked around for some shade from the sun. It would be a long day, perhaps too long for the innocent and the trusting.

And when the time came, the menace would still be there.

201

CHAPTER TEN

'JUST GET ME TO THE BLOODY SEA!'

Blackwood licked his dry lips and felt the sand grate between his teeth. It took physical effort to shut the temptation of water from his mind, and every time he moved to ease his limbs or use his binoculars he could feel it swilling inside his flask. It was a long day, and with the sun high in the sky there was little relief. Like the rest of the marines he had already consumed his small pack of rations, leaving the chocolate to the last. He could taste it now, and thought of the sailors giving their nutty rations to the children on the Greek island where they had handed over the rifles and ammunition.

He had intended to work his way around all the positions; some of the men would be feeling far more than personal discomfort. Inactivity was always the greatest enemy.

But Gaillard had refused to agree. 'Let the lieutenants do it. I don't carry passengers!'

He glanced at him now while he was checking his little notebook again. His eyes were red-rimmed and his face lined with strain. It was unusual to see him unshaven, like somebody else.

One of Despard's men had caught sight of a wireless aerial, for only a few seconds before it had been lowered again. Careful examination with binoculars had also revealed a hide at the top of the adjoining ridge. Invisible from the air, it merged perfectly with the crumbling brown rocks. A freak breeze from the Strait and it had shivered

202

very slightly, Blackwood had thought, like scenery in a school play. Probably painted canvas, but it was all the evidence they had. All they needed.

The tank stood as before, sometimes with the engines running, sometimes not. A few soldiers walked around between the barbed wire and the ridge, stretching their legs, smoking, only alert when they heard approaching aircraft. There were some collapsed and derelict buildings nearby, exactly as described in the intelligence pack, but nothing moved outside this small, desolate place. Even the Germans appeared unwilling to stray very far, and when one of them laughed the sound seemed to hang in the air like a taunt.

Blackwood peered at his watch. *How much longer?*

He thought of the house again. Of the swimming pool. The way she had looked at him . . . He jerked his head up angrily; he had almost fallen asleep. He glanced round as Archer moved slightly and raised one hand to his ear.

'Someone's comin', sir!'

Blackwood wanted to shake himself. *What is the matter with me? I should have heard it.*

Gaillard was dragging himself through a patch of scrub, his holster catching on the thorns.

He snapped, 'What is it?'

Sergeant Welland had joined them. 'Not another bloody tank, anyway!'

A few of the German soldiers had appeared from the ridge, buttoning their tunics, smartening up.

Somebody said, 'Must be Rommel payin' a visit!' He was glared into silence.

A small, open truck rolled up to the wire, dust

spewing from its wheels like great wings. Two of the soldiers were parting the wire with a crude but effective piece of tackle.

Blackwood watched, his mind recording every move, his aching fatigue forgotten. No mines in that gap; it was unlikely they would have laid many in any case. Two more Germans had joined the others now. He tried to recall how many he had seen, and if they were the same ones.

Gaillard must have been thinking the same. 'No more than twenty, I'd say.'

Blackwood tried to ignore him. What did it matter? With the tank there, and machine guns and armour to protect them, it would be very dicey.

An N.C.O. had stepped from the truck. Blackwood smiled to himself. *Not Rommel after all.* The soldiers stood listening intently to their orders, while the truck slowly reversed towards the tank.

He felt a chill on his spine, although he knew that his body was almost steaming in the heat.

The truck obviously visited here fairly often. *Routine.* His mind throbbed as he tried to recognise some kind of pattern.

Despard saw it first. 'Fuel, sir. For the tank.' It was so obvious that Blackwood wanted to reach out to him. 'Petrol, too. Two or three cans of it.'

Blackwood levelled his glasses, almost beyond his usual caution. A lot of fuel, so it must mean there might not be another visit for days. By that time . . .

He rolled over until his face was only inches from Gaillard's.

'It's got to be now, sir. If we blow the petrol, the explosion will do the rest.' Without turning his head, he knew that the fuel pipe was already connected. He dared not move. He had to make Gaillard understand, share it with him. But the major did not lower his glasses or look at him.

He heard Despard ask, 'Could you mark it down?' and somehow knew he was speaking to Archer, the crack shot of the company.

And then the brief, tense reply.

'Easy!'

Blackwood said, '*Now*, sir!'

Then Gaillard did turn his head, the dark eyes flat, unmoving.

'Before dusk?' He sounded neither troubled nor resentful; the word that came to Blackwood's mind was 'disinterested'.

Then he said, 'Pass the word. We're going in!'

Blackwood saw Welland lope away amongst the thorns, men coming to life all around him like a machine set in motion.

Archer eased his rifle comfortably against his cheek, but not before he had licked one thumb and then touched it against the foresight.

He murmured, 'Saw Gary Cooper do that once. An' it works, sharpens the image!'

He had small, square hands, like spades. Now they seemed almost gentle as he eased off the safety catch and took the first pressure around the trigger.

The sound of the shot was deafening after the silence. The seabirds rose flapping and screaming near the folly, and one of the Germans started to run even as Archer rammed another bullet up the breech.

A few seconds. Probably not even that long, just time enough for Blackwood to think the shot had gone astray.

Then came the explosion, like a grenade, but nothing worse.

He saw some of the soldiers running towards the ridge, another climbing up the side of the tank. The truck was sounding its horn, and Blackwood realised it must have been jammed by the exploding petrol. And then came the second detonation, muffled perhaps by the great column of black smoke, through which another fire was spurting like a welder's torch. The tank was ablaze, the weapon slits shining through the choking clouds, the air suddenly lethal with exploding ammunition.

They were all running, charging down the crumbling slope, heedless of everything but the need to hit the enemy first.

A Sten rattled off a few shots, and Blackwood thought he could hear one of Despard's Brens firing on another bearing.

Archer was pounding beside him, but managed to say, 'Told 'im, didn't I?'

Some of the Germans had been cut down by the explosions, and one was crawling on his hands and knees, unable to see. What Blackwood had taken for the unending shriek of the truck's horn was probably his scream.

On, on, through the wall of smoke, their faces set in masks of concentration, some with fixed bayonets, others with light machine guns.

Was this how it had been month after month for his father? For Vaughan, and all who had somehow survived those terrible days, but died a little each time they had gone over the top?

The smoke was everywhere, but from the corner of his eye Blackwood could still see the blazing tank, a soldier sprawled beside it in a pool of flames.

Shots came from ahead and above, and he knew two of the marines had gone down. He ran on, his throat raw, tensed as if for the next bullet. Nobody could stop. Not now. Not yet. Even if it was a friend, someone calling your name.

He swerved and almost lost his balance as a soldier appeared directly in his path. He vaguely realised that the man was fully equipped and wearing his helmet, and that he had a bayoneted rifle aimed and steady. A sentry perhaps, grateful only a few seconds earlier that he had been excused from the working party.

Something seemed to scream at him. *What does it matter! He's the bloody enemy!*

He saw the rifle buck, and imagined he heard the bullet ripping past him. He levelled his Sten but someone else was there, Sergeant Welland, perfectly balanced on both feet as he parried the German's blade, like an instructor with a raw recruit. The blades clashed, and the soldier lost his footing. Mere seconds, but they were all Welland needed. He drove his bayonet into the man's armpit, and as the soldier fell, gasping, he wrenched out the blade and kicked him aside and ran on after his section.

More shots, and then he saw Archer pause to scoop up a German grenade, the familiar 'potato masher', and fling it beyond some rocks where it exploded instantly. Another second ... He waved the Sten and yelled, *'Good lad! Keep at it!'*

There were only a few shots now, and as he followed two of his men up a makeshift ramp and through the torn canvas screen, he knew they had done it. The equipment was right here, two men standing on either side, hands in the air, knowing that just one stupid move would be their last.

There was another hide right behind this place, with more equipment and some camp beds. His hand steadied the Sten as he saw a further opening to the rear. Someone had escaped, might even now be running for a field telephone or wireless; the torn canvas flapped slightly as if to drive the point home.

He should have known. It had happened often enough. *Nobody had escaped.* He swung round, but fell to his knees as he took the full weight of the attacker on his shoulders. The oldest trick in the world ... He struck out, but the Sten had been knocked or torn from his hands.

Like living a nightmare, but this was real. The man was strong, and was grappling at his throat, choking him.

Instinct, training, fear, it was all and none of them. He allowed himself to fall, fingers dragging at his commando dagger. In a moment he would black out completely. The blood was roaring in his head, and he could feel the man's saliva on his upturned face.

It was like hearing the instructor all over again.

Thumb on the blade, sir, and stab upwards!

He felt the blade jar against leather and metal, then the great shudder as the soldier arched his back, the agony too great, too instant even for a final cry.

Hands were lifting him, pulling the dead weight from his body. Despard was here, hard-eyed, ready for another trick. But there was nothing.

Archer helped him to his feet. 'Nice one!' He

208

studied him searchingly. 'All right, sir?'

Blackwood picked up his helmet and looked at his attacker. A contorted face, eyes bulging, but only a man after all.

He replaced his dagger, and said, 'Let's get on with it.'

He did not glance at the men who had surrendered. 'We'll take them back with us.' He saw Welland's bayonet move slightly, and said with greater emphasis, *'I mean it.'*

Despite the drifting smoke the air seemed clean outside. It was over.

He saw Gaillard reloading his revolver, three marines being dragged away from the collapsed hide. Two were dead; the third would not live much longer.

Gaillard shaded his eyes as if it were still bright sunshine, although dusk came quickly here, and parts of the ridge were already in shadow.

Blackwood said, 'Set the charges, and round up any prisoners.' He knew Gaillard was watching him, but he said nothing.

Despard called, 'Mr Robyns has caught one, sir!'

It was not over.

Two marines were holding the lieutenant on the ground, another was trying to bind a dressing around his leg. There did not appear to be much of it left.

Despard said, 'Booby-trap, sir.' He gestured angrily to the wire.

'He should have known.' He sounded bitter, as if he were blaming himself.

One of the marines held up something in his filthy hand. It was an Iron Cross, probably from a body close to the barbed wire. Just one touch. It was all it needed.

Gaillard said tersely, 'Fetch a stretcher for this officer. The prisoners can carry him. Keep them out of mischief!'

Blackwood knelt and waited for Robyns to open his eyes. He looked very young, and suddenly helpless.

Blackwood stared over him and saw the sea. The Strait was marked in shadows, each slow movement like breathing. Their ships would be able to move in safety from now on, until the final retreat. It had been worth it. It had to be.

Robyns clenched his teeth until blood ran from his lip as the first agonising pain lanced through him.

Blackwood stood and walked away, unable to watch. It had to be worth it . . .

'Ready with the fuses, sir!' He almost expected the man to salute. He sounded alert and confident; discipline was already replacing the wild urge to kill.

Robyns screamed as the Germans lifted the stretcher, and Gaillard snapped, 'Keep him quiet! We've got fifteen miles to cover, remember!'

But Despard was shaking his head. Blackwood said quietly, 'Put the officer down,' and accompanied it with gestures. They lowered the stretcher, almost fearfully, he thought. Then he thrust his hand into Robyns's shirt, and remembered him grinning from the deck of the M.G.B. after the raid.

'He'll not make any more noise, *sir.*' He walked towards his men with their fuses and detonators, unable to conceal his contempt. *Ever!*'

They made the German wounded as

comfortable as they could, simple acts carried out in a wary silence. Help would come for them tomorrow.

They moved from the ridge even as the charges began to explode, all perfectly timed.

Blackwood watched the marines forming into sections for the return march. They had lost five killed, but as they headed away from the sea once again, he could not shake the feeling that they were still all together. Once he felt himself touching his commando knife, and knew it was not the time to reason, to question. This was today.

It was enough.

*   *   *

Lieutenant David Falconer stood wedged in one corner of his tiny bridge and swung his night-glasses in a slow arc. A veteran of Light Coastal Forces, if there could be such a creature in this fast-moving war, he was more used to darkness than the daylight which could leave them so vulnerable, easy prey for anything more powerful. M.G.B. 49 had been at action stations for most of the night, with only quick, stealthy gulps of glutinous cocoa, ki, and sandwiches so thick you could hardly get your teeth around them. Falconer's small company were used to it, as they were to one another; and he had come to know every one of them as so much more than mere names and ratings.

Crouched over the wheel was his petty officer coxswain, the core of any small warship. On parade or being visited by the brass, everything was always pusser and formal, but here, in the cramped, box-

211

like bridge, he was a reliable friend. Most of the others were like that now. Only the first lieutenant seemed unable to cross the plank, not completely.

He said, 'They're bloody late! I thought it was too good to last!'

The coxswain glanced over at him. 'Quiet enough, though. No signs of an alarm.'

Falconer grunted. He had not even realised he had spoken his thoughts aloud. *Getting past it.*

He moved the glasses again. Imagination, or was the undulating water already lighter? The dawn would be sudden, and they would have the sun dead astern. A perfect target. He could not see their consort, the other M.G.B. That was some comfort, but not much.

Maybe the F-lighter had broken down. He pictured the base engineering officer and decided against it; nothing got past his eagle eye.

And when the Germans eventually did pull out of North Africa, what then? Another flotilla, or some other special group. At least they were more co-ordinated now. At the beginning it had been almost impossible to know who was doing what. He heard someone curse as the boat dipped and rolled uncomfortably in the offshore swell. It would be nothing in a destroyer, or the 'big ships' which they always viewed with a sort of proud contempt. But in the motor gunboat, with her engines stopped, it was enough to turn the strongest stomach.

He felt Sub-Lieutenant Balfour hovering near one of the machine gunners.

Falconer said, 'Check our position, Number One.'

'I did, sir.'

Falconer restrained the sudden anger. It was not

Balfour's fault. It was just . . . He said quietly, 'Do it again.'

He heard Balfour lurching down the ladder to the privacy of the chart space. *Thinks I'm a real shit.*

Aloud he said, 'I could move further inshore. If the Royals have knocked out the radar we'll be safe enough. If not, we can still offer a good turn of speed to get us out of it!'

The coxswain felt the wheel bucking slightly in his hands. The skipper was right. She could go like bloody hell when the throttles were opened. He listened to the boat's distinctive noises, and the sluice of water beneath her flared hull, the persistent rattle of signal halliards, the restless sounds of her company. Good men and skivers, and those who would have spent most of their time at the defaulters' table in any other kind of vessel. He glanced at the lieutenant's broad shadow in the dimness. Or maybe with any other sort of C.O.

Falconer was thinking of the commandos, and in particular of Mike Blackwood. Not the sort of marine he had been used to, more like someone who was doing the job only because it was expected of him, and there had never been either doubt or choice. A regular, too. He considered his own previous life as a schoolmaster. He had never wanted anything but to get to sea. What war offered to one, it had seemed to take away from another.

A seaman called, 'Boat at Green four-five, sir!'

He grunted an acknowledgment. You must never show relief, not to those who were relying on your every action, your every gesture. But it was good to know that the other M.G.B. was still on station. If this were the North Sea or the English Channel, with their swift and perverse currents and tides, you might have been anywhere. In the Med you had some consolation in . . .

He froze, his mind clicking into place like a breech-block.

'Engines, sir!'

The coxswain had swivelled round. He did not need to say anything. The engines were fast-moving. And from astern. The wrong bearing.

Falconer said, 'How many, Dick?'

'Two. Maybe three.' His Tyneside accent seemed more pronounced; it always did when danger was near. 'Not bothered about the bloody din!'

Falconer said nothing. Maybe the attack had been tumbled. Or maybe Blackwood was lying out there somewhere with his men, like all the others he had seen. He tried to concentrate, to remember who the F-lighter's skipper was, but nothing formed.

He knew Balfour was on the bridge again, intent, afraid to intrude. He said, 'Company, Number One.'

He felt him nod. He would do his best, he had proved that. But there was never enough time to learn in this bloody game.

He said, 'We can stay put. Make off when those buggers have passed. They're not looking for us. They have other fish to fry.'

Why bother? He felt the anger again. Because it mattered. Especially to someone who might be dead before he saw the sun again.

Balfour said, 'The lighter might have been delayed. In that case . . .'

Falconer gripped his arm, and realised that he still had his unlit pipe jammed between his teeth. It

214

was a wonder he had not bitten right through the stem.

'In that case, John Balfour, they'll be needing us after all!' He found he could listen to the distant engines without anxiety. *Thrum-thrum-thrum.* E-Boats, bigger, and better armed than any of ours.

But he could see the swaying shape of the compass card, like something floating in darkness.

He said, 'Pass the word and tell Sparks to be ready to make the signal!' He touched the coxswain's oilskinned shoulder. 'At least the bastards will have the sun behind *them!*'

Balfour stared past him and saw the faint hint of dawn, where there had been only night. The guns were swinging round, belts of ammunition like snakes against the grey steel.

He almost ran the last few feet to his action station by the Oerlikon cannon.

He gripped the safety rail and held his breath. He could hear the enemy engines, and yet, above it, there was also the gentle sound of the seaman whistling to himself, strapped in his harness, waiting to begin.

Balfour wanted to remember the skipper's rough confidence, the way the small group which were this gunboat's crew looked up to him. But all he could think of was the girl he wrote to whenever he could. The smile, in the only photograph he had of her.

'Oh God, help me!'

But the Rolls-Royce engines roared into life and the deck tilted over to the thrust of rudder and power, and his plea went unheard.

*   *   *

215

'Over here, sir!'

Blackwood recognised Sergeant Paget's voice and quickened his pace to join him. The silence and utter desolation only added to the unreality, he thought. After the fury of the attack, the forced march back to the rendezvous had seemed an even greater strain.

The marines sat or squatted in small groups, clutching their weapons, snatching this brief rest while they could. Blackwood had already noticed that the pickets were in place, nothing left to chance.

Paget said quietly, 'It's Corporal Sharp, sir. Taking it badly.'

The man in question had been wounded in the leg by a bullet, and his shin bone had been shattered. Unable to walk, he had been carried by the German prisoners and his own marines. He must have been in great pain, but had not complained.

When someone had asked him how he was managing, Blackwood had heard the corporal gasp, 'Just get me to the bloody sea, chum! I can make it then!'

He stared at the stars, paler now, or so they appeared. But they were on course. The sea could not be more than a mile or two away. He thought of the corporal's words. Still more sailor than soldier, no matter what the Corps said about it.

He knelt beside the wounded man and his bearers. Even in the gloom, he could see the Nazi eagle on the tunic of one of them.

'It's the Cap'n, Ernie.' Paget sounded on edge.

Blackwood unclipped his flask and handed it to

the corporal. 'Drink this.' He heard the German's stomach rumbling. Thirsty, or fearful, it did not seem to matter out here. There were no sounds or reflections of distant battle, only the sky and the land.

Sharp muttered, 'Much further, sir?'

Blackwood laid his hand on the man's chest, feeling the anguished breathing, the despair. Like Robyns.

'A mile or so. You'll make it.' With prompt treatment, the leg could be saved.

Sharp tried to raise himself. 'Nothing to it, sir!' The effort made him fall back against the German.

Archer, who had been standing behind him, said, 'Major's comin', sir.'

Blackwood tested the bandages, the wounded leg bound to the sound one. The dressing was damp. Perhaps the bleeding had stopped.

'What the hell's going on?' Gaillard leaned over them. 'I said a short break, not a bloody banyan party!'

Blackwood stood, and felt the throb in his own wound.

'We're ready to move again now, sir. Corporal Sharp is doing his best.'

He felt Gaillard drag at his sleeve, drawing him away from the others.

'We'll have to leave him. Slowing us down. Make him understand. Can't risk the whole mission at this stage!'

'Is that an order, sir?'

Gaillard had begun to turn away, but stopped dead as if he had misheard.

'It is. Do you question it?'

'You know what will happen to him if we leave

him, don't you?'

Gaillard smiled thinly.

'You're a good hand, Mike, but don't rely on your luck. Not with me, right?'

Blackwood nodded. 'Thank you, sir.'

Gaillard strode away. 'Ready to move! Jump about!'

Blackwood let out a deep breath, and when his hand brushed against his commando dagger he felt suddenly nauseated. He thought of the blade catching on the soldier's belt and equipment, and then driving into his flesh. *Today I killed a man.* Not some hazy target, but a living human being.

Sergeant Paget said, 'Pick him up, lads!' He touched the makeshift stretcher. 'Easy, Ernie, this is going to cost you a tot when we get back!'

But he was looking at Blackwood, and Archer, waiting a little apart from him. The watchdog.

Captain Blackwood had been about to disobey an order. On active service, even from a Corps family like his, it would have meant disaster. And yet somehow Gaillard had realised it, and had changed his mind.

Paget was like Archer in one thing; he had served many kinds of officer. But Gaillard was different from all of them. He was dangerous.

Training, discipline and loyalty seemed to join as one, and scream, *stay out of it.* As on board ship, wardroom and messdeck don't mix.

He fell into step beside the stretcher, his rifle slung on one shoulder. He couldn't stay out of it now, even if he wanted to. He knew what had happened in Burma. He touched Sharp's arm, and heard him murmur something. *And it could have happened to you, Ernie.*

And Blackwood knew it also.

The lighter was turning, preparing to leave in the last, lingering shadows before dawn, when the weary marines with their wounded and ten German prisoners waded through the lapping water, and were hauled aboard without further delay.

Gaillard went straight to the bridge, and waited while the lieutenant in command laid his awkward vessel on course and increased speed.

Despard found Blackwood with the wounded, as the lighter's two sickberth attendants examined and changed dressings with the skill of any surgeon.

Men laughed again, and somebody was busy pouring tea from a pot the size of a watering can.

Despard chose his words with care. 'Heard about Corporal Sharp, sir.'

Blackwood turned quickly, like a cat. 'What did you hear?'

Not the proper way. Despard tried again, with greater caution. 'I thought he wasn't going to make it back there.'

Blackwood looked at him, still faceless against the paler patch of sky.

'Would you have left him, George? Tell me that.'

Despard saw his hand on the knife, and recalled his own surge of relief when he had seen him pulled clear of the body.

'I could say no, sir, but I'm not that certain. Not any more.' He turned away as the air quivered to far-off gunfire. He was almost glad of the interruption.

Gaillard shouted down, 'E-Boats, engaging two of ours!'

The marines forgot their wounds and apprehensions, and pressed against the side to watch the vivid flash of short-range weapons, tracer, green and scarlet, criss-crossing and knitting together against the first horizon.

Blackwood heard the skipper say sharply, 'We could give assistance, sir. What *they're* doing for us.'

Gaillard was watching the flashes; there was smoke visible now. It was going to be another fine day. For some.

He said, 'We could lose everything we've won. Think of that, eh? We have prisoners who will be interrogated by our intelligence people, wounded to be treated.'

There was a more intense flash, and seconds later the explosion rolled across the water like something solid.

Blackwood watched until his eyes watered. The destroyer escort had made its appearance, and shells were already falling amongst and astern of the E-Boats as they speeded away from another unexpected attack.

The feeble sunshine explored the sea. It was a common enough scene in this hard-disputed Strait. One of the motor gunboats had vanished, the second was badly down by the bows.

The destroyers were wheeling like thoroughbreds, and a diamond-bright signal was flashing in recognition and welcome.

A seaman at one of the gun mountings exclaimed, 'Jesus, just in time!' Blackwood watched the smoke, and remembered. He said quietly, 'For us, anyway.'

CHAPTER ELEVEN

ON ACTIVE SERVICE

Wren Diane Blackwood ran a soft cloth over the car windscreen and lowered the wipers. It was a powerful-looking vehicle, a Wolseley 14, barely four years old, and despite the drab camouflage paint it still turned a few heads when she drove it past the sentries at Eastney Barracks. It was used mostly by the Colonel, a courteous and correct man in every sense. She smiled at her reflection. So far.

She barely heard the tramp of booted feet across the parade ground now, or the snap of rifle-bolts at yet another inspection for new recruits. All in all, she had settled in well, although she still found it odd when some of them tried to explain the Corps and the mystique to her. They usually gave up in embarrassment when someone mentioned her family, as if Colonel 'Jono' Blackwood was still keeping an eye on her. She hoped so.

She looked up at the flag whipping out above the old red tower, and imagined she could feel warmth in the air, although the Solent was as grey as ever, with a hint of mist towards the Isle of Wight. Spring seemed possible, and there was new hope and excitement on the wireless, and in the scanty daily papers.

GERMANS OUT OF NORTH AFRICA. THOUSANDS SURRENDER TO VICTORIOUS ALLIES. ROMMEL ON THE RUN. It was heartening and infectious, like her thoughts of spring. People you didn't know grinned and spoke;

marines gave a thumbs-up to one another. Each a part of it in his own way.

She smiled again. *As I am.*

There had been letters from Mike, but as usual he seemed more interested in how she was getting on than with his own problems. No mention of his wound at all, not that that would have slipped past the censor.

A trio of Spitfires roared overhead, their familiar whistle making a few glance up. *Brylcreem Boys. Showing off as usual.* But she had learned to differentiate between resentment and pride. You soon did. On mornings like this it was almost impossible to grasp that the enemy was so close, and so vast. Just across the Channel, only a short flight to those three young men.

The whole of the promenade, the Front as the locals called it, was one great mass of tangled barbed wire, a constant reminder of the enemy's nearness. But the wire was rustier now, and the grim notices like *IF THE INVADER COMES— TAKE ONE WITH YOU!* or Churchill's now famous *WE SHALL FIGHT THEM ON THE BEACHES!* seemed less final.

Security was good, but not beyond personal involvement. There had been a party of Royal Marines here in Southsea, training night after night in nothing more warlike than cockleshell canoes, preparing for some secret operation 'over there'. It was all so secret that information only leaked out long afterwards that those same marines had carried out a daring attack up the Gironde to Bordeaux against enemy shipping. It was now known that only two men had survived; the others had died on active service.

The old sweats in Eastney knew better: they usually did. Many of those marines, despite their uniforms, had been put against a wall and shot. Inevitably, she thought of Mike when such subjects were mentioned.

And he worries about me!

And there was her second officer, too. She had gone to see her about clothing issue, and had been so surprised, so shocked, that she had forgotten the purpose of her visit.

The fierce, grey-haired guardian had been alone in her office, and in tears. Diane was not sure which was worse, her distress, or her anger at being unmasked as a human being. Someone she knew, or had once known, had been reported missing, presumed killed. It happened every day, every hour, and you made light of it. But not when it touched people like their second officer.

'Ah, here we are then! Wren Blackwood, I believe?'

She turned, still remembering a lonely woman's hurt and loss.

The second officer even had a word for this one, she thought. Colour-Sergeant Harwood, the recruits' nightmare, and tipped to be the next sergeant-major. Big, impeccable, the perfect Royal Marine.

She kept a straight face. 'Colour-Sergeant?' But all she could hear was the second officer's blunt summary. *Carries his brains between his legs, that one. I'm told even the sheep weren't safe when he was in Scapa!*

He ran his eyes over the car, and then her. 'I don't need to tell you about what's proper and what isn't, you bein' no stranger to the Corps.'

223

He always began like this. *What would he say if I told him to get stuffed?* A serious breach of discipline, or worse. She would certainly lose her driving job, which was a sort of freedom as well as being useful.

He rocked back on his iron-shod heels. 'There is an officer enquiring for you, Wren Blackwood, an *officer* no less! Rules are for everybody, and you should know it.'

She waited. He was enjoying it, and her initial fear was past. Even Colour-Sergeant Harwood would not keep her dangling if it had been bad news. It was said he was married. She wondered what it must be like for his wife.

He nodded severely. 'Fun an' games is one thing, but discipline is discipline!'

She said, 'What officer?'

He seemed vaguely disappointed. He probably imagined he had stumbled on one of the affairs she had heard about. *Against the dockyard wall,* as one girl had crudely described it.

He said, 'A lieutenant. A pongo, to all accounts.'

He glanced round, startled, as a door in the office wing opened a few inches and a voice said sharply, 'The Colonel will need the car in one hour.' It was the adjutant, who had told her about Mike. The voice added, 'The *pongo* is with me, Colour-Sarn't, so if you have other duties, I suggest ...'

It was enough. A stamp of boots and a smart salute, and he was gone.

She climbed the steps to the offices; they were curved and worn by the passage of many thousands of feet which had come this way over the years.

The adjutant picked up the telephone and
224

glanced over it at her. 'In my office. A Lieutenant Blackwood, of the Royal Engineers.' Then he said, 'Just thought I'd check.' And, as she hurried to the other door, 'How's the Wolseley running?' He saw her remove her cap and push her hair into place, and smiled at the telephone. She had not heard a word.

He was standing by the tall window, framed against the washed-out sky, like that day in the Long Room at Hawks Hill. She had often thought about their meeting, had even wondered if he might try to call her from Portsmouth, if he was still there. She had told herself to forget it; he obviously had. But she had dared to hope.

He took her hand, uncertain, unprepared.

'You look marvellous!' He grinned. 'Both feet, as usual!'

She released her hand and realised how cold hers had been. 'Is something wrong?' She wanted to use his name, and was angry with herself.

'No.' He tried again. 'That is, I wanted to see you. I'm moving out shortly.' He glanced at the wall and winked. 'Safe in here, is it?'

'When?' A warning seemed to say, drop it. *He's going. Don't make a fool of yourself.*

'Soon.' He walked away from her, perhaps deliberately. 'I needed to see you. To talk. To get to know you.' He looked at her, suddenly very unsure. 'If we could meet, I thought . . .'

Let him talk. Don't commit yourself. But she said, 'Something is wrong, isn't it?'

He turned towards the window again and she could see a squad of marching marines beyond it, as though it were a painting in stained glass. Like that day in church . . . was it really only six months

225

ago?

'I had news from Auckland, from the lawyers. Your father the Colonel made a will, but of course you know that. He provided for me in it, *me* of all people. He didn't even know me!'

'I've not heard yet. It all takes time, and I've been here.'

He nodded, but his thoughts were somewhere else. 'Shares in the estate, that kind of thing. Took me all aback, I can tell you.' He gazed at the adjutant's desk, neat and tidy, like the officer. 'Shares. I thank God some people think our little country will still be here after the war!'

She stood beside him and slipped her hand through his arm. Maybe he hadn't even noticed it. *Our little country,* not his home in New Zealand, where the sheep outnumbered the people. *Here.*

She said, 'I could get away and meet you, if you're sure . . .'

His hand closed over hers, although he would not look at her. 'I want it more than anything. Just to talk, nothing which might offend.'

She did not smile. It sounded so old-fashioned for one so young. And it suited him.

'I know that, Steve. I *know* that.'

How long they stood there, not speaking, not even aware of the life and movement beyond the window, she could not tell. Was it always like this when it happened, as it was supposed to happen? Not brash or cheap, but something so private that it was too strong to contain. Like the girl Mike had met somewhere. No name, no description, but all the more real because of it. He would tell her when he was ready. But he was vulnerable, especially now.

He said, 'It might be a while before we meet again.' He tried to lighten it. 'Like the song. You've only met me once, when you needed me to carry your bike.'

She was gripping his arm tightly but could not help it. Did not want him to stop.

'I want you to be my girl. Have something to live for. If I had more time . . .'

She said, 'I can meet you tomorrow.' It was the Colonel's day in London, and he always stayed overnight at the Club.

He stared at her. Disbelief, surprise, and then a smile, which was the first she had seen in this spartan office.

An orderly was in the passage, stamping his feet, coughing unnecessarily. She did not even know his name, but he always did it to warn her that the Colonel was on the move. An hour? Had it been that long?

She put on her cap and saw his eyes linger on the brightly polished badge, another memory of that day at Hawks Hill.

She said, 'Tomorrow.'

He gave her a scrap of paper. 'My unit. I can be reached there.'

He opened the door for her. She hesitated, and then kissed him lightly on the cheek, like friend meeting friend in a street somewhere.

He watched her go down to the car. She did not look back.

The adjutant saw her pass, and thought about the soldier with the same surname as hers.

He hoped it would be all right for her. He smiled. Anybody who could face the adjutant and Colour-Sergeant Harwood simultaneously must be

227

pretty special.

He pressed the bell on his desk. The spell was broken.

*   *   *

Major-General Ralph Vaughan sat as comfortably as he could on a hard-cushioned chair, and wondered if it was all part of the mystique. He could hear the murmur of traffic in Whitehall, and found himself comparing this suite of offices with his own H.Q. in the Pit. Perhaps because it lacked personality, and gave no indication of the kind of man who sat directly opposite him, his face partly hidden from the filtered sunlight.

Was that, too, part of the mystique? Merely setting the stage? Or was it because he disliked this man, and felt awkward in his presence?

Sir Clive Burgoyne, who always looked as if he had just enjoyed a hot shower, whose hair was never long or short, as if it was something vitally important to the man himself. Like his suit, Vaughan thought; grey and unassuming, but he guessed it had cost far more than anything worn by a mere civil servant, no matter how senior. Clothing coupons would not even come into it.

He was a departmental head of Intelligence, an expert on both Special and Combined Operations, and, perhaps more to the point, he was known to be close to the Prime Minister. Neat, clean and alert. Only his bitten fingernails, which he was careful to conceal, showed it was not all quite so perfect. Despite the power and easy confidence, Burgoyne was a worrier.

Vaughan could recall exactly their first meeting

in this same office, shortly after the fall of Rangoon.

He had said, 'I'm still not used to generals. May I call you Ralph?'

Vaughan remembered his own slight, short-lived sense of relief, and had asked, 'What may I call you in return?'

The little, deceptive smile; he had got used to that, too. '*Sir Clive* will suffice, I think—'

Burgoyne said, 'Hitler was wrong to replace Rommel with General von Arnim. It took the spirit out of the Afrika Korps. They probably felt betrayed. And now North Africa is clear of the enemy.' Again the gentle smile. 'The current enemy, at least. Your marines did a good job on the radar site. We could have suffered heavy losses during the final German exodus. As it was . . .'

Vaughan tried to relax, but it did not work. One battle was over; another was about to begin. A vital one, the first step back into Europe. *The soft underbelly,* as the Prime Minister had termed it in his inimitable way.

Burgoyne glanced at his hand, and then thrust it out of sight beneath the desk.

'If there are obstacles, this is the moment to remove them. Strategy, implementation,' he hesitated, 'and leadership at all levels, are of paramount importance.' He looked at the solitary, thin folder on his blotter. 'I know of your concern about certain allegations made by a marine named, ah—'

Vaughan tensed. *Here we go.*

'Marine Finch, Sir Clive.'

'We have to weigh the consequences as well as the bare facts.' He gazed at the wall, and Vaughan noticed his eyes. Pale blue, almost colourless.

Burgoyne waited, but when Vaughan remained silent added, 'There was an unfortunate episode in occupied France this year. A junior member of your combined staff was inadvertently arrested by the civil police in Marseilles—do I need to enlarge on it?' He nodded. 'Good. I thought not. It was a whole chain of unforeseen incidents, an act of sabotage carried out by some local, unofficial group, leading to the immediate involvement of the German authorities, and the consequences, the Gestapo. The woman in question was lucky—she was freed by members of the Resistance, the Maquis, who have been working closely with us. The woman was a courier, and as such would have revealed little of importance . . .'

'Even under torture?' Vaughan did not attempt to hide his bitterness.

The pale eyes studied him thoughtfully. 'Even so. But in that same police station there was already a prisoner who had been interrogated by the Gestapo, and was due for another interview, shall we call it, that day. I can tell you now, that man was a fully trained and trusted member of the organisation. He was, in fact, a police officer himself. It was of the utmost importance that he should be freed, or prevented from suffering further. I can tell you, Ralph, nobody can withstand that kind of inhumanity for long. He knew too many names, codes, contacts, even points of drops for arms and explosives.'

'What happened to him?'

'When they got into the station they found him too incapacitated to be moved. His body was broken, but his mind was still clear, fighting back.'

230

'So they killed him.'

Burgoyne looked at the closed folder. 'It was the only solution. The woman courier was rescued as a result.'

'Otherwise . . .'

'Otherwise. What a span that word covers.' He became restive, perhaps impatient. 'It is often claimed by senior officers, men of your calibre and experience, that one quality of leadership is to not risk the lives of many for the sacrifice of a few. I have heard others describe it in similar ways—my father wrote some poetry on the subject.' He did not blink. 'Before he was killed on the Somme.'

Vaughan thought of Major Porter's secret report, and its potential danger to future operations at this crucial stage of the Mediterranean campaign.

He said, 'Marine Finch was badly wounded. He could have been mistaken. Gaillard is an officer of high repute and experience in the Corps.'

Burgoyne smiled. 'And that means everything to you?' He held up one hand. 'I mean no disrespect. Quite the reverse. Values, they are what matter here. The next move will be against Sicily, and soon after that, if the weather holds, the Italian mainland, and your Commando will be in the spearhead!' He had raised his voice, which was unusual.

Vaughan said, 'I've thought of little else. In war, everybody is expendable. But when we put our people ashore they expect to be *led,* not driven like lambs to the slaughter!'

Burgoyne slid the folder aside. 'Or like the Somme.'

Vaughan wished someone would come with an

231

urgent message, or that there would be an air raid alert. But there was nothing, only silence. And a sense of betrayal.

Burgoyne said, 'The young woman has returned to her regular duties. That was your idea, I believe?' As usual, he did not wait for an answer. 'I'm glad of that. Commander Diamond was largely responsible for her assignment as a courier; they needed someone who would be known and trusted by the parties concerned. I think he was hasty, or perhaps he, too, was weighing the values of duty and sacrifice.' He seemed to tire of it. 'Diamond has been transferred to more rustic responsibilities. Commander St John, whom you already know, has been appointed in his place.'

'I see.' Vaughan thought of the girl named Joanna Gordon, so determined, so eager when she had accompanied him to the Middle East. The doctors had told him about her private struggle to put her ordeal behind her. He considered it, coldly, as the man opposite him would. If she had been too badly abused to escape, they would have killed her also. He could not accept it, condone it. In this austere office, it seemed a different war entirely.

'That's settled, then. I shall complete my report. I am certain the P.M. will be satisfied.' Burgoyne watched him almost curiously. 'After all, it was his idea to give your people the title of Commando. His own experiences against the Boers in South Africa, I believe?'

'Yes. We're very proud of it.'

He could picture their faces in the Alexandrian sunshine. The sergeants and the corporals, and the ordinary marines. Young Blackwood, and the tough ex-ranker Despard.

232

Perhaps Burgoyne's was the way to think, to place things in order of their value.

He thought of the old friend he would be meeting at his club for lunch; he could find no way of getting out of it now. Lieutenant-General Robyns had once been well known throughout the Corps, both ashore and afloat. The family. Now he had lost his only son, on that same raid they had just been discussing like doctors invited to witness an operation.

He realised that they were both on their feet, although he did not recall any movement.

Burgoyne was saying, 'You're a bit like me in some ways, Ralph. We have to think of our own future, too. When this war is finally over we might need to find a challenge elsewhere. It's worth considering, I'd say.'

The door closed, and another senior officer stood up and stared past Vaughan as if he were invisible. It was his turn next.

Vaughan jammed on his cap and strode to the staircase. Burgoyne's gentle comment stayed with him until he reached the street.

Whichever way you looked at it, it had sounded like a threat.

*   *   *

The little pub was well off the beaten track, and across Portsmouth Harbour on the Gosport side. It was almost impossible to reach for the ordinary serviceman or woman, unless transport was available.

Diane Blackwood guessed that he had chosen the place with great care, and he had somehow managed to obtain the use of an army car. As they got out of it she looked again at the scarlet-painted wings, which revealed that it belonged to a bomb disposal unit. When she had first mentioned it, he had brushed it aside. 'It's all okay. I've been doing a few jobs while I've been in Portsmouth.' She had not pressed him, and he had seemed almost nervous once they were alone together.

She had even toyed with the idea of asking for a sleeping-out pass, but had reconsidered. She was still uncertain if the decision had been a precaution against things getting out of hand, or against herself.

They pushed through the heavy blackout curtain, which smelled of dust and tobacco, and she was surprised that the bar itself was so welcoming. A lot of pubs took advantage of servicemen on a run ashore, knowing they were too eager to be away from discipline and duty to care about the finer points.

There were a few uniforms here. A.T.S. girls, probably from one of the anti-aircraft batteries, with their friends, and an army lieutenant who glanced at her companion with something like panic until he saw the New Zealand flash on his shoulder. A few moments of privacy. Escape. An old dog was dozing by an empty grate and she wondered how the one at Hawks Hill was getting on, surrounded by landgirls and Italian P.O.W.s.

He bought two gins at the bar and carried them to a table in the corner; he had been in England long enough to realise that you never asked for a Scotch any more. The landlord would probably call the police to say he had a German spy on the premises. Apart from senior officers, she had often

234

wondered what happened to all the whisky.

He said, 'Thought you might change your mind. Not come, after all.'

She smiled and sipped the gin. The other girls would ask her how she got on. It was like that in their convent, as it was nicknamed.

One of the Wrens had told them of an exploit in a restaurant where she had been having an evening meal with a shy sub-lieutenant. He had almost fainted when the manager had sidled up to their table and said there was a fine double room upstairs, with a coal fire to make it even more attractive.

They had all wanted to know what had happened. She was rather a brash girl and had enjoyed their curiosity. 'Well, there's a war on, and coal is rationed. We couldn't waste a good fire, could we?'

It was probably just a story.

He said suddenly, 'You look great. I saw all the eyes when we came in.'

She touched his hand. 'You're leaving soon? Tell me.'

He put the hand over hers, and again she sensed his uncertainty, a shyness which was only too rare.

'Next week. You know how it is.' He glanced around. 'But I'll probably be seeing your brother. There aren't so many Royal Marine units, are there?'

She looked at him directly. 'The Med, then ... You said you were doing something with explosives. H.M.S. *Vernon?* I wish I'd known.'

'Does it make any difference?'

She smiled. Afraid of what she felt, of what it might do, to both of them.

235

She said, 'The Colonel sent for me today. It's no secret, anyway. Mike is being decorated, the Distinguished Service Cross. I was so proud when he told me! I just wish I could be there when they pin it on him!'

He watched her, feature by feature, a very young girl again, unable to hide it, any more than she had in the Long Room at Hawks Hill.

'Lucky bloke!' They both laughed, and two of the A.T.S. girls looked over as if to share it.

She dropped her eyes, and studied their clasped hands. 'That car outside, Steve. Bomb disposal. Is that what you do? I'd like to know.'

His fingers tightened slightly. 'I want you to. It's not the main part of it, but it does involve explosives.' He grinned, perhaps relieved. 'Safe as houses, if you know what you're about!'

She looked at him again. 'I'm glad. You see, I care. Quite a lot, as it happens.'

Someone had switched on the news, and she saw his frown.

'During the night our bombers raided the marshalling yards at Hamburg. Fifteen of our aircraft failed to return.'

The landlord switched it off. His little pub was surrounded by naval and military establishments; they did not need to be reminded.

The interruption seemed to have given him confidence. He said, 'After the war, I mean if things are still the same, I'd like to come to England. For good. What you told me about Hawks Hill, and what I saw, well, I know I could offer something. I'm used to farms and to agriculture. But maybe your brother wouldn't care much for that idea?'

She watched the quiet desperation. She said

236

lightly, 'You'll have to ask him, when you meet. And write to me afterwards, won't you?'

He did not seem to hear. 'But it's not really that, either. I wanted you to know me, just a bit more, so that you might consider . . .'

'Ask me, Steve, if that's what you want.'

He looked at their empty glasses. 'No. It's not right. You don't know my prospects, and neither of us knows what might happen.' He glanced at their hands as she repeated, 'Ask me.'

'I don't want to lose you, Diane, not now that I've found you. I think we'd be fine together!' He smiled and shook his head. 'I don't even have a ring to give you!'

She disengaged her hand and stood, then she walked deliberately to the bar and ordered two more gins. She heard her shoes clicking on the uncarpeted floor, and counted every step like a heartbeat.

She brought the glasses back to their table, but remained standing, looking at him.

'I believe there are some nice shops in Chichester.'

He stared at her and said, *'Chichester?'* Then he jumped to his feet, his respirator haversack clattering from the chair. 'You mean it?'

She nodded, barely able to appear calm. 'And I'll give you a lift next time. The Colonel won't care!'

A small, rather dingy pub, which like most places could do with a few coats of paint, but there could have been no finer proposal. People were slapping them on the back, the landlord was refilling glasses and beaming.

When they eventually left and groped their way into the darkness, searchlights were sweeping the

237

sky, and in the distance they heard the insane shriek of a destroyer's siren. The war was never far away.

Then they kissed, and she was surprised that she could let it take control of her in a way she had never expected. He held her firmly but gently, as if he were afraid of hurting her. Not once did he attempt a deeper intimacy, and she found that she could still be shocked, mostly to discover that she would not have resisted if he had.

The following morning she was still thinking about it, while she prepared the Wolseley to collect the Colonel from the harbour station.

The grey-haired second officer came down the steps and said, 'There was a message for you. I had to take it. He's gone. Change of orders.' She studied her impassively. 'Sorry about that.'

Diane stared at her, suddenly cold, empty. 'Was that all? Please—I must know!'

The second officer nodded slowly, satisfied. 'He said that he loves you.'

She stared around, seeing nothing but the little bar, their hands on the table . . . the touch of him . . .

'I'll get one of the other chaps to take the car if you like?'

'No.' Then, 'Sorry, ma'am, didn't mean to snap.'

The officer smiled. 'That's the ticket, my girl. Powder your nose, straighten your cap, and don't keep the Boss waiting!'

As the girl walked away, she added softly, 'And bloody good luck to you! In this regiment, you need it!'

But the hurt remained, as if it was part of her own.

CHAPTER TWELVE

THE FINEST DAY

Although it was a different room, the view from the high, dusty window was exactly as she remembered it. The gravel path, the small outbuildings with unmatching tiles. But there was colour, too, leaves stirring in the bright sunshine where before there had been bare trees. And roses, only a few, which had defied the winter and the garden's general neglect to make patches of red and yellow.

She saw her own reflection in the glass, the pale blue uniform which should have been her defence against this place and its memories. It was not. She could have been naked, like that first time here. She shied away from it. Like before.

The same doctor sat on what could have been the same chair, her white coat probably her own form of protection.

She had let her talk without interruption. She had not even glanced at her watch to imply that she had more important things to do, more deserving people who needed her help.

Strange how easy it was to talk about Mike, to try to explain. When they had been together for that brief time at Alexandria, they had barely touched. There had been so much going on, so many people around them, the major-general, his foxy servant Percy Archer. Perhaps Mike had not noticed. *It was beginning again.* Like an ache. A recurring nightmare.

The doctor said, 'Perhaps you left here too soon.

239

I did warn you what you might expect. The mind can do funny things. Like a sorting office ... keeping things from you, dropping them on the mat when you're least prepared for them.'

Joanna Gordon stared at the gravel path. 'You see, I love him so much. People might find that hard to believe. We were together for such a short time.' She clenched one fist. 'But I knew. That I wanted him, that he needed me.'

'He is a Royal Marine Commando. Captain Blackwood?'

The girl swung towards her, then relaxed, second by second. 'Sorry. Yes. I told you all about him, didn't I?'

'Some people would find it difficult to understand. But in war, in times like these, the process is speeded up.' Then, abruptly, 'But you were in love before?'

'No.' She shook her head. 'I had a lover. I know the difference now.'

The doctor nodded. 'And you're afraid that your experience may have taken something away? Something of you, and that he will sense it, when you meet again?'

She walked to the opposite wall and looked at the neatly made bed. The hospital where everything was done, where nobody was ever seen doing it. Even the silence was physical.

'I have the chance to go back to North Africa. Briefly—but I must see him.'

'He's getting a medal?' She was prompting gently. It was as if the girl in W.A.A.F. uniform had come to an invisible barrier. To a dead end.

Then Joanna said, 'I'm so proud of him.'

'And he is of you.' She kept quite still, aware of
240

the frailty, like the most fragile glass. 'Let your mind go back. There's nothing to fear. You told me everything, all you could recall each time we spoke. You suffered enough; I doubt if many could come through that unscathed, undamaged.'

Joanna had removed her cap and tossed it on to the bed without noticing it. It was like giving in, surrendering all over again.

She said softly, 'The *gendarmerie* . . . it was there that I first realised what had happened. What was going to happen. I wanted to resist, to fight, but I was terrified. That *femme-agent* or whatever she was wanted me to provoke her.' She held out her arm as if expecting to still see the raw, burned skin. 'All the time she kept talking, talking, making me look at things, instruments, while she was searching my body.' She moved to the window again and stood quite motionless in a shaft of sunlight. 'She was hurting me, enjoying it. I used to see her every night when I closed my eyes. But I fought it, and fought it, until . . .'

'Until the rest came back to you?'

'Yes. I still can't remember exactly what happened. There was an explosion, and some shooting. I was just putting on some of my clothes and trying not to give in to the pain, when all the lights went out, and I was picked up and dragged out of the building. They put a pad over my face, like the smell here .. .' She stared at the doctor suddenly, but was seeing something else.

The doctor said, 'Ether. It will knock anybody out. Can be dangerous if wrongly used.' She knew her words had gone unheard, but it gave her time. The girl was reliving it, calling back a picture so misty in her mind that it was like another part of the puzzle.

'I was in a vehicle of some kind. A van. I could smell fish. Tar. But my mind kept sliding away. All I could hold on to was that I was free of the hideous place, from that *bitch.*'

The doctor waited, remembering her examination. The deep bruises, scratches on the shoulders where she had been held.

'And then we were in a boat. I knew we were in danger—he had a hand over my mouth. There were voices, men marching.' She shuddered, 'Soldiers.'

'And they hid you. To help you escape.'

She did not reply for a full minute. The silence seemed to surround them.

'We were in a sort of hold, like a storeroom under the deck somewhere. There was no space to stand, and I had to lie on some canvas, and I think some sacking, while he lay beside me, holding my mouth. Listening. My head was swimming, I could scarcely breathe, and I'm sure now that he drugged me again. But I heard the boots right overhead. The voices, one of them shouting. Angry. Like a barking dog.

'I missed the next part, and when I could breathe again I heard the boat's engine, water against the side. I didn't know where we were going. I didn't care. *I was free.*

'I kept drifting off. I just don't know . . .'

The doctor did not move. One word now might destroy everything.

'At first I thought he was trying to cover me up, I was cold, most of my clothes were still at the *gendarmerie.* I tried to feel my legs, but his hand was there. I tried, I tried . . .'

The doctor stood up, and joined her by the window without touching her.

'You could do nothing, Joanna. Nothing.'

'He was saying something. He was careful not to touch my burned arm. I wanted to scream but I was too drugged . . . I wanted to be sick. But I knew he was doing it, raping me. When I had recovered myself he was gone.' Her hand moved to her groin as if powerless to resist. 'But I could still feel him. *Feel him.*'

They both watched in silence as a tall figure in a blue dressing-gown appeared on the familiar gravel path. Walking slowly, as she had once done. A male nurse was following a few yards behind him, as if by coincidence.

Joanna said in a small voice, 'I'm afraid of what it might do to Mike, if he found out. He might think . . .' She glanced down as the doctor gripped her arm. 'He needs me. I couldn't bear to be the one to destroy him.'

They both looked at the path again. The man in the dressing-gown was kneeling on the grass, peering at one of the roses as if it was some personal miracle. The male nurse remained motionless.

'Only you can tell him. If he needs you, he will understand. If not, then he's not worth it.' She patted the arm, very gently. 'I can have you taken off that duty, just by picking up the phone. Nobody would blame you, no one would know. You should never have been there—you're not the first, or the last, I'll wager!'

The tall figure in the dressing-gown had turned and was pointing down at the rose, his grin very white in his tanned face.

243

The doctor glanced at her profile and watched a smile emerge for the first time.

Joanna said, 'I shall go.'

They walked together into the corridor with its cream-coloured telephones and numbered rooms.

The doctor took one case at a time, if only to preserve her own sanity. It was pointless to give in to the horror of what might have been. That happened too often here.

She said, 'You'll not be needing me any more, Joanna.' She saw the furtive movement of a white-jacketed orderly, trying to catch her attention. 'You did it on your own, always remember that.'

At the gatekeeper's lodge Joanna Gordon paused to look back at the big, rambling house, the windows like dark, hostile eyes in this bright sunshine. She nodded, as if to someone else. The nightmares might return . . .

The gatekeeper touched his cap as she passed and did not see her take a deep breath.

There was hope now. It was enough.

*　　　*　　　*

Captain Michael Blackwood was officially awarded the Distinguished Service Cross on June twelfth, one month to the day after the last of the Axis forces in Tunisia had been either evacuated or captured. Compared with the great events which were to pave the way for a combined invasion of Sicily, already codenamed *Husky*, the ceremony was a quiet and simple sideline, for which Blackwood and four other recipients were both pleased and grateful. The Commander-in-Chief, Mediterranean, made the presentations on behalf of the King, before he too was whisked away to his headquarters in Malta. That in itself was another visible proof of the victory in North Africa: Malta, bombed, mined, blockaded for so long, with only her people's determination and a handful of fighters which had been required to fly almost around the clock, was now a symbol of success. So many ships had been sunk trying to force supplies through to that beleaguered island, so many men lost, that it had seemed almost inevitable that Malta, too, would fall. But it had not fallen, and *Husky* was not a dream; it was a reality, at least to the British and American planners and staff officers whose responsibility now was to co-ordinate the movements of hundreds of ships, thousands upon thousands of tons of supplies, tanks, vehicles of every size and class, and men.

Even in Alexandria the change in atmosphere was apparent. Landing craft were arriving daily to transport men and tanks: *shoe boxes* as they were called, because of their limitations in handling and speed in anything but perfect conditions. Big supply ships too, and troops of every description. *Not even got their knees brown,* as Archer had been heard to comment.

The C-in-C had spoken to each of the recipients while the Chief of Staff had read out the citations.

Blackwood was touched by the simplicity of it. No bands or bugles, and only a guard of honour for the C-in-C. There were a lot of faces he knew, and many he did not. And there were absences, like Lieutenant Falconer, who had gone down in his M.G.B. after fighting his last battle with the E-Boats. It was still hard to accept, a bitter memory after their return to Alex in triumph, with their

245

German prisoners paraded on the deck of the lighter like trophies.

But Lieutenant Terry Carson was there, almost unrecognisable in perfect whites, and clean-shaven, with an unlikely appointment now in Cairo as Small Craft Adviser, and a half-stripe in the pipeline if he behaved himself.

He had said almost dreamily, 'Still, not too bad, Mike. Lots of relics in Cairo!'

It was hard to set the stiff wording against the events and the stark memories. *Showing extreme courage underfire.* When men had died with brutal suddenness. *Over and above the line of duty.* Where there had never been any choice.

A handshake, and a searching look from the slight figure who, more than anyone, had held these ships and these men together when they were most needed.

He had hesitated, the ceremonial taking second place. 'I was sorry about your father, Captain Blackwood. A very fine man and a great loss.'

And then it was over, as quickly as it had begun. More handshakes, and a general movement towards the mess.

It was a proud moment, or should have been. The admiral's mention of his father brought it sharply home to him. The tradition, the Corps; there never could be any doubts.

And in any case, how could she have been here, even if she had wanted to? Major-General Vaughan was in Malta for conferences on *Husky*, and 'beyond that', as Gaillard had put it. Gaillard himself had gone to Cairo to collect some new uniforms; his promotion had been brought forward. Lieutenant-Colonel Marcus

Gaillard, D.S.O., Royal Marines, was to command the new force of commandos, *Trident*, which was to be among the first to land on Sicily.

And yet, like the mention of his father, the prospect had left him feeling empty, and alone.

He saw Lieutenant Despard talking with one of the new officers who had come from England with *Trident*.

Some of the others were applauding, and he saw Brigadier Naismith nodding with approval.

Despard came up to him and said, 'It's all right, sir. I don't want to talk about it. Not now, anyway.' They shook hands as all the others watched in sudden silence. 'This is *your day,* sir. You deserve it.'

Blackwood said, 'I was always brought up to think of the Corps as a family. But at times like this, I'm not so sure it's a good thing.'

The message had arrived just before the C-in-C. It would have been Gaillard's task to tell him, but, feeling Despard's wordless despair, Blackwood had been thankful that he was away. It was never explained how bad news always got priority, but it did. Despard's mother had died in the Channel Islands almost unnoticed, much as she had lived.

He said, 'We'll have a drink later.' He smiled. 'Suit you?'

He watched Despard stride away, most likely to the sergeants' mess. *Escape.* He faced the others; even the Chief of Staff was grinning, and they meant it, all of them, as he had done often enough when someone he knew had 'made it'.

'Congratulations, Mike!' The Chief of Staff shook his fist at his secretary. 'Not now, for God's sake! We have a hero to celebrate!'

247

The secretary shrugged, and then moved up beside Blackwood while his lord and master broke into a carefully prepared speech.

He murmured, 'That girl you met, at Rosetta.'

Blackwood gripped his arm.

'What about her?'

'She's coming to Alex. I got word from Malta.' He tapped the side of his nose. 'Friends in high places!'

'Are you sure?' His mind was reeling, as if he had already had too much to drink.

'Tomorrow. She's flying in. I have to pick up some papers for his lordship. I could give you a lift.'

He nodded, her face very clear in his thoughts. Like the moment when he had last seen her, here in Alex; they had been surrounded by people, but somehow he remembered only the two of them.

It might be just another brief meeting. But she was coming, probably with Vaughan's blessing.

It did not do to dwell on the growing lines of landing craft, and the mounting piles of provisions and ammunition. That was tomorrow. They had to seize what they could, while they could.

They were all applauding again, and then there was an expectant silence. He could see a shadow by the door; Despard had waited after all. To share it, and rightly so.

He said, 'This is certainly the finest day for me.'

Across the smiling faces and the raised glasses he caught the Chief of Staff's secretary's eye, and saw him wink.

And it was true. *Now.*

*   *   *

The car's progress seemed slower and slower the closer they got to the harbour. Noise, service vehicles taking their chances with local donkey carts, dust, and choking exhaust fumes often made the journey difficult to endure.

The Chief of Staff's secretary was driving, one elbow resting on the opened window, probably to show how nonchalant and detached he was. Blackwood noticed that the front passenger seat was occupied by the lieutenant's briefcase and the small bag she had been carrying when they had met at the airport, so they could sit together in the back without attracting undue attention.

He knew her hand was beside his on the worn seat, but they did not touch. Like that time in the café; it seemed so long ago.

She had seen him as soon as she had finished showing her documents, had looked straight at him as if she had known he would be there. An over-attentive flight lieutenant, probably impressed that one so junior in rank could travel in a priority aircraft, could have been invisible. She had not even noticed him.

She was wearing the khaki drill he had bought for her in the souk, and she was holding her injured arm at her side as if to hide it from him. As if she were ashamed of it, as his father had seemed ashamed of his wounds. She wore a loose bandage over it, and had even tried to make some sort of joke on the subject, but he had sensed the tension immediately, and was troubled by his inability to identify or understand it.

She had told him that a billet had been arranged for her at the old yacht club, now used for officers in transit. It was comfortable enough, in a place which was teeming with servicemen of every sort, but certainly not private. He laid his hand over hers almost before he knew what he was doing, and felt her flinch. Surprised, embarrassed perhaps? But she did not pull the hand away.

'How long will you be here, Joanna?' Even the sound of her name seemed different.

She said quickly, 'Two days. Then back to England. It's all arranged.' She turned to look at him. 'It's not long, is it?'

'I've been worried about you. I keep thinking about what happened.' He glanced at the driver, but he appeared intent on an army truck directly in front of him. It was full of grinning soldiers, and someone had chalked on the back, *Berlin or bust!*

She said, 'I saw all the ships. It was like that in Gibraltar when we flew out, and Malta's filling up as well.' Her hand moved slightly. 'It's all coming to a head, isn't it, Mike?'

He realised it was the first time she had used his name. Was it that bad?

'I think so. Glad I don't have the job of organising it. Must be a real test of allied co-operation!'

She lowered her voice so that he could barely hear her. 'You'll be going over, Mike? It's what you've been preparing for, isn't it?'

'Yes.' How flat and empty it sounded. If only he could hold her, tell her. What it was like, really like. But how could he? There could never be any doubts for him.

She leaned closer, and he could smell her hair, perhaps her perfume.

'I recognise that place, the mosque! It's where

250

we got this uniform!'

For those few seconds he saw her as he had held her in his memory. She had momentarily put her anxieties aside; she was even gripping his hand again.

'It suits you, Joanna.' She looked directly at him, and then, surprisingly, lifted her hand to his face and held it there.

'I worry about you, Mike. About us. What it's doing, has already done to our lives.'

He said, 'I love you. That's all I care about.'

The lieutenant must have heard; he would be inhuman not to be listening. But this was important. The old yacht club was in the next street. Too important to lose. To spoil.

She said quietly, 'You will write when you can, won't you? Just so that I know you're safe.'

Blackwood tightened his grip on her fingers. 'You know I will.' But all he could think of were the dead marines lying by the burning tank, and Robyns's last cry before he had died, and Gaillard had walked away.

The lieutenant said brightly over his shoulder, 'Here it is! Supposed to have been quite a smart place to be seen at one time.' It was something to say, his attempt to help. Two servants were already hurrying into the road, and Blackwood saw several uniformed figures in chairs, with drinks in their hands. There were one or two women, probably nurses awaiting transfer, or passage in the next hospital ship.

The lieutenant said, 'I'll stay with the car, Mike. They'll steal the wheels otherwise!' But he did not smile. Perhaps he felt guilty at intruding upon something so painful, and so private.

251

They walked into the lobby together, where an orderly made a display of checking his records before handing the girl a key.

'The boys will get you what you need, miss.' He glanced at Blackwood. 'You can use the lounge, sir. The rest is Residents Only.' He smiled. 'Rules, I'm afraid.'

Blackwood had the feeling he was enjoying it.

She took her bag and said, 'Can you wait? I'll only be a moment.' She reached out as if to touch him again, but withdrew her hand. 'I'd like a drink if you can manage it.' She turned her back deliberately on the orderly. 'No rules about that, I hope!'

Blackwood found two empty chairs and signalled for a steward. Two days, in this place? He avoided the curious eyes, and tried to shut them from his mind. Something serious had happened, and in two days she would be gone. Maybe this was her way of saying good-bye. *Never get close to anybody in wartime.* Another stupid rule, obviously made by somebody who had never been in one. He looked at his clenched fists, seeing again the German's contorted face when he had driven the knife into him.

He stood up quickly, scraping his leg against the table. She had returned, and was looking at him, with concern and what he wanted to imagine was something else.

'Your wound—is it bad?' Then the hand came to rest on his arm. 'Please tell me, Mike.'

They sat down, facing one another, the tall glasses having appeared unnoticed.

'It's fine. Really.'

She reached out once more. 'You wouldn't tell
252

me anyway. I know you so well!' She could not keep it up. 'I want . . . *I want* to know you so well.'

Blackwood sensed the glances, and the more blatant stares.

'And I you.' He tried again. 'Is there somebody else?'

She shook her head, so vehemently that she almost upset the glass.

'You must never think that! When we had those hours together, in that funny house with the swimming pool . . .' She broke off, almost visibly composing herself. 'I wanted you then. When I saw you at the airfield I was afraid you might have changed . . . towards me, don't you see?'

He gave the glass to her and watched her trying to swallow some of the contents; he had no idea what he had been drinking. It did not matter. Nothing mattered.

He said, 'When I heard you were coming from Malta I could hardly believe it. And now,' he watched her holding the glass, skin tanned against the khaki drill. She was afraid, and the realisation filled him with sudden anger. 'Tell me what happened. What they did. Everything. *Just tell me*, share it with me.'

She looked at him in that searching, direct way, her breathing quite calm, her eyes steady.

'You will be going to fight again soon, Mike. All those ships, all the troops I've seen here and in Malta. I'll not just walk away from you, leave you worrying, doubting . . .' She looked past him, and he saw a small pulse moving in her throat, making her semblance of composure a lie. 'Your friend. The one who drove us.' She stared across the room, as if she were trapped. 'He seems to know his way around.'

He held her hand across the table. 'In his job, he needs to.'

She looked at him again, as if to make certain he was not making a joke of it. Then she said, 'Ask him, will you, Mike? Find us a room, I don't care where it is. I just want to be alone with you.' Then she smiled faintly. 'Only you with all your private troubles would understand. You know that, don't you?'

He stood. He had not released her hand.

'I'll tell him it was my idea.'

She watched his mouth, his eyes, searching for something.

Then she said, 'I love you.'

She watched him leave the room, and saw two officers at the next table whispering to each other.

She recalled what Major-General Vaughan had said when he had invented a reason for her flight under his orders.

'Tell them all to go to hell, my dear!' His battered face had bent into a grin. 'And tell Captain Blackwood, from me, that if I'd been a year or so younger he wouldn't have had a bloody look-in!'

He was back, gazing down at her, his eyes full of questions, of longing.

'You were right. He does know a place. Not that far.' He hesitated, as if afraid she had changed her mind.

She stood up and reached for her shoulder bag. 'Let's go. I've got all I need here.'

He saw the way she was looking at the two officers at the next table. Defiance, contempt; maybe they had made some remark to her in his absence.

254

She turned to him and almost smiled. As if she had made a decision, or one had been forced upon her.

Two days. He opened the door for her. It was more than some people discovered in a lifetime.

*   *   *

The Chief of Staff's secretary certainly knew his way around, and even the sight of several military police vehicles did not deter him.

'The chap who owns this place does a lot of work for the base. Boat repairs, carpentry—useful man to know.' He returned one of the redcaps' salutes and added, 'Bit noisy. But it's safe enough.'

The girl had walked between them from the car. There were servicemen everywhere, in the narrow streets where the balconies almost touched each other, in the bazaars and the cafés. But the heavy military police presence suggested something else: brothels, which, despite having been ruled off-limits, would be a ready temptation for the innocent.

The lieutenant said, 'He's Dutch, by the way. Left the sea to live here, of all places.'

She asked, 'Is it private?' It sounded so silly she almost laughed. She felt light-headed, reckless. Impatient with herself for being afraid, and angered by the rude stares at the old yacht club.

'It's okay.' He pushed open a gate and led the way across a small courtyard. 'Oh, he's in Cairo at the moment.' He sensed Blackwood's hesitation, and knew it was because of the girl. 'Really. It's all right. Believe me.'

Up an outside stairway and into a low-ceilinged

room which faced over the harbour. An untidy room, a masculine room. There was a large and severe portrait of Queen Wilhelmina of the Netherlands on one wall, an engraving of Rotterdam on another. A man a long way from home.

The lieutenant glanced at his watch and waited until the girl had gone to the other door before he said, 'Pick you up early, Mike. Back to the old yacht club, I'm afraid. There's a servant here, a dozy Greek; he'll look after things. There's food and wine.' He grimaced. 'The sanitation is somewhat primitive.'

She called across the room, 'Thank you. It's fine.'

Blackwood looked at the small balcony, a feature in most of these waterfront buildings. The sky was darker, with a hint of red in it, like the reflected fires over London. So soon? Where had the time gone since he had waited for her at the airfield?

And Gaillard would be returning tomorrow. Perhaps he could . . .

He turned as she came to him and put her head against his shoulder. The lieutenant had gone, and he could imagine the M.P.s nudging one another while they waited for the evening brawls and drunken disputes. Like the two officers at the yacht club. All right for some . . .

Together they walked to the table; it was surprisingly neat, and simply arranged. The lieutenant must have telephoned somebody, or maybe he used the place himself.

She said, 'I think we should eat. But I'll go and wash first.'

He said, 'I understand it's a bit crude!' They laughed together for the first time.

She picked up her bag. 'We don't all have marble bathrooms, you know!'

Blackwood poured some wine and tasted it. It reminded him of the resinous wine Carson had taken from the island, with a definite bite to it.

She came from the other room and picked up her own glass. 'I suppose I should feel sinful, wicked.' She gazed at him over the rim. 'I don't. We're on our own.' She turned slightly as a roar of laughter came up from the street, then she took his arm and they walked out on to the balcony and leaned on the sun-flaked plaster. The heat of the day lingered here despite the shadows, and the great spread of fire across the sky. Angry, unmoving, defying the coming of night.

Blackwood could smell the place: cooking of every sort, people, dirt. He slipped his arm around her shoulders, and realised that she had removed the protective bandage. He could feel the intensity of her eyes as he held the arm and studied it in the fierce sunset.

It had been a terrible burn. The marks of the fire bars were still livid, the seared skin in brutal contrast with her body.

'I'll kill whoever did this!'

She was shocked by the depth and pain of his emotion, but said nothing. He held her closely, and felt the warmth of her shoulders, her spine, like that time in the empty house in Rosetta.

He felt her stiffen and turn her head, alert, like a frightened animal.

'What is it?'

She whispered, 'That smell.'

He sensed her sudden resistance against his body. 'Tar. For the boats.'

She nodded, as if she had heard someone else's voice. 'I know. Like the van. And later in the boat. It took me by surprise.' He would have released her. 'No, don't stop, Mike. Not now. Especially not now. I need you so much. I must know, you see. I don't want to spoil it . . .'

He unfastened her belt and let it fall, and as his fingers paused and then opened the buttons on her jacket, he knew she was naked underneath. Why she had said at the awful yacht club, *I've got all I need here.*

She stood against him as he slid his hands around her waist and up over her breasts. She was trembling, barely able to control it, and yet so determined, as if something were driving her, forcing her.

Once she said, 'I'm all right. They told me. But I have to *know*, for your sake.'

He half-carried her through to the other room, her jacket falling to the floor, her face against his; somehow he knew her eyes were tightly closed. The bare shoulders were stiff and unyielding.

He laid her on the bed and unbuttoned her khaki slacks. He had to lift her to pull them from her; she made no move to help or resist him. He straightened and stood over her, her body motionless on the unknown bed, her arms outflung, like an exquisite carving.

She said suddenly, 'I want to be yours. You must know that. I need to find it again, to give it.'

She moved her head from side to side as if in pain.

'I've been so afraid. I was terrified when it
258

happened. I still am, because of you. Because of us . . .'

He realised that her eyes were open, but he sensed that she saw something or someone else, at once a spectre and a terrible memory.

She said, 'Take me, Mike.' He had to bend over her to hear her voice. So small, so afraid. 'I don't care what you do, I want you to *take me*. Then I'll know.'

He lay beside her, his hand on her breast, then the tightened muscles of her stomach, wanting her, and yet afraid.

She said, 'Your hand. Put it there. Take me.'

He sensed resistance as he knelt over her, and then felt her entire body denying him. Then, like the madness of battle, caution was gone. She was writhing beneath him, her body wet with sweat, her eyes still tightly shut as he found her, sensed her pain, her strength finally breaking as he entered her and their bodies came together.

She had one hand over his mouth, perhaps to reassure him as she responded to his need, suddenly aroused, freed from doubt and despair.

They lay together, not wanting it to end, not wishing to withdraw one from the other. She could feel his heart, his joy, his need of her. Something so strong and so demanding, so pure, could never be soiled. And when she touched herself again, she would feel him and no one else, no matter how many miles lay between them.

Somewhere beyond the shadows a ship's siren vibrated over the hidden water.

But she could listen to it now without fear.

CHAPTER THIRTEEN

A BIT OF HELP

Captain Mike Blackwood returned the salute of a seaman in webbing belt and gaiters, with the familiar mail bag slung over one arm. The postman was the all-important link for servicemen and women overseas, vital at times like these. He wondered if there might be a letter waiting for him in the mess, but decided not to hope too much.

He strode into the wooden building which had been allocated to Force *Trident*, until the next owners moved in. Units, specialised or not, shifted in and out of Alex with barely time for a signboard or company crest to be erected.

Lieutenant Fellowes, one of the new officers from England, made to rise from the desk but Blackwood waved him down.

'Too hot to jump about.' He looked back through the open door, where marines in full kit were paraded for weapons and kit inspections. It was bloody hot out there; he could still feel it across his shoulders. There was a wind, too, that seemed to scorch the skin.

Beyond the jetty and the moored craft he could see landing ships taking on stores. Soon now, very soon. You could feel it, although it was something nobody spoke about any more.

Sergeant-Major 'Bull' Craven's voice rasped across the inspection; it never seemed quiet for long. In a barracks or a larger base, Craven would have had other warrant officers for company. Here he was alone, and it seemed to suit him. Craven was no common drill-pig, a tyrant of the barracks square. He was the epitome of the fighting man, hard and lean, as if all the surplus waste had been sweated out of him. He seemed tireless.

A disgruntled recruit had asked how Craven had acquired the nickname of 'Bull'. One of the older hands had answered cheerfully, 'Cause he's full of it, that's why! Surprised he hasn't got brown eyes!'

But here, with a new unit like Force *Trident*, Craven was necessary, the buffer between young officers like Fellowes who, because of their rank, often remained remote from the men, and because they were in awe of old sweats like Craven. Necessary, too, for the sergeants and other N.C.O.s; they were dealing with somebody who knew all the tricks and skives in the Corps, which might otherwise be used against the officers without mercy.

They were out there now in the searing heat, checking through weapons and ammunition, although every single man present was certain he knew it all already.

Lieutenant Despard was with them. Nobody would try to work something past him. And Craven would know it.

He moved to the desk and leafed through the signals pad, aware that Fellowes was watching every move. Young though he was, he had managed to take up acting just before he had joined the Royal Marines. You could see it in him sometimes, an intent curiosity, as if he were learning a part.

Blackwood sighed. *Like the rest of us.*

Sergeant-Major Craven had been making his

261

displeasure known to some marines, almost where he was standing now, when Blackwood had finally managed to get the switchboard to find a connection to the old yacht club. The day she was leaving. The day Gaillard had decided to mount a practice boarding of some landing craft in full battle order.

He had tried to picture her in the club, probably waiting with her bag for a car to take her to the airfield. Maybe the same faces all around, watching, listening. He was being unfair and knew it, but it did not help.

Perhaps they had both known it was too much to hope for. Two whole days? It had been only a dream. He would not have been surprised if the Chief of Staff's secretary had dined out on the story, although for some reason he had known he would keep it to himself.

When he had spoken to him about payment for the room, the lieutenant had brushed it off. 'Bottle of gin will do, Mike. The Dutchman owes us a few favours, remember?' When they had parted he had added, 'You're so lucky. I'd commit murder for a girl like her!'

The strange thing was, Blackwood could not recall his name.

She had sounded quite calm on the telephone, had shown neither surprise nor disappointment.

'Nothing can change for us, Mike. I'm your girl, any way you want me. I'll be waiting.'

During that single night, with the ebb and flow of noise from the street below, the buzz of insects against the lamp, she had held him as if she would never let go when daylight found them. She had told him some of it. The rest he could imagine.

They had loved again, slowly, and with a gentleness so different from her earlier demands, her need. To break the memory, to disperse thoughts he could not contemplate.

And she had gone. He had even called the airfield to ask if she had been delayed, perhaps for another day. They had refused to tell him anything. *There is a war on, you know!* The refusal to disclose information had told him as clearly as any words.

When would they meet again? Was it meant to end there, in that airless room above the place where boats were repaired?

He smiled. It was a beautiful room; and once again they had eaten nothing before they had parted.

His eyes focused on the signal flimsy. Officers' meeting this afternoon. Lieutenant-Colonel Gaillard and Brigadier Naismith would be expecting an early start.

Was it really possible? Only eight months since he had stood in the old church for his father's funeral, and had kissed his sister good-bye. Only two months since the invincible Afrika Korps had quit Tunisia. How could so much have happened?

So many faces. Terry Carson and his dreams of Greek islands. Falconer, the ex-schoolmaster, who had seen most of his little squadron perish before suffering the same fate with his eager first lieutenant. Blackwood frowned. Balfour, that had been his name.

With a photo of his girl beside him as he had written to her. And so many others. *Had been his name.* Like an epitaph . . .

He thought of the corporal named Sharp, who had been badly wounded in the leg during that last

263

raid. A bunch of them had gone down to the hospital to see him leave for England, and had joked with him about the cushy time he would have on the hospital ship with all the nurses.

Sharp was glad to be alive and in one piece. Given time, he might be sent back to another unit or ship, but not as a commando. His wound had been a close thing, and yet he had not wanted to go. That had been the hardest part. He had gripped Blackwood's hand, as he had on the night when Blackwood had confronted Gaillard, and had refused to leave him behind.

'Glad about the medal, sir! I'd have given you one, just for doing what you did for me . . .' Neither of them had been able to continue.

So it was something special. *Something special*, no matter what the barrack room sceptics and Whitehall warriors claimed.

And Joanna understood.

Fellowes broke into his thoughts.

'Can I ask, sir, is it going to be hard graft?'

Blackwood looked at him. *How many years between us? Four at the most. A lifetime.*

'Just so long as we don't forget. We know why we're fighting this war, so let's not forget *how* we do it, right? Tom Paget's your sergeant. Don't be too proud to share your thoughts with him.' He heard 'Bull' Craven's voice fading into the distance, until the next time, and smiled. 'He's a good man. I know. Not like some.'

Fellowes was observing him solemnly, the actor again.

Blackwood saw Gaillard striding towards the building, and added quietly, 'They'll be looking to you. Not to see how tough you are, we all find that
264

out soon enough. It goes deeper.' He thought of her voice in the night. Reassuring him, after all she had gone through herself. 'They need to know how you feel. They need to know that you care.'

As he closed the door behind him, Lieutenant Fellowes walked to a window and saw him greet the colonel in a patch of shade.

He had never met anyone like Michael Blackwood before, and it surprised him. He would write to his parents when he had a moment, and tell them about it.

He half-smiled, self-conscious, even though he was quite alone. The actor came to his aid, and he said aloud, ' "And Conscience doth make cowards of us all." '

He turned to face the door, ready.

And I would follow him without question.

The door banged open and Gaillard said, 'Nothing to do, Fellowes?'

Fellowes seized his beret and almost ran from the room.

Order and discipline were restored.

*   *   *

Lieutenant George Despard waited patiently while the last section of marines stowed their kit. He had been right through it, and had cursed it often enough in his time. But these tough, eager young men would learn the sense of it for themselves, if they lived long enough. Getting the feel of it, the weapons and the tools of their trade, the ammunition, strapped and pouched about their bodies until it felt like part of themselves. And the weight was crucial; it had to be considered at every stage. These men were trained to the limit, to land on an unknown beach anywhere, at any time. Like the Corps motto, *Per Mare, Per Terram,* by sea, by land. But even the most rigorous training could not prepare men for every contingency, like a landing craft dropping its ramp too soon, caught, perhaps, on a submerged wreck or some deliberate obstruction. They could curse Sergeant-Major Craven all they liked, it was what he was there for, but they had to remember every detail. *The weight.* Apart from the steel helmet, uniform and heavy boots, the ammunition weighed a ton, or felt like it. The Bren gunner's pouches weighed ten pounds each, plus the clips of bullets and entrenching tool, and the rifle and bayonet, which added another ten pounds to the load. It made the haversack or pack seem modest by comparison, a mere five pounds including each man's link with normal life: washing and cleaning gear, mess tins, a change of underwear and shirt, and survival rations. It was not much on which to exist.

But, added together, it was all quite enough to carry him to the bottom if he was called upon to ditch.

The balloon was about to go up, and Despard was surprised to discover that he was almost glad of it. The news about his mother had not been unexpected, but it had still come as a shock. There was nothing now to stir the memories of his youth in the Channel Islands, nothing to hold him. He stared at the long grey hulls and the bustling harbour craft. There was only the way ahead. What he did best.

He heard Sergeant 'Sticks' Welland's boots approaching. One of the hard cases, good with his men and usually reliable. Always ready to carry a new recruit until he was confident enough to fit in. Despard almost grinned. But give him an inch, and he'd steal the shirt off your back.

Welland stamped his feet together. 'The last section's finished, sir.'

'They can line up for their dinner soon.' Another memory. Aboard ship, the pipe was always *Hands to dinner*, and the quartermaster would invariably add, '*Officers to lunch.*'

Welland said, 'Heard a buzz that there's an officers' meeting this afternoon, sir.'

It was probably true. He had seen their newly minted lieutenant-colonel in conversation with Blackwood. Welland would know; the sergeants always did.

'Can't be too soon for me.' He thought of Blackwood and the W.A.A.F. he was rumoured to be seeing, and wondered if she would ever know the man he knew, whom he had seen kill one of the enemy.

Welland watched him curiously. He, too, knew about the captain's girl. It was too interesting not to know, especially in this mob. Bloody good luck to him, he thought. He was a decent bloke, as far as you could tell with any officer. Welland had never been really serious about anyone for long. He just liked women for what they were. There was a solitary exception, Pam, a N.A.A.F.I. manager at Plymouth. She was married to some bloke stationed in India, so he was no bother. She was not exactly beautiful; she wasn't even as young as most of the scrubbers who hung about the barracks and dockyard gates, but she had something more than all the rest put together. No promises, no ties,

267

and he guessed he wasn't the only caller at her door. But she was special, and she was always glad to see him, no matter how long in between. And each time they parted she made no demands. Welland was a great admirer of Henry Hall's band, which played regularly on the wireless. He always signed off the air with the same song, *'Here's to the next time!'* It could have been just for Pam.

He asked carefully, 'D'you reckon Captain Blackwood will get made up to major? I mean, with promotion flying about in every direction?'

Despard shrugged. 'Probably not. You know what it's like. I'm glad he's with us, that's all.' He put it down to the heat. He would never otherwise discuss another officer with Welland, or anyone else.

Welland nodded, a frown forming between his eyes as he saw Sergeant-Major Craven striding amongst the dismissed marines, one hand jabbing here or there as if to reveal some fault. Welland had known Craven as a colour- sergeant. Even then he had been bad enough, full of bullshit, and always shooting off about himself. Of how *Dickie Mountbatten himself turned to me and praised the turnout of my section.* Or the admiral who had died in harness at Whitehall, and Craven had been part of the burial detail. *The admiral's wife was all over me, I can tell you! Soon forgot about her old man!* A right bastard.

'I'll carry on, sir.'

Despard watched him march away, and knew why.

Craven came up to him and saluted, his heels making little horseshoes in the hard-packed earth. *If it moves, salute it. If it doesn't, paint it white.*

268

'A good turnout, Sar'-Major.'

Craven eyed him as if considering it.

'They're learning, sir. Most of 'em. Still need some more time.'

Despard said, 'We don't have any. They look ready enough to me.'

The eyes flickered only slightly. 'If you say so, sir.' He waited a few seconds. 'You must have seen the changes yerself, sir? I mean, when you . . .'

'I know what you mean, Mr Craven. Yes, I still do. I can live with it.'

He relented, slightly. The next weeks, less for some, might decide everything. And the Royals would be on the knife-edge of it, that was bloody obvious with all the top brass scurrying around.

He said, 'They're the best we've got. I hope they think the same about us!'

He turned as the orderly sergeant approached from the wooden building. He did not see the triumph in Craven's eyes, as if he had discovered a flaw, a weakness. Nor would he have cared.

The orderly sergeant said, 'Just posting this notice, sir.' He held it up for Despard to read.

All leave was cancelled, indefinitely.

It was on.

*　　*　　*

Lieutenant Steve Blackwood of the Royal Engineers leaned on the guardrail of the troopship and feasted his eyes on the grand array of vessels which seemed to fill the bay. Tiny launches darted amongst them, frothing moustaches churning the water, midgets among giants. He had never seen so many ships anywhere, and he guessed that it was

269

probably the greatest armada ever yet gathered in one place for a single purpose.

Danger and uncertainty did not intrude into his thoughts. This was an adventure, and he was a part of it.

Most of the larger troopships had once been luxury liners, and he could well imagine this same deck thronged with excited and light-hearted passengers, making the most of it. He ran his hand along the fine teak rail, now carved and disfigured by hundreds of initials and even the full names of many of the servicemen this liner had already carried to war.

The stays and rigging of most of the ships were filled with khaki clothing hung out to dry in the brilliant sunlight, giving a certain jauntiness to the grey and dazzle-painted hulls, as if, in their own way, they were dressed overall for the occasion.

And yet, in spite of the great assembly of ships, the Rock of Gibraltar managed to dwarf them all, huge, imposing, eternal and strangely reassuring.

He turned and shaded his eyes to stare at the Spanish shoreline, almost hidden in haze. Algeciras, like the other historic names he had seen on the bridge charts when the soldiers, lesser beings, had been allowed to visit that hallowed place in small, manageable parties.

Yesterday they had passed Cape Trafalgar, and right there was Algeciras, of which the little admiral had written before his last battle, 'Yonder lies the enemy.'

Many a glass would be trained now, as in those days, on this formidable show of strength. Spain was neutral, in name at least, but Franco was known to favour Hitler. No horsemen; a few telephones would carry the news more swiftly. Security was tight. For us. But the whole world must know by now what was happening.

He rested his elbows and peered down at the deck below. Men like himself were drinking in the sights, others were cleaning their kit, playing cards, yarning. A mob of soldiers. It was hard to see them separated into units again, platoons, companies, battalions. Riflemen and despatch riders, tank drivers and cooks. He caught sight of some of his own men. And sappers.

They were no longer just faces, or *name, rank and last three* as any N.C.O. might label them. They were individuals. He could see his sergeant, Larry Godden, sharing a map with somebody, his bright red hair marking him out. But Godden stood out anywhere, once he allowed you to know him. A slight, watchful man; unsoldierly would be a fair description. But on the last course they had done together in Portsmouth he had seen even the experienced instructors, blasé in matters of explosives, observe with approval Godden's nimble skill with wiring and fuses.

Godden wore a single medal ribbon on his battledress, one so rare that Steve Blackwood had not recognised it. It was the George Medal. They had had a drink together one night after a full day of instruction, and he had asked him about it.

Godden had given him that searching look. 'Bomb disposal. In the London docks area.' He had not wanted to continue. 'Anywhere they needed us.'

Blackwood had asked him why he had transferred to an active service unit.

He had said quietly, 'I wanted to get back at those bastards. Let *them* feel what it's like for a change!'

They had had another drink together when leave was cancelled, and he had lost his chance to see Diane again. Too many drinks, probably, but he remembered asking where Godden had first learned how to use explosives so skilfully. Another sapper had started as a quarryman in Yorkshire.

Godden had laughed until his eyes had run with tears.

'You must have had a really nice upbringing, sir! You an' me are going to get along just fine!'

It turned out that Godden had been a peterman, a safe-blower, as he had patiently explained; one of the best.

'But the war started, so I thought to meself, why not?'

He realised that Godden was looking up at him, and wondered what he would say if he knew he had tried to propose to a 'sort of cousin' after meeting her only twice. He walked to the rail again and stared up at the Rock. *If only you were here.* If only he could tell her things. Explain. He had heard some of the others talking about their exploits, their sexual conquests, and had been unsettled by his own anger. *Old-fashioned, that's me.*

And yet when he had met her and she had shown him around Hawks Hill, which had seemed a palace after the house in New Zealand, he had not felt like a stranger or an outsider. Maybe his father, 'the galloping major', with all his faults, had been responsible for that. Despite the New Zealand shoulder flash on his uniform, he knew he belonged. He smiled. Even if his men did call him 'Kiwi' behind his back.

There was the severe-sounding Wren officer he
272

had been put on to when he had tried to call Diane at the barracks. It had been like trying to open an oyster with a bus ticket to get past her, until she had said coolly, 'Oh, you must be her friend from New Zealand.' It seemed to change things, and she had asked him if he had a message she could pass on.

Standing in the lobby of a naval wardroom at H.M.S. *Vernon*, where they knew more about mines, torpedoes and sudden death than almost anybody else, with the telephone pressed to his ear to shut out the din of laughter and some idiot playing a piano, he had said to his unknown ally, 'Tell her I love her. Very much.'

Surprisingly, she had responded, 'I'm so glad.' Just like that.

He saw one of the other liners preparing to leave, smoke trickling from three funnels which had once proudly borne the White Star. They were all Canadians in that one, and he had heard that the entire contingent had been convoyed all the way directly from that country. The next place those troops would walk on solid earth would be Sicily.

A flight of Spitfires thundered overhead, which they did several times an hour, their sleek shadows flashing across the ships like darts.

It had to be different this time. England was full of memorials from the Great War, and even in the little village near Hawks Hill he had seen one that bore more than a hundred names. In a sleepy retreat like that.

She was moving now, very slowly, her bow wave barely breaking the surface. Deck upon deck they were waving and cheering, and every ship in the bay seemed to be answering. Destroyers were waiting to take over the escort, for even with the enemy out of North Africa there was still danger all the way.

An officer he had met a few times in the mess came over to join him.

'Quite a moment, isn't it? I just hope we go through with it.'

'How d'you mean?' He turned and looked at him. An ordinary face. *An English face*, as his mother would have called it.

'I heard the ships' officers discussing the weather. Bad signs apparently, for this time of the year. That would really put the ruddy lid on it!' Like a man who has been told that a cricket match has been cancelled because of rain.

Blackwood smiled. 'Not our worry, fortunately.' He looked out at the ships, and the others which were already mustered and waiting, and was aware of an intense excitement, something he thought he had outgrown, or which had no place in war.

He had met a girl, one he had felt instantly that he had always known or been expecting. That, above all else, brought it home to him. He might never see her again.

He said, 'We'll make it this time!' But the other soldier had gone.

*   *   *

Joanna Gordon awakened suddenly, violently, every muscle straining as she stared into the darkness. For a moment longer she imagined it had been the same nightmare, the return of something she had learned to fight, if not to completely dispel.

274

Something she had believed gone from her life.

She held her breast, her heartbeat already slowing. Her skin was damp, as if she had been dreaming of him, and of that unbelievable night above the noisy street in Alexandria.

It was completely silent, and the air in the room was oppressive. She switched on the bedside light, her mind alive again.

On one chair lay her uniform, its buttons gleaming softly in the lamplight, a clean shirt and collar on top of it in readiness for tomorrow, if she had all the time she needed. On the other chair her dark battledress, her 'anonymous rig', was also laid out, in case she had no time at all. But there was no siren wailing along the river, no muffled crump-crump of anti-aircraft guns. A quiet night over London, for a change.

She switched off the light, and after a slight hesitation threw her legs over the side of the bed and walked to one of the windows, her bare feet careful to avoid something which she might have forgotten.

She opened the blackout curtains and took down the screen, and looked out across the darkened rooftops. There was a lot of cloud about, fast-moving and angry, so that the moon showed itself like a spotlight, reflecting in windows, giving even one of the bombed houses a kind of stark beauty. She could see the river, too, like black metal where it curved round from Chiswick Bridge. She felt her lips move in a smile. Where the Boat Race had always ended, in those times before the war. It must have been a pleasant place to live, neat houses like this one, trees and gardens, Richmond Park not far away. She allowed her mind to reach out. Not so far from that other sweeping bend in the Thames, where the commandeered block of flats was situated. Where they had met.

If only it could have been then. A place without personality, where ordinary people had once lived and planned their days. But they would have been alone, safe, while they found and discovered one another.

She shivered and pulled her thin nightdress around her body, remembering.

She saw a car moving along the road, its shaded lights like tiny eyes. The police, or a doctor maybe. Few others would have the petrol.

She thought of the other women who lived in this house, officers of all three services, most of them working, like herself, in operational planning departments, or attached to some ministry or other. They hardly met except to hand each other letters, or when they were waiting to use a bathroom. Self-contained, separate lives, holding on to something, or trying to hide it. As she had done at the hospital.

She gasped, startled, as lightning flashed across the houses, and a clap of thunder shattered the silence.

She closed the screen and the heavy curtains, shutting it out. So that was what had awakened her.

She sat on the bed again and switched on the light. In the yellow glow the scars on the branded arm were distinct and, to her, repulsive. But all she could remember was his tenderness when he had caressed it and kissed it, his anger and concern controlled for her sake.

He would be waiting right now, with all those others, the ones she had seen crowding around him. When he had looked beyond them, at her. *I felt you watching me.*

At the underground H.Q., the Pit, she had sensed the changing mood, the initial exultation giving way to anxiety as the date for *Husky* drew closer.

Supplies, machines and men; it was endless, like hearing about a film second-hand, and not being able to follow it in its entirety.

She was seconded to the R.A.F. Operations section. It was largely a question of keeping records. There were now bombing attacks by the R.A.F. and the Americans around the clock, a far cry from that time not so long ago when enemy planes controlled the North African skies, and had made the approaches to Malta a killing ground.

She had heard the senior officers discussing the change in the weather, and what it would mean to *Husky* if conditions worsened. At a meeting of the Chiefs of Staff an expert had suggested that the whole invasion could be reversed, even aborted, up to twenty-four hours before H-Hour, as it was known. That would be a formidable feat in itself. After that time had elapsed, there could be no turning back, weather or no weather.

She walked to the basin and rinsed her face with cold water, remembering the room above the street, the 'somewhat crude' arrangements. They had even laughed about that. And the stares she had received when she had returned to the yacht club to prepare for her flight. If only they knew . . .

Another roll of thunder, but further away now.

And he was there. The man she loved beyond hope or reason. He would be waiting.

She could recall when he had opened his heart

to her, on that other night. Their only other night.

All the things which had contrived to make him what he was. Name, tradition, duty. He had said, 'But when the time comes, I feel nothing. My mind is empty. Like somebody else.'

It pounded through her mind like a voice. *And he was there.*

She could not even share it with anyone. She thought of her last visit to her father. How old he had become, still grappling with the death of his son. She could not recall his asking how she was, or what she was doing. She had been hurt rather than angry, and most of all saddened by what had happened to him.

Perhaps it had been wrong of her not to tell him what had happened to his daughter.

She flinched as the telephone jangled noisily. Then she faced the door, testing her breathing. There was one telephone in the house, and six women lived here.

She saw the light under her door. How could she have known that it was for her?

Her neighbour from the next room rapped on the door and said huskily, 'For you, Jo.' She always called her that, although they hardly knew one another. Except one night when she had returned to the house after a few days' absence. She had been very much the worse for wear that night, and she was a reserved sort of girl; it had seemed somehow unfair that she should be so drunk.

Joanna had taken her into her room, had undressed and bathed her, and had eventually got her into her own bed. But not before she had seen the weals on her shoulders and thighs, the marks of a parachute harness, when a body is dropped

278

without protective clothing or flying gear. Simply because the parachutist would have no time to hide them.

She had never mentioned it, but, in her silence, she had shared it.

It was Major Porter, alert as usual. Did he never sleep?

'Glad I caught you up.'

She peered at her new watch. It was past midnight. What did they think she got up to at this hour?

Porter said, 'Could use a bit of help, if you can spare the time.'

She stared at a crack in the wall until it seemed to move.

A bit of help. The code. The invasion was on.

'Still there?'

She shook herself. 'Sorry, sir.'

He laughed. 'There'll be a car. Twenty minutes suit you? Good show.' He hung up.

She dressed unhurriedly and with care, and was ready when the car drew up outside the house. Before she left she opened her cupboard and held the khaki drill uniform for several minutes, until the doorbell rang.

Then she closed the cupboard and picked up her small bag.

A quick glance around. This was different. It was not only a dream.

She put on her cap and looked at her reflection in the mirror. She was ready.

CHAPTER FOURTEEN

SMILE BEFORE DYING

Under cover of darkness the invasion fleet, with the landing and support craft which carried the Royal Marine Commando, finally reached the lee of the Sicilian coast. Maintaining formation had been a nightmare for every watchkeeping officer and lookout, and in a gale which had raged all day many had given up hope of proceeding with the landings.

Hampered by their weapons and equipment, the marines suffered in silence, while around them seamen ran cursing through the darkness, replacing lashings, hosing away vomit, and generally making it known that they would be glad to see them leave.

Lieutenant-Colonel Gaillard had held a conference to which even the senior N.C.O.s were invited, which had put paid to any more doubts. *Husky* was on. Another lengthy examination of maps and photographs followed; every man must know exactly what to do once he got ashore, and others must be prepared to take over if the first attack was too costly.

Blackwood had watched his companions, eager, serious, troubled, and some with blanched, perspiring faces on the verge of seasickness, who were too wretched to care very much what happened. The contrasts were stark, from Despard, who had seen and done it all, to young Fellowes, preparing for his greatest role yet. And Sergeant-Major Craven, as smart as paint in spite of his weapons and combat uniform, and remaining quite apart from everyone else.

Gaillard had seemed different in some way, no less thorough with his briefing and details for his officers, but at times almost jovial, which was unusual if not unique.

Blackwood thought he knew why. At the final officers' conference in Alex, Brigadier Naismith had made it clear that Force *Trident* would be kept in support of his main assault group. Quite suddenly, that had changed. While an unheard-of north-westerly gale had whipped the sea into a raging barrier of waves severe enough to pose a real threat to some of the low-slung landing craft, Gaillard had received new orders. In his mind's eye, Blackwood could see the map. The U.S. Seventh Army was to land on the south-west beaches, which would favour their small, fast-moving troop carriers. The British Eighth Army would land on the south-eastern coast, then strike inland to capture any airfield which could be used for supply and reinforcements.

One other landing area remained between the two major armies, on the southernmost corner of Sicily. The First Canadian Division would overcome all opposition, believed to be Italian troops, and press inland to Ragusa and Pachino. The planners had considered everything, the suitability of the various beaches, the experience and, of course, the rivalry of every major unit. The Canadians were well trained, but without combat experience. In addition, Intelligence had discovered a last-minute obstacle to the line of advance from the beaches where the Canadians would be landing, and several carefully prepared strong points had been located on the headland to the west of those same beaches.

The weather had been bad enough, and nobody would know the full extent of the confusion it might have caused until the nakedness of daylight. The Americans' landing should have been a sheltered one; the gale had changed that. With strict communications silence imposed, it was impossible to assess the damage to ships and to morale.

Gaillard had exclaimed, 'History, gentlemen! Once again, the Royal Marines will be the first to land!' He did not mention Naismith. He did not need to.

Now those same faces were scattered throughout the ship. Watches checked, weapons and equipment ready to move. The human brain could only stand so much preparation.

Blackwood heard the sea sluicing along the hull. The gale had dropped soon after sunset, leaving a steep and heavy swell. It would make the final approach no less hazardous.

Gaillard joined him by the chartroom.

'Any ideas, Mike?'

Blackwood knew it was no casual question. He was sounding him out. Testing his nerve, his combat attitude, as the instructors termed it.

'Being swamped will be a major risk once we embark, sir. We should leave more space for them to work the pumps if need be. They're difficult little craft at the best of times.'

'Good thinking. Tell Mr Craven, he can deal with that. I want our people to be on top line, not waddle ashore like seasick day-trippers at Eastbourne!'

Blackwood could not see his face in the shadows. Was he so certain, so confident? Nobody could be sure of anything at this stage. Half the invasion fleet could have been scattered, or swept miles away from their allotted positions. And if the enemy knew they were coming it would be a hard slog. He almost smiled. Not a bit like Eastbourne.

Gaillard said abruptly, 'Been so busy lately, I've not had much of a chance.' He seemed to be making up his mind. 'Meant to ask you, Mike. When we were in Burma giving the Japs a bit of stick, did you have anything to do with a marine named Finch?' One hand tapped impatiently on a chart cabinet. 'He was sent with a landing party from the cruiser *Genoa*.'

Blackwood thought of the men he had met, most of them for the first time, except for the few like Paget. Faces stamped with strain and fatigue, shocked by seeing friends killed. Holding together because of what they were, because of what, in their different ways, they were all proud of.

'I don't think so, sir. Is he joining this commando?'

Gaillard sounded surprised. 'No. I just thought you might remember the fellow.'

'I could ask Sergeant Paget, sir. He was there. He might know.'

Gaillard snapped, 'No. Forget about it.'

A bell tinkled somewhere and he said, 'Midnight.' He seemed to take several deep breaths, like a sprinter on the blocks. 'Time to go!' He strode away to speak with the ship's commanding officer, and Blackwood saw marines getting out of his way. Like him, hate him, it made no difference now.

He found Craven and told him about the pumps.

Craven listened intently and said, 'I remember my colonel in the Norway caper, sir. Keep 'em busy an' keep 'em smart, they'll do the rest!'

Blackwood joined Lieutenant Fellowes on the starboard side and found time to marvel that men could work so smoothly in total darkness while the ship dipped and swayed around them as if bent on self-destruction. Beyond the rail it was black, with only leaping spectres of spray to show the sea's heavy motion. The landing craft were alongside, their screws and rudders painting the water with streams of phosphorescence.

'All right?'

Fellowes tried to smile. 'Nearly threw up, sir. But I'm more bruised than sick in this rust-bucket!'

Blackwood touched his arm. He spoke like a veteran already.

He looked towards the land. If the calculations were correct the ships were some eight miles south-east of the Sicilian coast. He tried to recall the map. The jutting spike of the peninsula, Punta Castellazzo. The cove almost adjoining it on the western side. Just like one of those hairy exercises, except that this time they would be shooting back.

He said suddenly, 'Keep with Sergeant Paget. If he says hit the deck, you do it. Don't ask questions.' He smiled and hoped Fellowes would see it, and that it might reassure him. *Blackwood's not bothered, so it must be okay.*

He could hear the marines slithering and kicking out with their boots to lower themselves into the little landing craft. No time for mistakes now. He hoped they would all remember what Despard had told them about falling into the sea fully loaded.

284

Nothing left to bury.

He said, 'You might feel scared.' He waved down the protest he knew would come. 'Don't let it throw you. The first time is always a sod. It'll pass.' He thought suddenly of his father. It must have been the last time he had seen him. 'Remember, they'll be looking to you.'

A voice called, ' "A" Troop embark! Come on, move your bloody selves!'

The marines, half crouched beneath their loads and wary of the heaving motion, hurried past.

Someone muttered, 'I'd like to move that big-headed bastard!'

A companion laughed. 'Never volunteer, Taff!'

Fellowes had gone, and the deck seemed empty of armed marines.

Percy Archer stood watchfully by the cargo port, having heard most of it.

'All set, sir?'

Blackwood nodded, and thought of the garden at Hawks Hill, where he had walked and talked with his father. For the last time. There had been roses there.

He heard what Archer said, but could not move. He remembered what the girl had told him about the hospital, the officer whose mind had almost been broken by his experiences. How a solitary rose had saved him.

She had told him in the night, her breath warm and unsteady across his shoulder.

He put his hand on Archer's arm.

'Keep your head down today. We're supposed to make history, remember?'

Together they clambered down and were guided the last few feet by some of his men.

The moon was in the first quarter, but now it was gone.

'Bear off forrard! Get under way and take station!' That was Gaillard, already in position.

He felt Despard beside him, and heard him say quietly, 'Like a needle in a haystack.' He might have been grinning. 'I reckon we'll have the jump on them with any luck!'

He knew the others were listening, straining their eyes in the darkness, although they were all shadows, without substance.

Everyone would know about it. Vaughan and his patient aide, the men and women at headquarters in Alex and in London. And she would be one of the first to know if the worst happened.

H-Hour was two forty-five in the morning, about two and a half hours from now. Before that time Force *Trident* would be overrunning the first objectives. Or wiped out.

He thought of his words to Fellowes. Really, there was no choice at all.

*   *   *

The course to steer for the selected cove was north-west. Had the gale still been blowing they would have been butting head-on into it, probably unable to forge ahead.

Blackwood felt the spray dash over his shoulders like rain; it seemed ice-cold after the heat of the day. It could hardly have been much worse. The swell made accurate steering impossible, lifting the landing craft's stern and causing the blunt ramp forward to plunge dangerously near to the surface. The tightly packed marines were soaked, huddled

286

together, glad of their steel helmets for once, if only to keep their faces free of water. Within twenty minutes of embarking two of the landing craft had had to turn back, one with engine trouble, the other so filled with water that it was unsafe to try and hold formation.

The land was no longer invisible. One horizon was eerily lit by drifting fires, followed by the flash and rumble of bombs. The R.A.F. were playing their part and keeping to time, lighting up the town of Pachino, a ready marker for the troops once they were ashore.

Blackwood could feel the tension as every lurch and stagger carried them closer to the land. But still no challenge, no devastating bombardment from shore batteries. Perhaps they were waiting for the last moment, when there would be no room to turn and claw away.

Gaillard came up to the forepart of the craft, and clung to a stanchion while he tried to peer ahead whenever the ramp dipped down into another welter of spray.

'God damn! Where the hell is it?'

Blackwood saw his eyes and face light up as a vivid flash revealed the nearness of land, and for an instant he believed they had been sighted, that their presence was no longer a secret. But there were more flashes and explosions, from somewhere beyond a cliff, the shells bursting far away, in the opposite direction.

Gaillard exclaimed, 'Shooting at the Raf, not us!' He swung away. 'Got that, Cox'n?'

Blackwood felt the hull turning slightly; they had not been so far off course after all. It was incredible. He wiped his streaming face with his sleeve and saw the land. He also saw the other craft, black, anonymous shapes, low down on the heaving water. He heard pumps working wildly, in this vessel or the other he did not know. The sound was deadened, and he could sense the nearness of the spike, Punta Castellazzo, reaching out like an invisible protection. He tensed, the rattle of one or maybe two machine guns probing through the din of trapped water and the irregular crash of the bows into solid rollers.

The marines had ducked down at the first sound of gunfire. He did not have to look to know it. Instinct, training, guts.

But no bullets cracked against the hull or whined off the thin plating. Someone else was getting it; there was no time to think about them.

Blackwood called, *'Ready!'* They were pressing behind him, and somewhere abeam the other craft would be doing their best to cover the last few yards. The ramp was being lowered; it always left you feeling naked, ready for the sickening, crushing blow, or worse, the realisation that you could not hide it from those who followed.

There was a great lurch, followed by several more which seemed to shake the hull from ramp to stern.

Blackwood knew that the landing craft had beached crookedly, that water was surging past him, flooding the hull, choking the pumps.

He felt his boots slide, and would have fallen but for his hand on the ramp. 'Forward, Marines!' Did he speak, or was it all in his mind? But he was wading waist and sometimes chest deep through the water. When he glanced back he saw the others following, in sections, as they had been trained to do, without panic, and remembering to hold their weapons high. Others carried cans of drinking water, ammunition, grenades, the tools, as Churchill had called them.

Disjointed thoughts flashed through his mind. Robyns, the lieutenant who had died, who had been drinking his precious water just minutes beforehand. The wounded Corporal Sharp, who had not wanted to leave his unit. Pleading to stay with his friends. Even his words, 'Just get me to the bloody sea!' seemed to sum it all up.

He heard sharp, controlled orders being passed, men fanning out, weapons cocked and ready, probably not yet able to grasp what they had done. Another machine gun came to life, but again the sound was distorted. Not our party.

It was a shelving, sandy beach, but beyond it there was no cliff as described in the intelligence pack. Blackwood heard his men running up a hard slope of what felt like limestone. Maybe they had landed in the wrong place after all? He could almost hear Vaughan's rage all the way from London, or wherever he was at this moment . . .

Gaillard was beside him, staring into the darkness as more marines scrambled over the rough stone, child's play after what they had been trained to do. Most of them were carrying packs of supplies as well as their weapons.

Gaillard turned as one of the landing craft started frothing astern. Their part was done. This would be no place for an undefended 'shoe box' when daylight found them.

He said, 'Bloody good show, eh, Mike? Enemy soil, the first step into Europe!' It was like hearing a newspaper headline.

Blackwood said, 'And we did it.'

Gaillard was still looking towards the sea. 'Get the machine guns sited. We have to assume that nothing has changed, but I want to hit them where it hurts. We'll see what the youngest general since Wolfe will have to say about that!'

'Ready to move, sir!' That was Paget's voice. He hoped that Fellowes would remember his advice. 'M.G. section closed up, sir!' Despard and his beloved Bren guns, thinking of nothing but the job in hand, certainly not of the home he had once known in the Channel Islands. That might destroy him.

Archer was beside him again, his rifle in the crook of his arm, like a gamekeeper out for a stroll. Blackwood thought of the exploding fuel, and Archer's comment about Gary Cooper. Maybe more like a poacher . . .

Archer said quietly, 'You've got a smile a mile wide, sir.' He sounded surprised.

Blackwood watched a file of men climbing up the slope, where a cliff should have been.

He said, 'I'd forgotten. It's my birthday today!'

Force *Trident* had landed.

*   *   *

Sergeant 'Sticks' Welland flopped hard on the ground and winced as a sharp stone tore into his elbow.

'The bastards are awake now, right enough.' He groped down to fix his bayonet, wondering why he had got himself stuck with one of the new lieutenants.

Lieutenant Bruce Hannah said, 'Where are

they? I—I thought the other troop was covering that side.'

Welland strained his ears. He heard the muffled vibration of engines, the next wave of landing craft moving into the cove. He grinned into the darkness. *Well, we were bloody first.*

He ducked as several shots echoed around the headland. No flashes, so somebody must have blundered into an enemy patrol.

He said, 'We'd better get closer, sir.' It was all he could do to keep his patience. Bad enough when you *knew* an officer, but this one he didn't know from Adam. Straight from commando training in England, keen as mustard, and he heard he was supposed to cut quite a dash with the girls. They must be bloody hard up, he thought.

Hannah said, 'We'll send a runner to the Colonel.' He was thinking aloud. Like an exercise.

Welland heard someone shouting, Italian by the sound of it. He half-rose on one knee. 'Take too long. The first strong point is dead ahead of us. Remember the photos they showed us?' He could not recall them either, but he had to do something.

There were more shots from a different bearing, and he heard another Italian voice. It sounded like surrender in any language.

It was taking too long. He stood up, and sensed the rest of the section following his example, screwed up to the limit. Some of them were in action for the first time. He glanced at the lieutenant. *Like this idiot!* He shouted, *'Move!'* and broke into a run, his eyes everywhere, his finger already tight on the trigger.

The tracer seemed to rise from the ground itself, a heavy machine gun by its sound. It would explain

291

the delay in their response to the patrols meeting on the slope. It would take a good while to move a gun like that; there were probably several of them, sited and trained on that other beach where the Canadians would be landing.

He tugged the pin from a grenade and let the lever fly before hurling it over the slope. It sent splinters cracking and hissing past the crouching marines. Welland already had another in his hand when long streams of vivid scarlet tracer zipped past and raked the slope from side to side. He took a deep breath. Despard's Brens; that single grenade had given him all he needed. He nudged the officer. He should have known. 'Ready, sir?'

The lieutenant got up and ran forward, his revolver in his hand, a man already overtaken by events for which he was unprepared.

More shots, up, and from the left. Welland charged on, yelling at the top of his voice although he did not realise it. A shadow bounded to meet him and steel glinted in the sporadic gunfire. Welland parried the blade and swung his rifle butt, felt bone breaking as he found the other man's jaw. He ran on, and heard a brief, choking cry as one of his marines finished the job.

More figures loomed out of the darkness, arms raised, voices cracking in panic, as if they had just been roused from their beds. It was laughable. And then one of them dropped on one knee, a light machine gun already jammed to his shoulder. There was a savage burst of fire from two of the Stens, and the soldiers, those trying to surrender and the solitary, would-be hero, seemed to pirouette round in the flashes before falling together in an untidy embrace.

Welland peered round, every fibre alert. 'Good work, Tiny. Now reload, and watch your front!' He turned and looked for his lieutenant and called, 'Pillbox, sir! Better make sure!'

The lieutenant seemed unable to move as two of the marines lobbed grenades through the weapon slits, and watched as each lit up with a savage flash. There was one frantic scream, before or after the twin explosions his mind would not register.

Welland checked his rifle and grinned. *Mummy never told you about nasty things like this, I'll bet.*

He snapped, 'Advance!' Next objective. Just like they had planned it. He was the sergeant again.

Lieutenant Hannah followed him, the revolver still gripped in his hand. Some of them turned and stared up as a bright green flare exploded almost overhead, but most of them watched the uneven ground. Ready for anything.

Then there was another flare. Second objective taken. Welland could not restrain himself. He gripped the lieutenant's arm and repeated, *'We were bloody first!'*

Even when the flares were extinguished it still seemed a little brighter than when they had splashed and stumbled ashore. Resistance mounted accordingly, tracer drifting and intermingling, with the occasional thud of mortars. A runner brought news that prisoners had been taken and most of the fortified positions had fallen. When a marine shouted after him to ask about 'our lads', the runner had been vague. 'Some of "B" Troop bought it! They're still out there somewhere!' He had hurried away. Glad to be moving.

Welland waved his men down; they were right in position, or as far as he could tell. Others would be moving past or through at any moment. He turned and looked for his lieutenant again. Daylight would be something else . . . Hannah was having a drink. Welland frowned. It was too early to waste precious water, but officers like Hannah would not be told. Then he recalled what Captain Blackwood had said about sharing experience. *Giving a lead.* He relented. Maybe he was right.

He reached out to touch Hannah's arm and then stopped, motionless. It was Scotch, or something very like it, that Hannah was drinking. Welland was both angry and envious, and, more than that, he felt something like contempt. As if he had been let down.

Hannah seemed to sense it, and asked awkwardly, 'Care for a tot, Sergeant?'

Welland cocked his head, hearing more gunfire, single shots: men meeting in the darkness, acting out of instinct, out of desperation.

'No, thanks. It'd go to my head.' His inner voice said, *go to bloody hell!*

A marine murmured, 'Here comes the skipper, Sarge!'

Blackwood dropped on his knees beside them and tugged out his binoculars.

'Nice work, Sergeant.' He looked past him. 'You all right, Bruce?'

Welland tensed; he had never heard Blackwood quite like this. A proper marine, from a marine's family. Nice enough, and a lot better than some he had known, but like a ton of bricks if you broke the rules.

Hannah said, 'They were heavy machine guns, sir. Long-range jobs. Ready for the landings.' Like someone repeating a lesson, Welland thought.

Blackwood said, 'Tip that stuff away. I didn't see or smell it.' His voice hardened. 'If I catch you again, I'll have you broken!'

He stood up as more men padded along the ridge. It was clear. Time to move on. Ready for the next flare.

Welland signalled to his two corporals. Near thing. Hannah had been lucky, this time.

Welland's father had been in the Great War, with the naval brigade, like Captain Blackwood's father and old Boxer Vaughan. He had heard all about it. Men stiff with rum, and officers so pissed they hardly knew which way to look, going over the top together. Together, that was the point. Hannah . . . he smiled grimly . . . *Bruce* would soon forget. His sort always did.

He shook himself. No room for bloody moaning now. Too dangerous.

He called sharply, 'Ready to move, you idle sods!'

Then he grinned into the darkness. *Oh, Pam, if only you could see me now!*

*　　　*　　　*

Sergeant-Major 'Bull' Craven said quietly, 'All in position, sir.' Blackwood looked over at Gaillard, who was leaning on his elbows while he trained his binoculars on the narrow road, and the pale shapes of houses beyond. The village, exactly as described. The last obstacle. Quiet, nothing moving, and yet somehow menacing.

Craven had been almost whispering, as if the enemy was only a few feet away.

But there was nothing wrong with Gaillard's

hearing or alertness.

He said, 'The stone emplacements are on the left. As I expected.'

Blackwood raised his own glasses carefully and saw one of the prone marines turn his face to observe them. It was much lighter now, enough to see the rough stone walls which had been thatched to make them look like farm buildings. Good cover for machine guns. Hard to shift, impossible with a frontal attack.

All the prisoners so far had been Italian, ready enough to fight, readier still to surrender if they got the chance. Blackwood knew that the Germans were strongest to the north-east, towards Syracuse and Augusta; some of them had been reported as being part of a crack airborne division. The best. Their high command probably considered that the narrow Strait of Messina was the obvious main objective for the invaders, a two-mile ditch before the Italian mainland.

He could smell the sea, and imagined the invasion fleet steaming towards the beaches, the Canadians poised for their first attack.

Gaillard was speaking to a runner, his tone clipped, positive.

'Tell Mr Despard. Rapid fire in five minutes, no longer. And I want Hannah's troop to move in from the left. We'll bypass that strong point if we have to, but I'd prefer to knock out those guns first.' He peered at his watch. 'Off you go, man! Fast as you can!'

Despard had put his machine guns on the slope to the right. Good for covering fire, and the only way to keep the enemy occupied.

Blackwood watched some chickens pecking at

the ground by one of the stone walls, and wondered if Hannah would be up to it. But he was there; there was no other choice. It was to be hoped that Welland would be able to support him. *There was no more time.*

Gaillard said suddenly, 'You go with the main section, Mike. I don't want to have half of the men cut down by our own crossfire.'

Blackwood crawled into a gully and knew without looking that Archer was close behind him.

More faces turned towards him as he reached the main section of the troop. There were a few quick grins, and a nervous wave from Lieutenant Fellowes.

The air quivered and they heard the rumble of gunfire, far away like thunder. Covering fire from warships, probably for the Eighth Army, meeting their first serious opposition.

The magnitude of this operation made him realise how vulnerable they were here, with the Canadians not yet in position and the nearest Allied troops fifty miles to the west at Gela, where the U.S. Seventh Army and their fearsome General Patton would be storming ashore, provided the gale had not scattered them beyond recall.

'Christ, what's that madman think he's doing?' Sergeant Paget watched with disbelief as a solitary figure broke from the remaining shadows and ran on to open ground.

It could happen to even the most experienced fighting man. The sudden change from half-darkness to the first watery sunlight had caught him unprepared, and he had simply lost his sense of direction.

Blackwood said, 'It's the Colonel's runner. I

hope Mr Despard can see who it is.'

The marine must have realised his mistake, and with a swift glance over his shoulder ran on again.

The solitary sound was more like something metallic, or a sharp echo, than a rifle shot. They watched helplessly as the runner fell forward near the rough road, and, clutching his arm, staggered to his feet again. The second shot flung him on to his back, his helmet rolling away like a dish. A heavy bullet. Even in the weak light Blackwood could see the blood, black against the dusty road.

As if to a signal the concealed Bren guns opened fire as one, the red tracer ripping away the fake straw roofs, striking chips and sparks from the stone walls.

Blackwood took Archer's arm. 'Go to Mr Hannah's section. Tell him to move in on the left.' He did not release his grip. *'Be careful.'*.

Archer looked at him and almost winked. 'I know, sir. That's a fucking sniper out there, or I'm a Dutchman!' Then he was gone, loping and weaving down the gully, his rifle gripped in both hands.

As the Brens ceased firing to change magazines Blackwood heard a new sound. Screams, women and probably children, from beyond the strong point, in the village itself.

He could recall Gaillard's words when they had had a final discussion before landing. *The village is the key. I want it taken and held, I don't care how. Street by street, house by house, room by bloody room if need be, but I want it done!*

It was certainly no place for women and children. Sergeant Paget was saying, 'Ready to move in, lads! Never mind what else is happening!'

But even he, the true professional, seemed shaken by the turn of events.

Fellowes lifted his Sten and stared at it as if he had never seen one before.

'You heard that!' He nodded to Paget. 'When you're all set, Sergeant!' It had cost him quite a lot, and Paget knew it.

Someone said, 'Christ, that poor bastard's still alive.'

Blackwood levelled his glasses and saw the wounded runner moving his arm, back and forth, as if he was gesturing to somebody. It did not seem possible that he could have survived.

He heard the click of bayonets, the sudden rattle of weapons. Now or never.

He said, 'I'm coming too, Mr Fellowes.' He heard the crack of the rifle again, and saw the dust spurt up beside the dying marine.

Yelling like madmen, the marines on the left flank charged towards the end of the stone wall. Despard's guns were firing again, ripping into the defences and through any apertures still hidden by the straw, some of which had burst into flames.

Blackwood saw one figure sprinting towards the dying runner, shouting something, his voice lost in distance. He knew it was Hannah, without understanding how he could be so certain.

Paget yelled, *'Now!'*

The marines broke cover and charged, each man expecting to be cut down by the concealed machine guns. Nothing happened: Despard's gunners had forced the enemy to take cover. Long enough, except for Lieutenant Hannah. The din of firing and the sudden bang of grenades masked the sound of a single shot.

Hannah had reached the man on the ground, and Blackwood thought their hands had touched when the hidden sniper marked him down.

Archer was here now, breathless, not with the exertion of running with Gaillard's message but from the intolerable tension, the closeness of death.

Blackwood said, 'Cover me.'

Archer stared at him, his eyes wild. 'What? Where the 'ell are you goin', sir?'

Blackwood tossed his helmet to the ground and ran on to the open patch of ground. Bullets whined close, dangerously low over his head, and somehow through it all he knew it was one of Despard's Brens, and that the big, withdrawn lieutenant was firing it.

He heard the metallic whiplash of the rifle and saw Hannah fall on his side, where the runner had been hit before being hurled down by the force of the second bullet.

His breath was raw in his throat and lungs, and his muscles were working as if he had lost control of them.

He twisted his head and saw a pile of cement bags and unused stones, some builders' tools. He heard the rifle, and saw grit spurt from the hard ground. *The same line of bearing.* The madness was almost overpowering, but he could remember Despard telling him that his father had been a builder in Jersey. How fussy he had been about money and not wasting materials. Of all the desperate, angry and frightened marines in this godforsaken place today, Despard was probably the only one who would see it. That the cement was stacked badly, where it would become as solid as

300

rock, costly to poor people like these Sicilians.

But the perfect hide for a sniper, even with a limited field of fire. He swerved away and ducked as another line of tracer cut into the pile of cement.

Then he ran to Hannah and dragged him to his feet, up and across his shoulders in a fireman's lift.

'Hold on, Bruce, you mad bugger!' He swung around, his eyes almost blinded with smoke and dust, his ears cringing against the next crack of the hidden rifle.

Hannah was gasping, unable to stop talking. 'He died—just as I got to him, poor chap! He smiled when he saw me coming.' He gave what might have been a sob. 'Then he died!'

Blackwood slipped and almost lost his balance. He saw Archer, rifle aimed and ready, and other marines running to help him. His leg was throbbing, and he knew he was calling out, praying that the wound would not go sour on him. 'Not now, *please,* for God's sake!'

By some rocks the others took Hannah from his shoulders. There was blood everywhere. But one of the marines, busy with a dressing, looked up at him, the wildness going from his eyes. ''E'll be okay, sir. Thanks to you.' The others muttered in agreement and Archer said hotly, 'If I'd done it you'd 'ave chewed me balls off, sir, and you knows it!'

Blackwood stared at Hannah's face, so pale now beneath its first North African tan.

Gaillard strode down the slope, Craven behind him.

'Want to show you something, Mike.' He saw Hannah and raised his eyebrows. 'Live, will he? Good show.'

Blackwood followed him to the road. Fellowes, the actor, would approve, he thought wearily. A perfect change of set. Women and children, some waving, others handing out grapes and cheroots to the exhausted marines. And beyond them, guarded only by a handful of Despard's troop, were lines and lines of Italian prisoners, some of them senior officers. Fellowes was here too, outwardly relaxed, some dried blood on his sleeve. He crossed quickly to Blackwood.

'Why did you take such a risk, sir?'

Blackwood stared beyond him and saw the sea, so dark in this brittle light. But no longer empty; it was crammed with ships, some of which were already beached and unloading men and vehicles. Unopposed. He looked at Fellowes, and Despard, who was speaking with Gaillard, but looking directly back at him.

'I owed it to him. If he'd been killed I would have been as much to blame as that sniper.'

Fellowes nodded jerkily, but did not understand. Blackwood smiled, his mouth stiff and dry. *Any more than I do.*

More marines were coming down the slope, rifles slung, marching with a jaunty swagger despite their weapons and packs.

They appeared strangely clean and fresh when compared with Force *Trident.*

They would soon see the sprawled bodies near the village, marines like themselves, perhaps even men they had known. The Corps was a family.

Despard came up to him and said, 'Got the bastard. He tried to make a break for it.' He hesitated. 'You all right?'

'Thanks for what you did. I knew it was you.'

A moment of warmth despite the smell of death and suffering. Like the sick officer with the rose, as she had described to him.

Men were already shaking themselves, mustering into squads and sections, grinning at friends, or staring around for faces which were missing.

The wounded were being carried away; the dead would have to wait a while longer.

It was time to move on.

Archer had recovered his helmet from somewhere and watched him grimly as he replaced it on his dusty hair.

It was the maddest, stupidest thing he had ever seen anyone do, let alone an officer.

He heard Bull Craven bawling out names and duties as if he was on a parade ground.

Now if it had been him . . . He grinned and fell into step beside Blackwood. *I'd have given the bloody sniper a hand!*

Blackwood looked once at the open stretch of ground where the runner had lost his sense of direction, and thought of what Hannah had said about his last smile on earth.

All the tradition and training in the world could not prepare you for that. He saw a girl with a baby waving at him, and somehow it was possible to wave back.

And these same men had done it. Together.

CHAPTER FIFTEEN

UP THE LINE

Flight Officer Joanna Gordon closed the door of the washroom and stared at her reflection in the ceiling-high mirror. She felt tired, strained to the limit, and dishevelled; her shirt, although fresh this morning, clung to her body like a damp rag. The Pit had never been properly adapted to conceal and contain so many people, and it was still hard to imagine London streets so far overhead.

She deliberately unfastened her cuffs and rolled up her sleeves and waited for the hand basin to fill with tepid water. Like everything else down here, the water and the ventilation seemed incapable of dealing with any emergency.

She studied herself in the glass, the shadows under her eyes from days and nights in this place since 'the balloon had gone up', as Major Claud Porter had put it. Then the reports had come filtering through, the setbacks and the early successes, one beach after another falling to the combined allied armies. She smiled at herself, but it made her look sad. And the Royal Marines. Major-General Vaughan, what little she had seen of him, had been almost as pleased about that as he would have been to be in Sicily himself.

And down here in the Pit, they had all shared it in their various ways. The disasters, some born of inexperience, like the pilots who had released their troop-filled gliders too soon, so that they had ditched into the sea. With the men burdened by so much kit and ammunition, it was unlikely that many would have been saved. And the landing craft which, because of the gale and misjudgment, had ground ashore on the wrong beaches, under heavy enemy fire.

Joanna had not found the time to return to the house near Chiswick Bridge. Instead, she had shared a rest room here, and slept when she could. She plucked her shirt away from her breast. The ventilating shafts merely stirred up the stale air. She glanced around the washroom, which the Wren officers in the Pit insisted on calling 'the heads'. She liked to listen to them; they seemed to bring her closer to Mike, who had once amused her by referring to a 'run ashore' in London.

She held out her left arm and stared at the burn. Sometimes she forgot about it, and with her sleeves rolled up in an attempt to keep cool she had seen several people glancing at it. But nobody ever asked. Not in this place, at least.

She often tried to imagine what it was like for him. And there was something else, which at first she thought was also imagination. Claud Porter had deliberately broken off a conversation with a Royal Marine officer about the possibility of regrouping the Commando in Sicily when he had seen her, as if . . . She pushed the thought away. Nothing must happen to Mike. Not now.

The door opened slightly and she saw one of the Wrens peering in at her.

'You're wanted, Joanna. Mother Beaufort's been asking for you.'

Joanna straightened her skirt, giving herself time. Was it like this for everyone, the terrible leap of the heart when the dreaded telegram arrived, or

305

some senior officer sent for you to give you the news?

But not Squadron Officer Anne Beaufort. She was the senior W.A.A.F officer in the Pit, and was confined to dealing with Special Operations personnel.

It was not a good idea to keep her waiting. She stared at herself almost defiantly. There was nothing she could do to improve her appearance, and, in any case, it was not exactly the Savoy down here.

A W.A.A.F. corporal greeted her nervously.

'Go right in, ma'am.'

Joanna smiled. *Ma'am.* She was probably younger than the corporal.

Squadron Officer Beaufort was on her feet, facing the door, when she entered. Joanna could not have described her, except to say that she exuded an air of complete self-confidence and control without seeming to make any effort. She wore, as always, a perfectly tailored service uniform, without a crease or a fold; nobody had ever seen her in battledress.

Her features were strong, elegant rather than beautiful. Joanna had heard some of the women discussing how she always managed to appear so perfect, her hair never unkempt or out of place.

'Ah, here you are, Joanna.' She did not look at the clock, but the implication was plain. 'I hope I didn't drag you away from something urgent?' Joanna felt her cheeks colour, like a schoolgirl on the carpet. 'No matter, you're here. That's the main thing.'

There were some flowers on the desk, and Joanna wondered who had put them there. Anne

Beaufort wore no rings, and she had heard no mention of a man in her life.

She said, 'I was asked to deal with someone's effects. One of our people lost his life recently. There are always loose ends, you know.'

Joanna waited, her heart suddenly pounding. Was Mother Beaufort really so cold-blooded that she could speak of a man's death so casually, as loose ends?

'I cannot tell you anything much about it, but then you are well aware of the need for secrecy. Otherwise you would not be here. Now.'

She opened a drawer and took out a small package. She laid it on the desk and then looked at the girl over it.

'What passes between us is private, Joanna. I am still not entirely sure that I should have taken it this far. However . . .' She unfastened the package and removed a wrist watch. 'I believe this belongs to you?' She did not hand it to her, but dangled it in the hard light like a piece of evidence. 'In fact, your name is engraved on the reverse. Rather careless to be wearing it on a top secret mission, I'd have thought?'

Joanna braced herself. *She's playing with me. Maybe enjoying it. Like that woman.*

She said, 'My father gave it to me for a birthday present.' She lifted her chin. 'In Marseilles, as it happens.' She could not keep up the defiance. 'I lost it when I was taken prisoner. I thought they'd stolen it.'

Beaufort nodded. 'As we thought. Apparently he was going to return it to you. You must have made quite an impression on him.'

The man she had never seen face to face, who

307

had saved and protected her, held her while German boots had scraped only inches above their hiding-place. The man she had wanted to destroy for what he had done when the terror had slowly ebbed away.

'He's dead, ma'am?'

'Yes. Another mission. The plane crashed—brewed up. No chance for him, or any of them.' She held out the watch. 'So here you are. Mystery solved.'

Joanna turned it over in her hands. Perhaps the last piece in the puzzle, just as the doctor had described. The final barrier. Two people flung together, escaping from terror and something too terrible even to contemplate. Like that woman, and the drawer filled with glittering instruments of torture.

Each of them had come through it, and had clung to the other for support.

Had she tried to fight him off, to scream as she had truly believed? Or had she allowed him to take her, out of gratitude, and perhaps for the sake of her sanity?

Only one man knew or guessed the truth, and he was far away, in Sicily with his men, men she had seen greeting him with such genuine pleasure in Alex.

She realised that Squadron Officer Beaufort had come around the desk, and had laid her hand on her shoulder.

'These things happen in wartime, Joanna. It's better this way. No sense in having some relative wondering about the watch, is there?'

Joanna moved away, and wished she could be alone for a few, precious moments.

'No, ma'am. No sense at all.'

Beaufort frowned. 'For God's sake smarten yourself up before you go back on duty. We have to hold up our corner here, so to speak!'

Her abruptness helped more than anything to save Joanna. It might never leave her, but it was over.

When she allowed her mind to explore it again, she felt only pity. Now she could understand what Mike and men like him were going through, and how they were expected to overcome what they dreaded most. Fear.

Squadron Officer Beaufort watched the door close. *Pretty little thing.* Courageous, too. She glanced at the vase of flowers and smiled. *But not for me.*

Then she pressed the bell and faced the door. Not a hair out of place. She was glad that she had gone against her better instincts for once. All the same, she knew Joanna Gordon would never wear that watch again.

*   *   *

'I've never heard of anything so underhanded, so bloody insensitive to the realities of war!'

Major Claud Porter was relieved that he had chosen the secret signals room for this meeting with his superior. It was in the deepest part of the underground complex, and was said to have the thickest walls.

He regarded the folder on the metal table, which had increased in size since his friend in Intelligence had first shown it to him, and was now covered with the rubber stamps and signatures of all those who had been privileged to see it. He frowned. Too many people. Even the First Sea Lord had gone through it, or someone in his tight little department had signed on his behalf. Not the Prime Minister, not so far. But he might well ask to see it; he liked to know a little about everything and in the end Sir Clive Burgoyne would make certain of it. No matter what Major General Vaughan claimed, there was no love lost between them.

Porter was tired, like everyone else in Special Operations, but not too drained to be unaware of the dangers to Vaughan and to the Corps, to say nothing of the men in the field. Two weeks had passed since marines and soldiers had stormed ashore, and the total collapse of German and Italian defences in Sicily was imminent. Not months but days, and almost every objective had been taken and held. The human cost had not been insignificant, but compared to what might have happened there was plenty of cause for pride at what had been achieved.

Vaughan exclaimed, 'And all because of some wild allegation, probably made out of spite, or to get some special treatment for himself!'

Porter waited. There was no point in going over it all again. At any minute a messenger might come, and he would be required to deal with some new crisis. He thought Vaughan was being unfair, and that, in his heart, he knew it: Marine Gerald Finch was crippled, half blind, and discharged from the Corps, the only life he had ever known, and he had not wavered in his allegation that the then major Marcus Gaillard had cold-bloodedly killed men too badly wounded to escape from the advancing Japanese. The Judge Advocate of the

310

Fleet had noted his story; very soon one of the less reputable newspapers would sniff it out. Like the hero who had won a Victoria Cross, and had been 'discovered' stripped of his rank and scrubbing floors in a canteen. The papers had made the most of that, as usual, and blame had been laid heavily and unjustifiably.

If Gaillard's actions were investigated, questions would be asked, not, perhaps, why he had taken the alleged action, but why he had been appointed to command in the first place. And, more to the point, who had recommended it?

Porter had explained it as cautiously as he dared. Major-General Vaughan himself would be the scapegoat, and would almost inevitably become a target for the popular press.

He said, 'The point has already been made, sir. Force *Trident* has achieved everything it was required to do. It is now proposed to regroup the two Commandos already involved, enlarge them, and prepare them for the next step, into Italy.'

Vaughan glared at him. 'I know that, Claud, but not yet! You've seen the reports. Morale is high, Gaillard is doing a good job with *Trident*. He has the tenacity and the drive to see it through to the end. And I *am* thinking ahead. The Commandos *will* be regrouped and expanded. It will be on to Germany before too long—we'll show 'em, eh?'

Porter persisted, 'Lieutenant-Colonel Gaillard could be withdrawn and brought back here, sir. Some new appointment can be found. The Judge Advocate might well be satisfied.'

Vaughan looked past him. 'It is *without honour*, Claud. Bring a chap back from the war he's helped to fight for so long, one with a D.S.O. to his

311

credit—how would you feel if it were you?'

Porter looked at the file. 'I'd be more concerned if it were you, sir.' He was aware of Vaughan's anger and anxiety, and felt only compassion for him. A marine's marine. But no match for the tactics of Whitehall and Fleet Street.

Vaughan said bluntly, 'What would you suggest? Speak as a friend if you like, no strings.'

'It is almost certain that a full colonel will be appointed to an enlarged Commando. In fact, I did hear that Colonel Fitzroy was in line for it.'

Vaughan studied him thoughtfully. 'Alex Fitzroy, eh? Knew he'd do well when he married his colonel's daughter.' He frowned. 'He could do it, all right.'

Porter relaxed very slightly. He always took great pleasure in seeing Vaughan at his best. No list or file could match his true strength, his gift for picking out a name or recalling a face. Or some cheeky subaltern who had married his colonel's only daughter.

Vaughan took a few paces across the box-like room. 'Now, if young Blackwood had a bit more seniority . . . He grinned. 'But he don't!'

Porter looked surreptitiously at his watch, and thought of what he had heard concerning Flight Officer Joanna Gordon, and the wrist watch which had been returned to her. A lucky girl. And so was Blackwood, given the chance . . .

It came to him quite suddenly. Blackwood had disliked Gaillard from the outset, ever since he had been appointed to the new company, and perhaps before that. Personalities clashed as often in the Corps as in any other organisation, and Blackwood had made every effort to conceal his true feelings.

But they had been revealed, however briefly . . .

He said, 'In all fairness to Lieutenant-Colonel Gaillard, I think he should receive some advance warning of a possible regrouping. Otherwise, he would think it out of line if he were left completely in the dark.'

Vaughan passed his chair and patted his shoulder as he went. 'I agree. *Trident* will be pulled back soon. They paved the way, they were the first. It's the obvious time for it!'

Porter sat in silence, impressed and saddened by Vaughan's struggle with himself, his sense of responsibility to those men, some of whom had probably died even as they spoke in this stuffy concrete box under London.

Vaughan said quietly, 'It was so different in that other war. Men you cared about, loved even.' He tried to smile. 'Some right bastards too. But you saw them every day, knew them, good and bad. And you were there when they bought it, so many of them that you stopped asking yourself how it would happen. You only wondered when.' He waved one arm, seeming to embrace all of them. 'Now I have to sit and watch from a distance, snug and safe. Different war, but the same men.' He reached for his cap. 'The weapons are dirtier, that's all, Claud.'

He paused in the doorway, filling it.

'I'll be at lunch with the admiral. You've got the number.' Still he lingered, as though uncertain. 'You'll deal with Gaillard, won't you?'

Porter picked up the file and looked at it, and murmured, 'I think he already knows, sir.' But he was alone.

313

Captain Mike Blackwood tossed the shaving water from his mug into a pile of wreckage and dabbed his face with a piece of towelling. It was none too clean, but, like the hot water Archer had scrounged from an army field kitchen, it seemed a luxury. He raised his steel shaving mirror and held it to the light. The first proper shave for ... he frowned, trying to remember ... ten days. Days of almost continuous vigilance, exchanging fire with a retreating enemy. He must not forget all that because of a few moments of rest.

He looked around the room. It had been a cottage, unremarkable, and no different from all the others he had seen. This village had been fought over in the first full days of combat, and it was little more than rubble now. He found himself thinking, not for the first time, about the people who had once lived here, and if they might one day return to rebuild their houses and resume those hard, simple lives. A shirt, still dripping from Archer's efforts, hung in a shaft of sunlight; it might still be damp when he put it on again, but it would be clean.

He heard Archer whistling quietly to himself as he completed his ritual of stripping and cleaning his rifle, and was amused by his apparent satisfaction when he had used the pull-through and squinted along the barrel. He bent down to replace the mirror in his battledress pocket. All the old sweats joked about it. *Over the heart to stop a bullet.* Not bloody likely, they said. But they all did it.

Force *Trident* had been pulled back from the line, wherever that was. In Sicily it could be any building, or any hill, day or night. You just had to keep going.

He had watched the danger weld his marines into something more than a weapon, had witnessed their growing self-dependence and determination, and sudden acts of incredible courage.

Now the war was at a distance, with only the far-off rumble of artillery and the vapour trails of friendly aircraft cutting across a clear sky. At a distance. Or so it seemed in this battered village with its unpronounceable name.

He had seen plenty of prisoners being escorted back to the beaches where they had first waded ashore; they had all been Italians so far. The only Germans they had seen had been dead.

Ten days. Was it possible? Since those first wild moments when they had linked up with Canadian patrols, and had pushed inland to occupy the high ground. By taking it at the very beginning of the attack, they had given a very necessary protection to the beach perimeter.

They had lost twelve men killed, and sometimes now it was hard to recall their faces, let alone their names. A pair of boots beneath a blanket, an outthrust hand. It was better that way.

Archer handed him a mug of steaming tea, the same mug he had used for shaving.

'All the comforts of 'ome, sir!' Nothing seemed to get him down.

Just three days ago they had received a supporting bombardment from the navy. A monitor, the *Roberts*, her big fifteen-inch guns mounted in a high turret like tusks, had fired her shells far inland to pound the enemy's artillery and armour into scrap. She could not be much different

315

from the monitors at Gallipoli, about which his father had spoken, slow, ugly, but, to the troops ashore, so reassuring.

His father had also told him of the moment when the fleet had been withdrawn from the peninsula because of the arrival of U-Boats in the Mediterranean. 'When we saw the sea empty of our ships, we knew there was no way forward for us and the P.B.I.'

Each time *Roberts* had fired, he had heard Archer counting off the seconds, and once he had said, 'Bit too close for comfort, that one!'

Most of the wounded had been moved to the beaches and were probably in hospital by now. Lieutenant Hannah had been given a hero's send-off, and was expected to make a good recovery.

Gaillard had mentioned the incident only once. 'He was a bloody fool to risk his life for a man already as good as dead.' He had looked up, his eyes like dark buttons in the sunlight. 'And you were an even bigger one for going after him! As my acting second-in-command you are important, not only to me but to the men who rely on us. Bear that in mind in the future!'

He was right, of course, and Blackwood knew it from his own experience. He also knew that he could not have acted otherwise.

There were reports of more reinforcements arriving shortly; there was never any shortage of rumours. Eat, sleep, keep your head down, and survive. The rest was rumour.

Archer watched him over the rim of his own mug. It was so quiet compared with the past few days he could hardly credit it. Like all the traffic stopping on Armistice Day in the East End; no matter what you were doing, you all stopped. He could remember his father in his police uniform, very erect and strangely sad. Bus and tram drivers getting down from their cabs to stand in silence. He had often thought about the Great War as it must have been ... not the war the boozers bragged about in the Salmon and Ball on a Friday night after they'd been paid, but the unspeakable truth. And the officers, what had made them different? Archer had once competed for a Blackwood medal at the barracks, and thought it must be quite a load to carry, coming from a family like that. He thought of his friend, Ted Pratt, whom he had seen earlier cadging food from the army. He smiled. Pratt ... it was the right name for him. But even he had his moments. Like the buzz he had started. Sergeant Paget had heard him going on about it, and had shut him up smartish. He knew that the sergeant and Captain Blackwood were pretty close. You could feel it. Like old mates, with only the barrier of rank which no outsider could ever grasp.

If it was something outside the mob, it was best to leave it there. Even in the Corps, and the navy too for that matter, there were always those ready to drop you in it, just for the chance of getting a couple of tapes for their sleeve. Or working a fast one to grab a nice cushy billet ashore every night, feet under somebody's table if you were lucky. Crawlers, too. He grimaced. Like Bull Craven.

Being a copper's son in the East End of London was sometimes hard to live down. Especially if, like his father, he was taking the drop from the local bookmakers.

But in this lot, the Commando, it was something else. They didn't care what you were or what you'd done. It was what you were now that counted. Who you could look to when the going got rough. Like Blackwood.

He said, quite suddenly, 'Somebody says the Colonel was askin' about some marine called Finch, sir.'

Blackwood turned with the empty mug.

'I'd forgotten. What about it?' He had not forgotten, but there had been no time for idle speculation.

Archer busied himself with his jug of tea.

'Burma, it was, sir. Where you was before you come to our lot.'

Blackwood rested his head against the wall, feeling the sun's warmth against his cheek. Burma. Just the word brought it back. Those ancient launches full of wounded troops and terrified civilians. Snipers and fanatical bayonet charges, the horrific sight of a soldier's head on a spike beside the river, hacked off by one of those Japanese swords so prized as souvenirs.

He thought of the girl in the *souk*, their pleasure at being together.

He said, 'Finch? No, I can't say I recall anyone of that name.'

'It's just that they say 'e went missin', or 'e might 'ave done a runner, o' course. But now e's puttin' it about that 'e was left to die, by an officer.'

Blackwood stared at his hands. Clean for once, But still one scar from the broken glass when he had pitched the grenade.

He should not even be listening to this. It was probably just another bit of gossip. Nothing had been posted about it. He looked away. *Don't be such a bloody fool.* Archer was all kinds of things,

318

but he was no muck-stirrer, except possibly where Bull Craven was concerned. It was no use.

He said, 'There was so much going on at that time. Marines joined us from various ships, from everywhere. All we had to hold us together was the Globe and Laurel, and that would never appear in any infantry training manual.'

Archer was satisfied. He had done the right thing. No matter what divided them, rank, class, breeding, Blackwood was all right. He had guts too, standing up for Corporal Sharp when the Colonel said he should be left behind. And poor Mr Hannah, thick as two planks, but he hadn't deserved to die. Not like that, anyway.

The past days had been hairy at times, but they had managed. Muddled through, as Tommy Handley would say. He felt the ground quiver. Miles away, but not for long. They'd be going back. Up the line, his father used to call it. He had been with the 60th Rifles in that lot, and had donned a police uniform when he had been released. He had said it was because he missed the army comradeship, not because he couldn't get any other work, like so many idle buggers claimed.

Archer understood what he meant now, in this shelled and fought-over village nobody would ever have heard of in Bethnal Green. He thought of the W.A.A.F. officer who was sweet on Captain Blackwood. In her perky little cap she looked about fifteen. A woman for all that . . .

A head poked through the shattered doorway.

Archer snapped, 'Can't you *knock*, Nobby?'

The marine grinned. 'Sorry to disturb you, sir. Mr Fellowes isn't sure what to do about some new arrivals.'

319

'I'll come.' Blackwood dragged the shirt over his head. It was bone dry. 'Have you told the sergeant-major?'

He knew that the two marines were exchanging glances. Archer said, 'Oh, 'e'll know, sir!'

He knew just how far he could go. Blackwood clipped his revolver around his waist. Like the buzz about the unknown marine. But not unknown to Gaillard . . .

He must forget it. Gaillard had been on edge that day. He was in command. *How would I feel if* . . .

He said, 'Lead the way.'

Archer picked up his gleaming rifle and jerked the bolt before applying the safety catch. He said casually, 'I'll stroll wiv you, sir.'

Their eyes met. The danger was always present. So was loyalty.

There were about a dozen tired figures, standing with their kit and looking slightly lost. Soldiers this time, not Royals.

One, a lieutenant, strode to meet him and was about to throw up a salute when Blackwood said sharply, 'No saluting here. Dead giveaway to any sniper. And I mean dead!'

He relaxed slightly and knew that Archer had turned away, apparently disinterested, but his eyes would be on the empty and shattered houses, a bullet already in the breech of his Lee-Enfield.

He said, 'Royal Engineers? I'm Captain Blackwood, Royal Marine Commando. Force *Trident.*'

The lieutenant smiled. 'I know, sir. Same name as mine.'

They shook hands, strangers, and yet with an

320

odd sense of recognition.

'You're the chap my sister wrote to me about?' He saw some marines emerging from the rubble to watch, to share this small link with home. 'Getting engaged, right?'

They fell into step, and Blackwood saw a red-haired sergeant who, like Archer, was staring around the broken village, as if very aware of the nearness of danger.

'I've written to her, sir.' And then, with sudden confidence, 'I love her very much.'

Blackwood smiled. 'Come into the mess.' He gestured to the cottage with half a roof and no windows. 'I'll open the bar!'

The meal, eaten from their mess tins with spoons, seemed to consist of hot mashed corned beef and some kind of powdered potato. But, washed down with the rough local wine, it hit the right spot, although at a guess the temperature outside the ruined house was up in the nineties.

Lieutenant Steve Blackwood found it surprisingly easy to relax with the marine officers who, on one pretext or another, had come along to make him welcome. Young for the most part, and showing signs of strain in spite of the jokes and the black humour common enough among servicemen.

One lieutenant, Despard, easily the oldest here, outlined to him the general layout of the marine force, and the various army units nearby. Without fuss or exaggeration, like the man himself, he suspected.

When he and his sappers had come ashore from the landing ship he had been astonished by the span of the operations on that and the adjoining beaches. Ships and landing craft of all sizes and for every possible role, soldiers working to lay out fresh tracks on the beach to withstand the weight of more armoured vehicles and tanks yet to come. Everyone appeared to know exactly what to do, so that the war had seemed almost an intrusion on their industry.

Until he had seen the wrecked landing craft, some upended by shellfire, others because of collision. There were graves too, many of them, with a bearded naval padre, hatless, smoking his pipe while he checked each identity disc and noted it in his book. Like a picture she had shown him at Hawks Hill. *Where no birds sing . . .* A different war. The same finality.

He looked at Diane's brother, catching his interest in what one officer was saying to him. Alert, intelligent. And the eyes, green like the eyes of the girl to whom he had opened his heart. *And she had listened.*

He realised with a start that the eyes had turned to him.

'How was she when you last saw her?'

The others might be listening, but they were excluded.

'She looked marvellous in her uniform. Suits her.'

He saw the slight frown. 'I've not seen her in it yet.' The other side of him. Wistful almost, suddenly somewhere else.

A marine peered in at them; it was Archer.

'Colonel's back, sir.' Just that, and yet Steve Blackwood could sense the change in this impromptu gathering.

The others emptied their mugs and said their farewells.

Blackwood watched them leave and remarked, 'A good bunch. I'm quite proud of them.' He smiled, and his face seemed young and vulnerable. 'They're all well trained, but nothing prepares you for the real thing.'

Steve Blackwood said, with feeling, 'I'm just finding that out!' There were voices. 'I'd better shove off, sir.'

Blackwood was looking at the broken door. 'Call me Mike, for God's sake. We're related, and likely to be even closer soon.'

Steve Blackwood watched him, perhaps looking for doubt or even envy, but there was none.

Then he said, 'No. Wait and meet him. I'd be interested . . .'

Gaillard strode in, his eyes darting around, missing nothing.

'This is Lieutenant Blackwood, sir. Royal Engineers. I'm not certain about orders . . .'

Gaillard thrust out his hand and said, 'I've only just heard myself. Got a whole clip sent across from the flagship. It seems they've nothing better to do!' He looked from one to the other. 'Two of the family, eh? I suppose I'm stuck with it!' He glanced at the wine jars and cigarette ends. 'Having a party, eh? Fair enough. Maybe the last for a bit.'

Blackwood watched him, surprised by his mood.

'Care for a drink, sir?'

Gaillard regarded him absently.

'D'you know, Mike, I think I will.' He waved Archer aside. 'No. In my kit. There's a bottle of Scotch. Thought I'd never get a chance to open the bloody thing!'

Blackwood waited for him to sit down. It gave him time to think, to fathom out what had

323

happened to change Gaillard. On edge, terse one moment, and almost flippant the next.

Archer filled a glass and was peering around for something to dilute it.

Gaillard snapped, 'No. As it comes. Christ, I think we've all earned this!'

He swallowed the neat whisky and gestured for Archer to refill the glass.

He said, 'We're going up tomorrow. It's all here in the intelligence pack.' He dragged open his tunic and pulled out the familiar envelope. 'Intelligence, they call this. Sometimes I think they couldn't find an elephant in an ashtray!'

Then he looked directly at Lieutenant Blackwood. 'It's why *you're* here. We're up against the German army this time. They've laid mines, booby-traps—you know the score, right?'

Blackwood said, 'We're under strength, sir. Brigade said we were to await reinforcements.' He watched for some sign, some hint of what had happened. 'Why we were pulled back.'

'Yes.' He gazed at the reflected glare, dust floating in it like smoke. 'Well, that's all changed. We move tomorrow.'

Feet grated on rubble, and Craven's shadow leaned into the room.

'Permission to take charge of them sappers, sir?' But his eyes were on the soldier.

'Carry on.' Gaillard waved his hand and some whisky slopped down his shirt. He did not appear to notice it. 'Show this officer where they're being quartered, and what to do in an air attack—not that there's much chance of one now, eh?'

Blackwood walked with him to the broken doorway and saw the red-haired sergeant hurrying

324

to meet them.

Steve Blackwood said quietly, 'He doesn't seem too fierce, Mike, after what I heard about him coming over.'

He looked down, surprised as Blackwood took his arm and held it very tightly. He was to remember it for a long time afterwards.

Blackwood said, 'Something's happened. I've never seen him like this, not even in Burma.' It was not what he had meant to say. It was nobody else's problem. Not any more.

He said, 'Just be careful. We've lost some good hands in this place. I want you to promise me you'll look after Diane if . . .' He forced a grin. 'What the hell! A fine welcome for my sister's future husband!' The mood eluded him. 'Sorry about that. Really. It's just me.' He did not even blink as a rifle shot cracked out like a whip. Not near, but close enough.

The New Zealander said, 'The same goes for you. I'd sort of like the chance to know you better.' He smiled. 'A whole lot better, as it happens, Mike.'

Blackwood returned to the room, and saw Archer leaving with the dirty mess tins.

Gaillard said, 'Seems a decent enough type, for a brown job!' He laughed, and then became quite serious. 'They're going to regroup the two main Commandos, Mike. *Trident* will be integrated.' He repeated it as if he had been mistaken. 'Integrated. It means the Royal Marine Commando is here to stay, no matter what bombastic blowhards like Naismith might have believed!' He moved as if to rise from the old cane chair, but the effort seemed too much for him. 'Nother drink, Mike. Have one yourself if you feel like it. That Sicilian muck will

325

rot your guts!'

Blackwood refilled the glass, and thought of Archer's expression as he had hurried out. The bottle was already half empty.

He said, 'We could see it coming, sir. We did what we came to do, and we were the first seaborne troops ashore. More than some people expected, I imagine.'

Gaillard had not heard him. 'All I've done, fighting one brasshat after another, dragging out weapons and the right facilities to use them. Like pulling bloody teeth! And now we're here, right on the threshold of the real events, when the whole world will see the part we've played, and what does some lame-brain decide? Integrate . . .' The word would not form properly and he took another swallow instead.

Blackwood looked at his watch. There was a meeting in fifteen minutes. He would tell the others about tomorrow; they had been expecting it. The Eighth Army might be at the Messina Strait within days. In Sicily, it would be all over.

He looked over at Gaillard but he was asleep, his head to one side, the glass still held in his hand. Empty.

He heard Archer by the door and said, 'Fetch the Colonel's M.O.A., will you?'

Archer answered, 'I'll deal wiv it, sir. Keep it in the family.'

Blackwood picked up his beret and banged the dust from it against his thigh. He could feel the wound. Where she had touched it while they had lain together, and had talked into the night.

He said, 'Thanks.' Some people might have seen it as a moment of petty triumph; he could almost hear it. *Guess what? The Colonel's pissed!* It might even have made him seem reachable, more human, instead of a faultless machine.

It was neither. It might even become a tragedy. The Corps meant everything to Gaillard. He could not recall hearing him speak of anything else.

Suppose the rumour was true? Gaillard might be recalled on some pretext or other. It had happened to others. It would destroy him . . .

He walked out into the sunlight, and felt it on his face like an open furnace.

He saw small groups of marines moving into patches of shadow; a few nodded to him as they passed. *No saluting here.*

Even that seemed to mock him. Only one thing stood out, stark and chilling.

What Gaillard carried in his mind could destroy all of them.

CHAPTER SIXTEEN

A MATTER OF TIMING

The nightmare was at its climax. She was calling to him, but there was no sound; he tried to move, but he was helpless. Being held down. They were dragging her away, to the room she had once, and only once, described.

He sat up, and would have struck out but for the grip on his wrist.

'Easy, sir!' Like another part of the nightmare. But as his breathing steadied he saw Despard's face in the torchlight, and realised that nothing had

327

changed.

He said, 'What is it? Trouble?'

Despard sounded very calm. 'The Colonel wants you, sir.'

It was all coming back now. Gaillard's strange behaviour, the Scotch, his anger. He felt his head and groaned. The local wine was stronger than he had thought.

Despard said, 'He was up half the night. Been on to Brigade.'

Blackwood peered at his watch. It was three o'clock in the morning. So quiet; even the distant artillery had fallen silent.

'I'll bet that pleased them.' He was already on his feet, fully dressed but for his boots and revolver.

He said, 'God, we're supposed to be moving out of here as soon as the lads have been fed.' He relented. It was not Despard's fault.

'It's off, sir.' Despard waited, as if to make certain the full impact of his words had reached him. 'Something else has come up.' He watched Blackwood grope for his belt and beret. 'He's got a visitor.'

He recalled Gaillard's sudden fury. *Integrated.* Was he being replaced? Surely not at this stage.

He walked out into the coolness before dawn. It would be like a furnace before they knew it. It was misty, too, haze or trapped gunsmoke it was hard to tell.

But so peaceful. In the gloom, even the shattered walls and rooftops lacked menace.

Gaillard had set up his H.Q. in the only part of an old chapel which had remained standing. It was very cramped, but the walls were thick enough to withstand a mortar, if anybody was so determined.

328

Maybe they were being pulled out, for good. To prepare for the next step, Italy? Or back to England to regroup?

Gaillard looked up from a table, his face very tanned in the lamplight. He appeared as fresh and alert as Blackwood had ever seen him, shaved, hair neatly combed, and wearing a clean shirt.

'Sorry to drag you here, Mike.' He waved a hand towards his visitor. 'This is Major Ellis, Intelligence.' As he made the introductions, his dark eyes never once left Blackwood's face.

Ellis was dressed in various articles of khaki clothing and a lambswool jerkin. It was filthy, and looked as if it was regularly slept in, and when he leaned over to grasp Blackwood's hand he could smell it, too. He wore no badges of rank or any divisional insignia, but his battered cap, which lay on the littered floor, bore the winged dagger of the S.A.S. Another of the cloak-and-dagger brigade. Blackwood could almost hear Terry Carson saying it.

But his credentials must be of the highest rating; he would not have got this far otherwise, nor would Gaillard have received him.

He looked from one to the other, more disconcerted by Gaillard's transformation than by his visitor's wild appearance.

Gaillard said, 'Tell him what you told me.' He tapped some papers. 'It's all here, but I want you to hear it first, Mike.' He even smiled. 'We'll have some coffee shortly. Muck, but drinkable!'

Ellis said, 'The enemy are pulling out faster than we thought. Right now, some will be crossing the Strait. When the last Germans leave, their Axis allies will fold up like a pack of cards.' He looked

329

directly at Blackwood. 'You've had some experience with battlefield clearance stores, I understand.' His eyes were very grey, the colour of the Channel across from Eastney Barracks, and cold. 'Well, we'll not get much joy here! Apart from weapons taken from surrendering Eye-Ties, most of the arms vanish as soon as their owners have no further use for them.' He shook his head. 'Not partisans this time, Captain Blackwood. This is for more personal use. The Sicilians hate the Germans because of their ruthlessness and their reprisals. The Italians they'll be glad to get rid of, simply because they represent the authority of Rome and Il Duce.' He made a slicing gesture. 'Here, the Mafia ruled. They intend to do so again!'

Gaillard cleared his throat and said, 'There is an operation for *Trident*.'

Blackwood sensed the S.A.S. major's irritation, but it was swiftly concealed.

He said, 'We've been gathering information for weeks. What the enemy would do when we invaded, how he might react when Sicily was in our hands. Invasion of the mainland must follow, and closely, if we're to avoid the consequences of winter. A whole army could be bogged down if it's left too late. The German High Command is well aware of our choices—I'm sure they've discussed them as much as our own staff. Landings, support, supply, the usual order of things. A severe setback at the beginning could give the enemy a breathing space, and make any hope of the Allies invading France and Germany next year out of the question.'

Blackwood watched Gaillard's fingers on the papers. *Tap . . . tap . . . tap . . .*

Ellis frowned, possibly at the sound. 'Just last month, the German vice-admiral commanding small battle units was in Naples. He's usually more concerned with the Channel ports and the Baltic area of operations. Also, he's known to dislike working openly with the Italian navy.'

Blackwood forced himself to concentrate, imagining he could still taste the coarse wine on his tongue. Not radar this time, but something else so secret that this man, major or not, had come in person.

Ellis glanced at the sacking-shrouded window. It would be light soon, and Blackwood found himself wondering whether he would take off the smelly jerkin in the heat of the day, or was it a permanent fixture.

Ellis said, almost casually, 'Do you recall H.M.S. *York*, Captain Blackwood?'

Blackwood saw Gaillard's fingers, still at last, press down on the papers.

'I was at sea. It was about two years ago. We heard about it.' He sensed that Gaillard was listening intently. 'H.M.S. *York* was an eight thousand ton cruiser. I visited her a couple of times, here in the Med.' His mind sharpened, like a prismatic gunsight. 'It was during the last days in Crete, before we had to evacuate. She was one of the most useful cruisers in the fleet at the time. It was all kept pretty hush-hush, but the story got out.' He saw Ellis nod, in agreement, or merely because he had given the right answer he did not know. 'It happened in the early morning. She was in Suda Bay.' He looked at each of them in turn. 'She was attacked by some Italian explosive motor boats. She was a total loss and had to be beached.

331

She's probably still lying there.'

They had heard the news with some disbelief when it had filtered down the chain of command. The Italians had always been regarded as a bit of a joke, indifferent as fighting men and quick to surrender, as they had shown in North Africa and here in Sicily. But as saboteurs they were suddenly less funny. They had been the first to perfect the use of frogmen and two-man torpedoes, and in Crete they had demonstrated that an explosive motor boat could be just as devastating, if suicidal for its solitary crewman.

The cruiser had been a sister ship of *Exeter*, of River Plate fame. She, too, had been sunk the following year by the Japanese in the Java Sea. If the navy was a family, the Corps was an even closer one, and there was usually some individual you could remember whenever a ship was lost.

Ellis said, 'They had a few more successes, but it took the German navy to see the true potential of such a weapon. Cheap to produce, and needing only a single volunteer to point it at the enemy.' He took out a packet of cigarettes and said, 'And they're here, if the latest intelligence is correct. About a hundred miles or so from where you're sitting, as a matter of fact.'

He looked at Gaillard. 'I can't tell you how to do it. I can only explain why it has to be done, and at once.' He ticked off the points on his fingers. 'At the first hint that we're on to them, their admiral will scatter the boats. We'd have no time to discover their new lair. Think of it. They're fast, but smaller than a ship's boat, and the forepart is packed with explosives. They can run beneath radar and be into their targets before a shot could be fired. Big landing ships, troopers, supply ships—I don't have to draw a picture, do I?'

Gaillard said slowly, 'And Brigadier Naismith believes we should wait for reinforcements?'

'I didn't say that, Colonel. If we had the time, I might support such a delay. But we do not have the time, nor do we have men like Force *Trident*, who are trained for this type of mission.'

'Right. Then give me all you can, photographs, defences, obstacles, anything of use.'

Ellis glanced at Blackwood. 'Any questions? I'm sure your colonel would not object.'

Blackwood said, 'If the target is so close, we will have no escort, am I right?' He saw the man nod, just as Gaillard's fingers began to tap again.

They were used to taking risks, and seeing men die because of them. Why should he feel any doubts this time? Because of Gaillard? *Or because of me?*

Ellis was saying, '*Trident* will be transported overland to Palermo. Security will be better this way. When you leave Palermo, it will be to attack.' He looked at the lamp, his face grim. 'An invasion of the mainland will make *Husky* look like child's play. If they get a chance to use those explosive motor boats, lentils, the Germans call them, we shall have to postpone the whole thing.' He regarded Gaillard for what seemed like minutes. 'It's that vital, Colonel.'

Gaillard bit his lip. 'It will be done. I shall tell Brigade myself.' He turned on his chair and said, 'Officers' conference, Mike. Put them in the picture. No dramatics, just the bones of it. We'll move today.' He laughed abruptly. 'In a different direction, but that's the war for you, eh?'

He was still laughing when Blackwood stepped outside, and found Despard waiting patiently for him.

They fell into step together. Despard spoke first. 'Rough, was it, sir?'

Blackwood thought of her, her infectious smile, the precious moments they had shared. So little time.

To some of the others he might have replied, *a piece of cake*, or *nothing we can't handle*. And they might have been satisfied.

He said, 'Yes. Rough.'

*　　*　　*

Blackwood looked around the hastily erected tent. The sun was so fierce that it was almost painful to touch the camouflaged canvas, and it was airless enough inside to dull anyone's mind.

They were all present, officers and N.C.O.s. The latter had been his own suggestion, and he had been surprised that Gaillard had agreed without question. 'Bull' Craven was as straight-backed as ever; rigid was a better description, even though his sweat-stained shirt made a lie of his stance. The younger lieutenants allowed themselves to sag in the heat, but each one was very aware of the urgency which had greeted their first call. They could hear some of the huge American trucks manoeuvring noisily near the winding, unpaved road, making a big show of it as if to demonstrate their contempt for British discipline and the King's Regulations. American soldiers were driving them, and at any other time it would have been good to see people who had been fighting their way inland, day after day since the first windswept landings.

Gaillard was standing by his map, which was propped on what appeared to be a schoolroom easel, and probably was.

'All present, sir.'

Most of the marines, especially the officers, were looking at Major Ellis, the stranger in their midst. As untidy as ever, and badly in need of a shave, he had caused a lot of speculation, and a certain amusement despite the formidable reputation of his regiment.

He saw Steve Blackwood at the other end of the tent, and they exchanged quick smiles; the New Zealander seemed to realise the significance of this meeting. Occasionally aircraft thundered overhead. It was sometimes difficult to remember that Malta was only eighty miles away, and that that small island, which had once been bombed and blockaded almost into submission, was playing its part again and providing full air cover whenever it was needed.

Steve had brought his sergeant with him, and in the hard light Blackwood understood the New Zealander's comment about 'unsoldierly appearance'. From his frayed and wrinkled webbing gaiters to the khaki forage cap stained with sweat or hair cream, he looked anything but an example to his men. But in the short time they had been able to speak together, Blackwood had sensed the very real bond between them.

Major Ellis stepped forward, squinting in the glare. He was still wearing the lambswool jerkin, which was even scruffier in daylight, his only concession to the heat being two unfastened tapes.

He pointed at the map, but kept his narrowed

eyes on his audience, seeming to assess them face by face.

'The Lipari Islands, *here*. About midway between the Italian mainland and Sicily, and forty miles north-west of Messina itself. Most of them are too small to be of any use, volcanic, waterless, bypassed by the war until now. Our island, Angelo, is *here*.' Blackwood wondered how his finger found the location so unerringly when he never turned his head. 'Probably once a volcano itself. Due south of Stromboli, and east of Salina, and avoided even by fisherman, because of rock ledges which can rip out the bottom of any boat trying to use a net.' He paused. 'A very dangerous place. The raid will have to be carried out at night, and because of the area no escorts will be available. The Germans would up sticks and be away before you got within miles of them. Angelo is little more than a lagoon surrounded by rocks and lava. In it, there will probably be some fifty or more explosive motor boats, of the type already mentioned, enough to cripple a fleet of supply and landing ships. Even if every man-jack of them were killed, the damage to our invasion plans would be disastrous.' He smiled, for the first time. 'Unlike the Italians who sank H.M.S. *York* at Crete. All six men were picked up on their little rafts, complete with shaving kit and a change of underwear, the latter probably very necessary!'

That brought some laughter. The safety valve, as always.

'It is a vital target, make no mistake. The Germans will withdraw the boats only when Sicily is completely in our hands. After that, it might be months before our agents can discover their new

336

hiding-place.'

Blackwood watched his words going home. The Germans had produced several new weapons, even an improved radar, not yet a match for British equipment. But given time . . .

When he looked again Ellis was sitting down, his eyes like glass in the reflected sunlight.

Gaillard took over. 'We will move to Palermo. After that, and provided I hear nothing to the contrary, we will embark.' He looked at the map. 'For Angelo. All kit and weapons will be inspected beforehand. Mr Craven?'

Craven seemed to bounce to his feet. *'Sir!'*

Blackwood saw 'Sticks' Welland lean over to whisper something in Sergeant Paget's ear. They both grinned hugely.

Gaillard regarded them distantly, as if he were already planning ahead.

'You will point out to your Troops and sections that they are not only making a vital contribution to this campaign, they are carrying on a tradition unmatched by any other fighting man!'

He nodded curtly and walked through the assembled marines without a further glance at any individual.

Could any man, even with Gaillard's record, be so confident? Or was it an act? If it was, it certainly seemed to have worked. They were all chattering again, calling out to one another as if it were all cut and dried.

Blackwood left the tent, grateful for the fresh air. Men were already waiting to dismantle it, until another meeting; different faces, another target.

Major Ellis was slumped in a battered scout car, frowning as the driver revved the engine in competition with the Yanks.

He beckoned to Blackwood and said, 'There might be nothing left when you reach the place. If so, it's someone else's problem.' He seemed uncertain whether to continue. 'You may be pulled back after this little lot's over and done with. You could do with it, I imagine. Make a change after this. Regrouping, new faces.' He prodded his driver's arm and the car lurched forward, spurting stones and sand in protest.

Blackwood stared after the cloud of dust. Merely being friendly? Or telling him because he was personally privy to some strategy of which the S.A.S., conducting their secret war, had been forewarned? His comments had been drowned by the scout car's engine, as he had probably intended.

But, in his mind, Blackwood had clearly heard the unspoken words.

A new colonel too.

Despard had joined him. 'Shall I carry on with the inspections, sir?'

'I'll come with you. May be the last chance I get before we embark.'

Despard watched him gravely. 'Better than hanging about, waiting for something to happen, sir.' He seemed to sense Blackwood's mood. 'Don't worry. They'll not let you down, you have my word on it!'

Blackwood looked at him, eyes keen in the hard light.

'I never doubted it, George. They deserve better, that's all.'

He did not explain, and Craven was already bawling at the marines to fall in for weapons inspection.

Despard turned to follow him, to allow routine and discipline to take over, as it had so many thousands of times during his service in the Corps.

They always said, *if it's got your name on it, there's not a thing you can do to stop it*. He sighed. Like the steel shaving mirror.

But somehow he knew that what he had just heard was very important. And it troubled him that he could be so moved by it.

*　　　*　　　*

It was to take another three days before Force *Trident*, frustrated and bewildered after being thrown about in the American trucks on appalling roads, was finally delivered to Palermo. General Patton's army had captured the town early the previous week, but so thorough had been the destruction and the sabotage of streets and bridges that progress had slowed considerably. It was said that the winding clifftop road eastward to Messina and the Germans' final line of retreat was almost impassable.

They had been the longest three days Blackwood could remember, with Gaillard's anger and impatience at each delay stretching everyone's patience to the limit.

As one American major had remarked, 'Your colonel sure as hell is eager to get his head blown off!'

But there were some compensations. After the usual verbal sniping and mutual distrust, the marines had been surprised by the warmth of the Americans' welcome. Even Craven's eagle eye could not stem the tide of hospitality, chocolate, 'candy bars', and gum that found its way into respirator haversacks and ammunition pouches. Even 'Sticks' Welland had conceded that the Yanks weren't a bad lot, considering . . .

Eventually five landing craft had arrived, not from Malta or Alex, but direct from Tunis.

Gaillard had leafed through his orders and said, 'Advance planning. That's a bit more like it!' He seemed satisfied, as if he had expected some last minute cancellation or change of plans.

The shipping was so congested and the air cover so complete that the little landing craft were virtually unnoticed.

Blackwood sat in a small American hut and went over the final plan for 'the Angelo raid', as it was now called. Everything would depend on surprise. Without it they would never set foot on the place. Provided the map and the photographs were accurate, it was not impossible. The Germans had chosen their haven well. Despite the lack of facilities, the explosive motor boats, the lentils, would be simple to maintain, and could be exercised without attracting too much attention from inquisitive aircraft, requiring only the one-man crews, some mechanics, and whatever troops were thought necessary to protect the approaches from any determined agents.

And suppose the birds had flown, as Major Ellis had warned might be the case? Blackwood looked at his folded battledress, the minimum of gear he would be carrying. In one pocket was the letter he had wanted, and had tried, to write. All it said was *My darling Joanna.* It was not much to be remembered by, if she ever saw it. But she had endured enough. A letter would not help if the

340

worst happened.

He allowed his mind to dwell on the operation itself. Not next week; not even maybe. It would be within the next twenty-four hours. He realised that he was gripping his hands together tightly, as if holding on to something. It had taken three days to cover the hundred miles from the wrecked village to Palermo. No wonder Gaillard had been so savage. One wag had commented, 'Three days? We could 'ave crossed the bloody Atlantic in that time!'

Steve Blackwood would be in the support section; a chance, maybe, to get away if it went sour. There had been a lot of talk about Major Ralf Blackwood in the family, although he had never met him. One thing was certain; had he been alive he would have been proud of his son, soldier or not.

He thought of the final weapons inspection, which they had carried out before climbing into the American trucks. It had been like so much of his time in the Corps; his father always seemed to be nearby in spirit, ready to lend his own experience, the very qualities people said had made him what he was. *Colonel Jono*. He had felt it then, pausing at each man, a smile here, a brief word to somebody else. It was always too late when the firing started. Never come down so hard on a man who is doing wrong that that same marine might, in the future, hold his tongue, and refuse to speak when he has seen something you yourself may have missed.

He stood, and pulled on the battledress blouse and fastened it, his hands moving without thought. Any spare kit would be collected and sent back. Back to where? Like the horizon he had heard his father and Vaughan discussing when he had been only a boy. *The horizon*, the lip of the trench. The first thing they saw each morning in Flanders, and, too often, the last.

He knew Archer was waiting outside, to make sure he had forgotten nothing. He tightened a webbing strap, and felt the unwritten letter inside the pocket.

My darling Joanna. He might even have spoken aloud.

It was time to go.

He saw Archer as he left the hut, and remembered his father's words. *Looking to you.*

He put on what he hoped was an American drawl.

'Say, Limey, you got any of that candy left?'

Archer laughed, as did some other marines who were carrying a Bren gun between them.

He could imagine it. *Just heard old Blackie cracking a joke! Not a bloody care in the world, that one!*

Blackwood walked out into the street, one fist so tightly clenched that it ached.

If only they knew.

He turned his face to the sea. My darling Joanna. It was too late now.

*　　*　　*

Major Claud Porter paused outside the door of the main lobby to regain his breath. He was surprised and rather annoyed that he should be so out of condition. It made him feel old, which was no help at all.

He considered the stupidity of the decision to shut the old lift shaft which led directly down to the

Pit. For cleaning and maintenance, the notice said. Of all the idiotic times to do it. He had practically run down flight after flight of stairs, each apparently steeper than the previous one; he had never realised that the one-time wine cellars were so far beneath the surface.

It had all started earlier, on his way back from the Admiralty, where he had gone to speak with Major-General Vaughan. There had been an important meeting of the Chiefs of Staff; everything was important in that place, he thought. Gieves must be making a fortune from all the gold lace he had seen.

Vaughan had listened without interruption. The signal had been delayed, had gone through channels, doubtless because of its contents. Marine Gerald Finch, last appointed to the light cruiser H.M.S. *Genoa*, who had been badly wounded and partially blinded during the retreat in Burma, was dead. It seemed doubly cruel when you considered it. So many of his comrades had died in the closing stages of the campaign; some had come through unscathed, physically at least.

Perhaps it had all been too much for him. In his mind, he had probably seen no reason for continuing when he had already lost everything. A nurse at the hospital had found him hanging from a tree. There had been no note or letter, no last recrimination. The police were satisfied that it was suicide. Porter thought it was a pity it had taken somebody so long to let them know.

Vaughan had shown neither surprise nor satisfaction. 'Poor bugger. He's well out of it,' was all he had said. And, as an afterthought, 'You'd better tell Gaillard. He's off the hook. This time.'

343

And then, on the way back here, they had run into a road-block. A policeman in a steel helmet had eventually reached their place in the line-up and explained that it was an unexploded bomb. Probably safe, but the sappers were making sure. Until then, et cetera, et cetera . . .

Porter knew then that he had been overworking; they all had. The delay had been the last straw.

He had said sharply, 'So the war has to wait, does it?'

The policeman had stared past the driver, taking in the rank, and some medal ribbons he would not have recognised.

'It looks that way.' He had smiled. 'Sir.'

It had been too much.

Porter had told the driver to find his own way back; he would walk. It was a lovely summer evening, and the air seemed fresh after what he had become accustomed to. But it had been farther than he had realised, and, on top of that, the bloody lift was out of order.

He straightened his back. *I'm getting past it*. Must be that, after all.

The familiar sounds greeted him: a radio somewhere, teleprinters, and a solitary typewriter. It was late; most of the day staff would have long gone.

A second officer in the W.R.N.S. was at the duty desk, and smiled as he strode towards her.

She was very attractive and very intelligent. A rare combination, he sometimes thought. And *very* nice legs; she was crossing them now beneath the desk. She always managed to obtain silk stockings, hard to get anywhere in wartime. Most Wrens would kill for them. Perhaps she had a boy friend

344

on the convoy runs to America. Or perhaps even a Yank.

He said, 'You remember that special signal I sent last week. To Lieutenant-Colonel Gaillard?'

'Yes, sir.'

She never forgot anything. 'I have a follow-up, same procedure. Check the code of the other signal . . .'

'I know the one, sir.'

He smiled. 'Sorry. I've been a bit pushed lately, Sue. We all have.'

Her pencil was poised over her pad. She probably guessed what it would be.

Porter said, *'Cancel my previous signal. Explanation to follow. You will remain in command. Ends.'* He watched her, glad it was done. They might never know what had really happened. It was all part of the equation, as Vaughan had called it.

He added, 'Soon as you can, eh?'

She smiled. She *was* very attractive. 'Flight Officer Gordon is waiting, sir.'

'My God!' He stared at the clock. 'She had an appointment. I'd forgotten all about it!'

'That's not like you, sir.'

He said, 'No. I'm beginning to wonder about myself.' As he reached for the door he turned. 'Don't forget the signal, will you?'

She smiled again, privately. He was a fine one to talk.

The girl got to her feet as Porter entered the office. She had been thinking that he had deliberately stayed away to avoid seeing her, although she knew he was a man who would never behave in such a manner.

It was hard to believe that she was leaving this

345

place. It was another part of her. A sheet-anchor, as Commander Diamond would have termed it. Especially after her kid brother and then her lover had been shot down. Until Mike . . . To leave here now would make him seem even farther away. Cut off. In her heart, she had known it would happen; she had only been on loan, but her work with the intelligence and operational staffs had not gone unnoticed, and there had been a signal from the A.O.C.'s office. She was to be transferred to a new R.A.F. unit outside Southampton. Porter had tried to make light of it. 'They've taken over one of the good hotels, I'm told. Not a bit like this dump!'

He had told her he would do everything he could, and she thought he had seemed quite pleased at her request to stay. He probably knew why.

Porter said, 'I'll lay on some tea. I'm terribly sorry you've had to wait. You were off duty ages ago.' He smiled sadly, remembering his coded message on the telephone. *Could use a bit of help* . . .

She gripped her hands together, unable to hide her anxiety.

'*Can* I stay, sir?'

He looked at her and wondered how Diamond could ever have consented to send her into occupied territory, simply because she had once lived there and was known to the so-called informant. He had seen the way she moved her arm if someone brushed against her, even though he had been told that it no longer caused her pain. Not bodily, in any case. He had seen the scars when she had forgotten to roll down her shirt sleeves; it had been the ventilation which had gone wrong on that occasion.

He said, 'They're lucky to get you.' He saw her shoulders droop and added, 'I shall try to pull some strings. You never know.'

She looked down at her clasped hands and said, 'Thank you for trying. And for helping me when things were so dicey.'

It seemed wrong in some way to hear an R.A.F. expression from her, although the Wrens used naval terms for almost everything.

He said, 'Next year, who knows, we might even be bashing our way through Germany. They'll need every experienced officer when it does happen.'

He tried to think of the attractive Wren called Sue, but it did not distract him. Perhaps he knew this one too well. It was personal, not a bloody job.

She must have read his thoughts.

'Can you tell me about Captain Blackwood?' The smile would not come. 'Without breaching any code of secrecy? I so want . . . to know.'

Porter was suddenly glad that he had forced his way into the Chiefs of Staff compound. Vaughan had often said that the progress of the war after Sicily was a matter of timing. Weather, supplies, men and losses. The equation again.

All the signals had made it clear that, despite the tremendous pressure mounted by the Allied forces, the enemy were resisting, fighting every mile of the way, aware of the inevitability of defeat, even more aware of the damage any delay would cause. Porter had seen the first, secret details of the next step, Operation *Avalanche,* to take place further north along the Italian coast, and a much tougher prospect than *Husky* had yet presented.

Fighter cover so far north was already perceived

as a problem, but with command of the sea and with round-the-clock bombing to soften up the defences, they could shorten the war, perhaps by months.

The Germans' stubborn resistance on their retreat towards Messina would help Gaillard if no one else. There would be time to send more reinforcements. He sighed. Time.

He said, 'Captain Blackwood's unit is in reserve at the moment. We should hear some more sensitive news before long.' He smiled. 'While you're still with us. The A.O.C. has agreed that you may stay for another three weeks. By then they may have chosen someone else, if that's really what you want.'

She nodded, unable to speak. *One step at a time.*

Porter smiled broadly. 'Might cost you promotion, y'know. Or maybe a drink, what d'you say?' He swung round as somebody rapped on the door.

The Wren named Sue stood in the doorway, her pad folded in one hand.

'Sorry to interrupt, sir. I thought you'd want to know.' She looked then at the girl in R.A.F. blue, as if she were speaking to her. 'Your signal, sir. It was disregarded. The unit is embarked.'

They sat in complete silence for a long time after the second officer had left them, or so it seemed.

Then Porter said, 'That drink, is it on?' He saw her nod. Fighting it. 'I may have to come back later.'

She turned her cap over in her hands. Remembering. 'A bit of help, sir?'

'Yes,' he said.

Vaughan was right. It was all a matter of timing.

CHAPTER SEVENTEEN

KNOW YOUR ENEMY

Blackwood gripped the protective shield of a machine gun mounting and felt the metal raw and sharp beneath his fingers: like everything else in these sturdy landing craft, no frills, built for the job.

After the final preparations, the uncertainty and then the urgency of getting each section of marines embarked, in the right order and with the allotted officers and N.C.O.s, this was almost an anticlimax. The steady, unhurried beat of the engines, the gentle rise and fall of the blunt bows, and an endless ceiling of pale stars from horizon to horizon above an empty sea. And yet, ever since they had slipped unceremoniously out of harbour and formed into line, they had never been far from land.

Blackwood had just been right through the hull, and was aware of the absence of tension. They were committed, but in most of them he sensed relief that they would be spared any further doubt and speculation. They were doing something. If anything changed, it was somebody else's problem.

They had even managed a meal, despite the cramped conditions. Hot soup, coarse bread and gallons of sweet tea.

There were five landing craft, two of which were now further astern after the last alteration of course. With limited navigational equipment, and not even a stern light to guide the helmsmen, it was surprising that they ever reached their objectives.

Until you met the crews of such craft as these. A mixture of seamen and marines, they seemed to work without giving or confusing an order, anonymous shapes moving in the crowded hull, dodging weapons and crouching figures as if they had known no other life.

The commanding officer was a tough, leathery lieutenant of the Royal Naval Reserve, who, like most of his kind, had been a merchant seaman in peacetime. A true professional, and one who would be quick to resent outside interference.

Ashore, in a crowd, you might not notice him, or if you did you might only see yet another older than usual lieutenant with interlaced stripes on his sleeves. But Lieutenant Dick Stuart, once of the Anchor Line out of Liverpool and Glasgow, was now in command of five unreliable shoe boxes, and entrusted with the destiny of one hundred and fifty Royal Marines and the task of making an exact landfall on a small, desolate island in pitch darkness. Blackwood smiled to himself. There was also the enemy.

He climbed on to a locker and stared into the darkness. The sea was calm, with hardly a feather of spray or a glint of phosphorescence to break the pattern. The two landing craft astern were invisible. He wondered how Steve Blackwood was faring on what must be his first real mission. He was carrying enough explosives to sink a cruiser. If he was troubled about it, he seemed well able to hide it. Blackwood had thought about him with Diane, and in his mind could see them together. Any jealousy or resentment he might have expected to feel was non-existent. Maybe he was the man she needed? He stopped it right there. It was dangerous to plan anything.

He climbed up into the wheelhouse; it was little more than a steel cupboard. A Royal Marine corporal was at the wheel, another lounged by the speed and revolutions gauges. They were both smoking.

'Come for a look-see?' Lieutenant Stuart, bulky in his stained duffle coat, eased himself from one corner.

He switched on the light above the sealed chart table. A tiny bulb, but after the sea and the empty sky it was almost blinding.

Stuart traced the pencilled course with a pair of dividers, and Blackwood noticed that the metal was stamped with the Nazi eagle and swastika. Another story.

'Course is east-by-north at the moment. Making a good twelve knots. I can crack on a bit more speed shortly.' He shrugged as one of the marines coughed politely. 'Another couple of knots, anyway.'

Blackwood was thankful when the light was extinguished.

'You know these waters pretty well?'

Stuart considered it.

'I served my apprenticeship out here. Gib, Suez, Port Said, mostly mail and passengers. It was a living.'

'*Light*, sir! Red four-five!'

Stuart turned his head and responded, 'Disregard. Shooting star.' Calmly said, Blackwood thought. The lookout would not be afraid to report something in the future which might not be a friendly shooting star.

Stuart faced him again. 'We'll not get much

trouble for a while. The Krauts stay well inshore if they move stores or evacuate troops at night. Our M.T.B.s and M.G.B.s have been playing hell with them this last week or so. But once we reach Angelo—well, we'll have to see.' He hesitated, assessing the man he had seen only briefly before getting under way. 'You're no stranger to this game yourself, I take it.'

'I'm still learning.'

Stuart seemed satisfied. 'Best way to stay in one piece!'

Blackwood said, 'We may have to face it. The enemy may have cleared out already.'

Surprisingly, Stuart laughed. 'Never. He always leaves it to the last minute if he can.' He made the enemy sound like one giant personality. 'If he's got all those explosive motor boats he'll want to see which way we intend to move *after* Sicily. Just look at the chart. Whatever the top brass decides, Angelo is well placed. No, he'll be there, by my reckoning.'

Blackwood wanted to yawn, but was ready to stifle it. Stuart's quiet, sailor's assessment seemed suddenly at odds with Gaillard's briefing before they had embarked. There had been no N.C.O.s present that time, not even Craven.

'You know what you're up against, you've studied the layout. The target must be destroyed.' He had seemed suddenly impatient, as if in some way he was not getting through to them. 'There will be no retreats, no surrenders and no bloody excuses, *right*?'

Stuart had been there, and must have wondered. But he had probably been on so many missions like this that he was unmoved by it.

A face appeared in a round hatchway by his feet, like a pale egg.

'Yer colonel's on 'is way, sir!'

The face vanished and Stuart said, 'Good lad. Well trained.' He sounded as if he was smiling.

Blackwood touched his grubby sleeve and went out into the cool breeze. Tomorrow would be another oven. *Tomorrow.* It would soon be today.

He felt the deck tilt slightly and heard an enamel mug clattering across the gun mounting. They were altering course again.

He could see it as if the chart were still lying, brightly lit, before him. North-north-east, with the tiny islands clustering in around them. Terry Carson would likely know all about them, and their history. The depths shelved to seven hundred and a thousand fathoms hereabouts, a world of darkness, a long way down if the worst happened.

He watched another shooting star and confronted the truth calmly.

If it went wrong, he knew that Gaillard would never submit. It would be suicide.

*   *   *

Lieutenant Steve Blackwood crouched in what must have been a storage space for mooring wires and fenders. It had been cleared to make room for their packs of explosives and fuses.

He had always loved and been around boats ever since he could remember, and one of his most cherished memories was that of his father teaching him how to sail. That must have been in Wellington.

He swallowed hard, and retched. After this trip

353

in the landing craft, he doubted if the sea would ever seem the same. The combination of smells, petrol, diesel, grease and crowded humanity, added to the motion, gentle though it was, were having their effect.

He saw his sergeant, Larry Godden, with one of the webbing packs open by a vibrating light fitting. He was showing a commando sergeant some of his tricks, as he called them. The sergeant was named Welland, and called 'Sticks' for some peculiar reason. He retched again. All part of the mystique which made these men different. But it was amazing how quickly you sensed an atmosphere, even a mood, when working in such close contact with people who had already risked their lives on this sort of operation. There was a Royal Marine lieutenant in this section too, a Lieutenant Capel, tall, good-looking, and apparently super-confident. He had joined Force *Trident* straight from England, and he had heard him described as a climbing expert, highly skilled at scaling cliffs, work which required not only strong nerves but a top level of physical fitness. Steve Blackwood had gathered, from his time among them, that Sergeant Welland also prided himself in that direction, and that he disliked the lieutenant intensely.

He had heard him say to another N.C.O., 'That bloody Hannah was bad enough! But at least he had guts when it came down to it!'

The other officer's name meant nothing, but Welland's contempt stood out like a beacon.

Godden was saying patiently, 'This is a Ready-*Safe,* okay? And this one is a Ready-*Set.* 'Ere, feel the difference. You can tell 'em apart when it's as black as a boot all round you!'

354

Welland felt the fuses doubtfully. 'Suppose you get 'em mixed up?'

Godden smiled. 'Bang!'

Welland sighed. 'Rather you than me, chum. Where did you learn all this stuff?'

Godden's eyes shone in the light as he glanced across at his officer.

'Oh, 'ere an' there. You know 'ow it is.'

Steve Blackwood felt the bond between them. Something they shared with no one else.

He pulled out his wallet and opened it with great care. It was the photograph she had given him that night when they had visited the pub across Portsmouth Harbour. She had wanted him to have it, had insisted, and, looking back, it was as if she had known they would not meet again. He swallowed, but not because of the motion. *Not for a while*. It must have cost her a lot to give it to him like that. She hardly knew him. She could have any man she wanted with her looks and her background.

He gazed at the photograph. Younger, the hair much longer, but it was her right enough. Like the portrait of her mother, which he had seen for himself at Hawks Hill. She was wearing jodhpurs, one hand holding her hair from her face, the other stroking the nose of a horse.

Sticks Welland heard the boots moving outside and said quietly, 'What's your bloke like?'

Godden did not look up. It was a precaution, something you did without thinking if a copper was watching you. Or you were protecting someone.

'Good as gold. Knows 'is stuff, too. Not bad for a Kiwi.'

Welland nodded. 'And a Blackwood. That counts

355

for a lot around this mob.'

He scowled as he heard the lieutenant's voice, having a go at some unfortunate marine. Throwing his weight about. Not like the first attack; he had been careful then, eager to show he was ready to learn. Afterwards they'd all been like men who had been on a binge, or had smoked something like the Chinks did in Singapore. But not him. Mister-bloody-Perfect. *Well, we'll see about that!*

He watched the New Zealander carefully replacing the photograph in his wallet. Poor bugger. As if there wasn't enough to worry about without that.

Like that first time he had asked Pam to go to the cinema with him. She had still been wearing her N.A.A.F.I. uniform, and she had not resisted or pretended surprise when he had put his arm around her in the back row of that notorious flea pit, which had since been bombed flat.

Just before the main film she had made an excuse, and had slipped away to the Ladies. He had half expected she would not return. She was probably used to something better.

But she had snuggled down beside him, her eyes fixed on the screen as the film had begun with a crash of thunder and lightning.

She had gone to the Ladies for one reason only. When his hand had reached the top of her stocking and touched cool, bare skin, he knew what it had been.

They all looked up as Despard lowered himself into the compartment, his face wet with spray. The craft had made another turn, and he had been up there, checking progress.

Steve Blackwood was surprised to see the big

356

lieutenant squatting beside him.

'All set to go?' He seemed to hesitate. 'Steve?'

He guessed it had never been easy for this man, who looked as if nothing on earth would ever defeat him.

'I think we've checked everything. A couple of hundred times!'

Despard regarded him searchingly, perhaps comparing. 'We go in after the others. The plan suggests a good position for setting your charges. A fall of lava rock—it should be enough.' Again the hesitation. 'Don't you agree?'

Steve Blackwood nodded. The sickness was leaving him, or maybe it had just been nerves.

'I'll have to rely on your scaling team. I'm not much of a hand at rock-climbing, especially in the dark!'

Despard glanced over at Welland. Still brooding. That was bad. Unusual, too, for a real pro like Sticks. Despard knew some of it, and could guess the rest. If it wasn't for the danger, it would almost be funny. At long last the sergeant had met his match, albeit an officer, someone as big-headed about physique and women as he was. He had heard Lieutenant Capel going on about the girls, 'gels', he had swept off their feet without even trying. That and his affected drawl had put up the backs of his fellow lieutenants, so Welland's silent fury was understandable. But dangerous. He would stamp on it.

He said, 'Just remember it's the Germans we're up against this time, not a bunch of half-hard Eye-Ties. They say they're not expecting trouble, but you can never tell. If they cut loose with those explosive boats, it could be nasty.' Almost distantly

357

he added, 'I had a pal in the old *York* when they attacked her.'

Had. He did not need to elaborate.

Not for the first time, Steve was glad that Despard was with this section, although he sensed that he hated and perhaps resented being away from the vanguard. He almost smiled at the term. He was already fitting in.

Despard said suddenly, 'I hear you're to be congratulated.'

He stared at him.

'I haven't said anything—'

Despard smiled. 'He told me. The Captain. He's quite chuffed about it. I'm glad for him.' And, quickly, 'You too, of course!'

The boat was slowing down. As if they were feeling their way.

Steve Blackwood said quietly, 'You're fond of him, aren't you?' and was aware of the instant guard, the last barrier.

Despard turned his head as a voice came through the opening.

'*Stand to*, sir!'

He wrenched his mind back from the moment, like the marksman easing the pressure on his trigger when every second is precious.

'You could say that. Yes. I'm no guvnor's man, saying it in the hope of another pip on my shoulder. I've got as far as I ever will in the Corps, as far as I want.' He looked down, surprised, as the New Zealander touched his arm.

'I know that.'

Despard moved his holster slightly and got up. The moment was almost past.

He said abruptly, 'He's in danger. I should be up

358

front with him.' He looked into the shadows and snapped, '*Stand to!* What the hell do you think this is!'

The two Royal Engineers were suddenly alone, the hull around them alive with metallic scrapes and hurrying feet.

Godden grinned at him.

'Like a bloody confessional, ain't it, sir?'

Steve Blackwood nodded and groped for his steel helmet.

If he lived after today, he would never forget it. Despard's intense loyalty made his own anxiety and uncertainty seem like nothing. Something he had seen in her brother's eyes when he had been with his men, and before they had slipped out of Palermo. *Pride.*

He shivered. And he was not even sick any more.

He said, 'Just don't get your bloody fuses mixed up,' and tugged the chinstay into position. 'Bloody bang, indeed!'

He was ready.

*　　　*　　　*

Marine Percy Archer cocked his head and listened to the changing beat of the engines. Slowing down again. He could imagine the tough-looking two-ringer in the wheelhouse peering at his chart, probably saying a prayer or two in case he had made a mistake. He doubted it. These R.N.R. officers might lack the polish and easy authority of their regular opposite numbers, but they were real sailors, not like some. Plus the fact that they knew their straightlaced companions would be quick enough to point out any failure on their part. At the start of the war, the regulars had smiled politely at the reservists. The R.N.R. had been labelled *Really Not Required*, and the part-timers, the R.N.V.R., had been made to suffer *Really Not Very Reliable*. Within a few months, that had changed. Oh, how it had changed. If anything, the amateurs were now the professionals.

He climbed carefully on to a bollard and peered towards the nearest island, or where it was supposed to be. Not even a bloody seagull. It was as if the landing craft was completely alone, ploughing on into nothing.

He went through his own practised routine again. Ammunition pouches, filled and fastened, and the stupid respirator also correctly fastened so that it was less likely to catch on something. The gas mask had got more blokes into trouble than any other single item. He grimaced. Except women. Railway station lost property offices were always full of them. Cinemas, buses, canteens: they got their owners put on charges every day of the week. They would never use gas, not after what they had said about the Great War: men coughing their lungs out, men blinded, the foulest death of all. As a kid he had known a bloke at the Green, heard him every morning, *cough, cough, cough*. The war, they said. Gas. Then one day the coughing had stopped. He'd lost, after all that time. It was strange to realise he had never once laid eyes on the man.

Everything clipped or taped down. He turned his rifle over in his hands. There were men all around him, some doing what he was doing, others chatting to their special mates. And a few staring into space. Archer was able to shut them out. Here, or on

360

some beach, or in a crowded ship's messdeck, it was a ritual, a must.

He was satisfied. Fairly. His fighting-knife would not slither out if he had to jump from the ramp, his rifle was loaded and ready, with one up the spout. Piling swivel and sling, taped, noiseless.

The steel helmet was a bloody nuisance. It distorted the sounds, clattered like a tin can if it touched anything. Once he had seen two marines duck when a shell came too close. The rim of one helmet had smashed the bridge of the other man's nose. Useless.

He heard Captain Blackwood speaking, probably to the colonel, who had been with the two-ringer for most of the journey.

It reminded him of the time when the colonel had gulped down his Scotch as if it was the last drop on earth. An officer who was always on top line, ready to crack down on any defaulter without mercy. Like poor Lieutenant Hannah. But Captain Blackwood had said nothing about it, and he had been the first one to risk his own neck and a sniper's bullet to rescue the silly sod.

He felt the sea surge against the flat side, and the tinkle of sand or gravel. God, it must be shallow here. Or else it was a sandbar.

They were all quiet now; he could see all of them, even though it was pitch dark. Faces he had come to know so well. To respect, to doubt, even to admire, and some he would never know in a thousand bloody years. But in this lot you had to trust somebody. So today it was Blackwood, tomorrow somebody else. He grinned, embarrassed. No, it wasn't like that with him. Whatever you were doing, he always made you feel as if you mattered.

But the colonel, he was something else. One of the corporals had overheard him giving the officers a pep talk just before casting off. Bloody eavesdropping would be nearer to the truth. But he had told him about Gaillard's final rockets about surrender and retreat. Nobody needed to say that sort of thing in the Corps, especially not another marine.

He sorted it over in his mind. Suppose it was true about Gaillard, and the buzz he had heard about people being shot. It made sense. Surrender, retreat, or being too badly wounded to escape from the enemy, they all amounted to the same thing in the end.

He felt somebody push past him. Sergeant Paget. Strict but fair, and would always forget a bottle after he had given it. A good bloke. For a sergeant, that was.

Paget peered at him. 'Must be close. I can smell the bloody place!'

'Reckon they'll be on to us, Sarge?'

Paget wiped the spray from his mouth. 'Would you be, in their boots? Stuck out here on guard duty, surrounded by rocks and bits of volcano poking out of the sea, while your mates are getting their arses shot off in Sicily? They should be so lucky!' He turned as if by instinct and said, 'Here, sir!'

Archer tried to relax, muscle by muscle. He had pins and needles in his left foot, and wanted to stamp it. That would make him really popular.

He saw the other lieutenant scramble past: Fellowes. Didn't have a clue, but seemed ready to listen to others who did. An actor, they said. *Just what we need in this regiment.*

Dead slow. Dead slow. The vibration made everything shake and rattle. Enough to wake the bloody dead. In fact, he knew that their approach would be almost soundless. He gripped his rifle. All the same . . .

'Starboard beam! One of them's in trouble!'

Another voice snapped, 'Silence, that man!'

Archer raised himself on his toes. It was probably a sandbar. *That's better.*

The flare exploded, a blinding, glacier intensity which made men duck or cover their eyes. There had been no sound, or if there had been it was lost in the growl of the engines. It was like a film suddenly jammed in the projector, motionless, although that was another illusion. The other landing craft had slewed round, almost bows-on, only her frothing wash, sandy yellow in the unwavering glare, betraying their frantic efforts to go astern, to free the hull from yet another treacherous spit of land.

Archer shaded his eyes and tried to see the island. The flare was already dying, and he could just make out the nearest hump of solid ground. Even that looked unreal, as if it had been transformed by the light; it was pale, like salt. He heard the clatter of ammunition belts as one of the machine gunners swung his sights towards the shining patch of water.

'Hold your fire!' Archer hurried forward. It was Blackwood's voice. In the blink of an eye, everything had changed. He kept telling himself it was just bad luck; they would tow the poor bastards off and try again. The third landing craft was somewhere to port. They must be wondering what the hell was happening.

Some of the seamen were already running aft; one fell headlong as the flare died, as if somebody had switched it off by hand.

Archer felt the sudden quiver of increasing speed, spray pattering over the side, hitting his helmet. They were not turning. Not going to help the other craft. It was so bloody dark after the searing light he could barely think straight.

And then came the tracer, angled down, but at a guess not from any great height, probably a ridge or a fold in the cliff.

Bright green balls of fire. Flashing above their own reflections on the heaving water, dead straight and flat trajectory: a small but powerful cannon.

Archer's experienced eye had time to take this in, to estimate the range and force of the shellfire, as the invisible gunners found and straddled the grounded landing craft.

Flashes now, and separate explosions, and then writhing banners of flame, fuel and ammunition, and there were men out there, too, burning and dying.

Archer stared until his eyes watered, until the boat turned again and steel blotted out the scene. Men he knew, like those pressed around him. *Like me.* Who believe it only happens to someone else. There was a loud explosion, and then hundreds of small feathers of spray as fragments rained down in every direction. There was another explosion. Then there was only darkness.

Archer had moved without realising it. As if, like the imaginary hand on the light, some greater force had taken over.

Somebody must still be alive back there. Even if

only one.

'Prepare to beach!'

Archer moved his rifle, something so familiar that it was almost a part of him now. It felt slippery, and he knew it was not from spray.

And Blackwood was beside him.

'All right?'

Archer tried to grin but his jaws felt locked. He knew it was important, perhaps for both of them.

He barely staggered as the ramp came down and water surged amongst them like surf.

He tried again. 'Never better, sir!'

Somebody only a yard away threw up his hands to his face and pitched into the swirling water. He did not move again, and Archer realised he had not even heard the shot which had killed him.

He ran after Blackwood and tried to empty his mind of everything but the job, stage by stage, as it had always been.

But all he could feel was the hatred.

*   *   *

'Get down!' Blackwood dropped on one knee and peered ahead and upwards as dark shapes spread out on either side, gasping for breath like old men.

'Second section, follow me!' That was Tom Paget, keeping his head. If he had doubts, he was giving nothing away to his men after the unexpected turn of events.

A few stray shots cracked and ricocheted from the rough ground, to be challenged instantly by a burst of Lewis gun fire from the landing craft. It was going astern; Blackwood could see it in his mind. The ramp raised like a drawbridge. No way

365

back.

Gaillard was beside him, dragging at his night glasses. 'How many, d'you think?'

Blackwood listened, thankful that his heart was steady again. He wanted to laugh. Steady? How could that be?

More shots, a light automatic, sparingly used.

He winced as someone called out, *'Oh, Christ! Oh, Christ!'* Another casualty.

He said, 'Only a picket, I'd say. My guess is that the main body are on the far side, watching the other craft or what's left of it.' Just something to say. To keep his nerve, to shut out the pitiful cries from the wounded man, rising and edged with fear as realisation drilled through the pain.

'Don't leave me, lads! *It's me, for Christ's sake!'*

Blackwood heard someone mutter, 'Stow it!' Then, as the man began to scream, he added almost savagely, 'Die, you bastard! For God's sake, die!'

It was Archer, of all people.

He heard Paget whistle between his teeth, his private signal. His section was in position, above and to the left. In daylight there would be no cover at all. They had to move.

He gripped his Sten, his mind cringing as the wounded man began to sob like a child. It was far worse than the screaming.

'Now or never, sir.' He was prompting him, could not help it. Gaillard lurched to his feet. He did not even flinch as another shot kicked grit from the ground.

He said, 'Different angle. The bugger's moving back.' He seemed to make up his mind. 'Advance.' He reached out to steady himself, and might have

366

fallen but for another anonymous figure. 'Now or never, eh? I like that! We'll show 'em!'

Blackwood waved his arm and felt the marines respond, as if they were all taped together. Show who, he wondered. Naismith, Vaughan ... ? He waved the arm again. 'Move, lads! *Move! Move!*'

The wounded man must have sensed what was happening and shouted, 'Don't leave me! You rotten bastards!'

The marines scrambled up the slope, shutting their ears, hating the unknown voice, and one another because of it.

'Down!' Blackwood gasped as he felt the rock grind into his knee. More shots, tracer this time. He watched it, like blood against the sky. The other landing craft had made it, had pressed on despite the noise and the explosions, and the fate of the third craft. It was little enough. He pressed his face to his forearm and contained his emotion. They were no longer alone.

He thought suddenly of Despard and the supporting party with the sappers and explosives. The whole place would be like a madhouse soon; Despard might stand away. It would be pointless to sacrifice men for nothing. He forced himself to his knees. Despard would never stand away at any time, orders or not. He recalled his own anger when Gaillard had made his little speech to the officers. It had been like an insult.

'*Move! Move!*' They were running forward again; it felt more like staggering. One man stopped in his tracks, his knees buckling. He dropped his rifle and fell beside it, as if he was praying. Another marine skidded to a halt, and reached out his hand towards him.

'Tim!'

That was all. Then he ran on, his friend already dead. Nothing. There were frantic shouts, muffled, shielded by a shoulder of rock, and then a wild cheer, drowned out by the concentrated rattle of machine guns.

Blackwood glanced at the sky. Was it lighter already? So soon . . .

The other landing party had jumped an enemy patrol, or perhaps one of the regular guard detail. He shook himself. *We would have blundered right into it.*

A figure darted around the rock and fell sprawling to a single shot, and he heard Bull Craven's hard voice.

'Not fast enough, my son!'

Almost matter of fact. And yet Craven had just killed a man, without even raising his voice.

'Spread out and find what cover you can!' Blackwood peered down a crumbling slope. He could see nothing, but sensed the water somewhere below him. The lagoon, the anchorage. What was probably an old volcano crater. The target.

They fell flat, faces and fingers pressing into the dirt, bodies tense and vulnerable as more tracer angled across the uneven ground. He saw it reflected in the unmoving water. To move forward would be suicide. To wait for daylight would only postpone the inevitable.

He had seen the close-fitting helmet which Craven's victim had been wearing. A paratrooper's helmet, just like the one in the recognition manual. *Know Your Enemy.* Hard men, who had proved themselves in Poland and Russia, in France and in Crete. They gave no quarter, any more than they would plead for it.

Gaillard raised his head and watched the probing bursts of tracer.

'The other two craft should be here by now! What the hell is Despard doing? If I thought for a moment . . .' He jerked upright again, oblivious or unaware of the spiteful burst of gunfire.

'Watch it, sir!' Gaillard had not even heard him. And then he knew what had taken and seized his attention like a claw.

The sound was magnified by the natural rock wall of the lagoon. No wonder the intelligence people had claimed it was impossible to destroy, even with fighter-bombers. Heavier aircraft would have been equally useless.

It was the sound of a boat's engine, spluttering at first, as if rudely awakened like the paratroopers who were guarding the place, then steadying into an even murmur.

Blackwood watched Gaillard's silhouette. Unmoving. Stricken. What did these boats do? Thirty knots, more? It could make no difference now. The Germans had probably exercised them over and over again. They would not hang about and wait to be destroyed or captured.

More tracer, feeling its way. As ordered, the marines remained in position, and left the field open to the snipers. It could not change things, but it might confuse the enemy as to their strength and deployment. A waiting game. He moved his Sten until he could see it against the pale rock. Two hours at the most. The stars seemed fainter, even though he knew he was imagining it.

They should have had a bigger force, more landing craft. The Germans would have gone anyway. He glanced at Gaillard again. He knew, must have known from the start. He thought of the S.A.S. officer in the filthy lambswool jerkin. *Warning me.* That Gaillard needed to carry it through, if only to save himself.

He thought of the screaming marine, and the one who had died with such quiet dignity. *Tim.* A cry of anguish, for all of them.

He knew that if he touched his pocket he would feel the crumpled, unfinished letter. Not even started. Like us. He did not; he knew it would finish him.

He said, 'I can take one section and go down there, sir. Now.' How could his voice sound so level, so devoid of doubt? His entire body was coiled like a spring; lose that, and he would crack wide open. It was what he had tried to explain to her. And she had understood. Had shared it.

'Death or glory, eh?' Gaillard seemed to be smiling. 'Let me see, how many V.C.s in your family? Two, isn't it? Out for the next one, are you?'

Blackwood clenched his fists, saying nothing, remembering his first thought when Vaughan had told him about the new posting. *I wanted him dead.*

Gaillard said, 'Might work. Diversion—anything to prevent those bastards from getting away. That must not happen!' Then he removed his helmet and wiped his face with his handkerchief. Blackwood heard Archer draw a sharp breath. A handkerchief, even a khaki one, like the movement of a rifle bolt, was a gift to any sniper worth his salt.

He began to back away. 'When the sappers arrive, sir . . .'

'Just do it! I'll decide on the final—' Gaillard

370

turned abruptly as a stray shot sang overhead like a hornet.

Sergeant Paget was waiting for him, as if he had been expecting him.

'Ready, sir.'

'Never volunteer.' He gripped his arm. 'Thanks, Tom.'

Paget hesitated, caught out by the use of his name. 'I've detailed some likely villains, sir.' He nodded towards another shadow. 'Marine Archer insisted, of course.'

Blackwood tensed as more stars of tracer floated over the wall of lava rock. Not now. *Not now . . .* And another voice. *It's what we do. What I am.*

'We go down now.' Paget had not named any of the others, and he thought it was better not to know. He gritted his teeth. *Tim.* 'We'll hold them inside the anchorage until the second party arrives. Sergeant-Major Craven will give covering fire if we have to withdraw.' Someone managed a faint but ironic cheer.

He added simply, 'I won't ask for questions. I might not have the answers.'

They started down the slope, weapons slung for balance as well as safety. If it went wrong from the beginning there would be no time to pull a trigger.

Paget remained in the rear. It did not need to be shouted out loud. *In case I fall.*

He touched his pocket and felt the letter, something he had tried not to do.

It was only her name, after all. He quickened his pace, his mind suddenly clear.

It was enough.

CHAPTER EIGHTEEN

WITHOUT QUESTION

Lieutenant Steve Blackwood held tightly to the side of the small wheelhouse and stared at the intermittent flashes, the occasional drifting balls of tracer. So deceptively slow, distance giving it a sort of cruel beauty.

His muscles were still bunched, unable to relax, to accept that the sudden stammer of machine gun fire and then the louder explosions were quite detached. *Nothing to do with us.* Was he the only one, he wondered, or had the others, the more experienced marines, known from the beginning that they were not the target?

He heard the other two officers talking to the landing craft skipper, a young R.N.V.R. subbie who looked as if he should still be in school uniform. Despard's voice was unhurried, measured. Making a point which he needed to know was understood. And Lieutenant Capel, a sharper tone, impatient, or perhaps less confident now.

One thing stood out above all else. One landing craft had been destroyed. That final explosion had demolished hope and doubt alike. He had even seen the outline of this small, desolate island named Angelo for the first time, albeit briefly, until the fiery glow had died, and men with it.

Suppose it had been the leading craft? Gaillard and Mike Blackwood together? He guessed that was what the young subbie was thinking. That his own superior, the tough Lieutenant Dick Stuart, had bought it.

Despard pulled himself hand over hand along a rail to join him.

'The rest of our main party must be ashore. It'll be light in an hour or so. They'll need all the help we can give them.' He gripped his arm. 'We can't beach the thing here, it's too rocky. Our skipper seems to think so, anyway.'

There was no anger or sarcasm. If anything, Despard was only voicing his thoughts, facing what seemed inevitable to him. It was his decision.

Steve Blackwood said, 'We've got the rubber dinghies.' He felt Despard's grip relax and then withdraw. Relief? Had he expected him to back down? To insist that they pull away while there was still a glimmer of hope?

He said quietly, 'I can do it.' Just like that.

Despard cursed as the hull rocked dangerously in the swell. *'We'll* do it! Just tell me what you need.' He saw that Capel had joined them. 'Get your climbers ready. We're going in now! Dinghies!'

Capel was staring at him. 'We don't know for sure that they're able to hold out! We could be walking straight into it!'

Despard groped past him and called into the wheelhouse, 'Close as you can!' The young subbie said something and Despard retorted harshly, 'And *I* say, damn your bloody orders!'

The engines increased speed. Where was the tail-end landing craft? Keeping well out of it, probably.

He saw Despard's powerful figure striding amongst the landing party, his voice rallying them, dispelling uncertainty. And hope. Despard had

373

known that this might happen, but had not known how to share it.

Winches squeaked, and he knew the two big dinghies were being swung outboard. He saw Sergeant Godden dragging one of his packs of explosives and said, 'I'm taking this one. You stay on board.'

Godden showed his teeth. 'What, miss all the fun? With respect, sir . . .'

They both stared at the sky as a flare exploded on the other side of a ridge of land. Like a moonscape, stark and vivid.

Godden exclaimed, 'There's our other boat! I thought they'd done a bunk!'

Despard was here again. 'I'll lead. Mr Capel will keep with you.' It sounded so formal that the closeness of danger seemed secondary.

Steve watched Despard leap into the long rubber dinghy and found time to wonder at the speed and confidence with which the marines used paddles to manoeuvre the cumbersome craft clear of the side.

He said, 'Over you go, lads!' He dragged his eyes from the fresh outburst of tracer which clawed towards the other landing craft. He saw sparks, and could imagine the havoc caused in such a small, overcrowded hull. But it was still moving, turning now, perhaps to follow them, an ancient Lewis gun firing blindly at the land.

Despard's dinghy slewed round and almost overturned as it drove over a low ledge of rock. Men were already scrambling out, some with packs of explosives, others dropping down to offer covering fire if the enemy was waiting for them. There seemed to be plenty happening on the far side of the ridge, small arms fire and some grenades, but nothing nearer. Steve Blackwood was flung on his back by the rearing dinghy, and felt hands grabbing him. 'Sticks' Welland was spitting out sea water and saying, 'Bloody pongos—I don't know, I'm sure!' He was actually laughing.

And here was the ridge. A cliff, a wall of rock. No wonder the enemy thought it was a good hiding-place for their boats.

The marines were already swarming up from the ledge where they had smashed unceremoniously ashore. When one of them reached the top he realised that he could see his head and shoulders silhouetted against the sky, when minutes earlier, or so it felt, there had been only darkness.

Heaving lines dropped like snakes, and the heavy packs were soon bobbing up the sheer rock face as if completely unaided.

Despard said, 'Now you, Steve. After this it's your show. I'll give you all the cover I can.' He did not turn as more machine gun fire clattered and echoed amongst the rocks. His eyes suddenly gleamed as an explosion boomed against the land like heavy surf. The other landing craft had been hit. Drifting now; he imagined he could smell the stench of burning, or high explosives. He added shortly, 'Either way, we're on our own, so let's make a good job of it!' He clapped him on his soaking shoulder and hurried after his men.

Lieutenant Capel said, 'Here. Keep with me. We'll go up together.'

Welland was coiling up a heaving line, but paused to watch them begin their ascent.

Even Capel's confidence did not touch him now. He had to admit that, for an officer, he was good at it. But he would die rather than say as much. He stared at the other marines, moving away like shadows, hearing the occasional click of steel. Trained fighting men. Special. He tried to push the rest from his mind; it had always worked in the past. Bash on regardless, was his motto. But this was different.

He realised that the untidy, red-haired sapper was watching him and said sharply, 'Well, let's be about it, eh, matey?'

Godden scurried after him. He believed he knew what was troubling the commando sergeant. He thought they were all going to be killed. Killed for nothing which he could recognise. Like risking life and limb to blow open a difficult safe, only to discover that it was empty. A waste of time. But petermen, even good ones, had no traditions or discipline to sustain them if things went wrong. It was all part of the game.

Welland, maybe for the first time in his life, felt cheated, without the prop he had come to take for granted.

A marine corporal who was following him up the rock drove his boot into a niche and called, ''Old on, Sarge! Can't afford to lose *you*!'

Godden blinked as grit fell across his face and mouth, and took a firmer grip of the line which had been dropped for him. Not what he had joined up for. Perhaps Welland was right after all. A grubby hand reached down and seized his, the dirt and blood of the climb sealing it like a bond.

The marine said, 'Cheers, Sarge! Bloody well done!'

It was crazy, but suddenly Godden was glad he was here.

Leaving cover, even the most precarious kind, was always a bad moment. Something you had to force yourself to get used to. Captain Mike Blackwood rested for a few seconds and looked back at the barrier of fallen rock. He could have been quite alone; Tom Paget and his collection of 'likely villains' had vanished. But he knew they would be watching him right now, and scanning the surrounding terrain for any sign of movement or danger.

He tried again. A few inches at a time, moving his head from side to side to try and assess the lie of the land. The sky was much lighter, but there was no hint of the heat soon to come. Individual rocks and clumps of rough gorse stood out more clearly with each painful movement. He felt an insect cross the back of his hand, and found himself hating this desolate place. There were a few bird droppings, but not many. Even the gulls had deserted the soulless remains of a long extinct volcano.

Here was the edge of the ridge, the headland which had appeared so simple on the chart and action-maps. And water. He thought of the wounded marine. *Just get me to the bloody sea.* Except that this time it was not an ally, but a trap if things went wrong.

He raised himself very slowly, waiting for his body to loosen up, to rid itself of the instant tension of breaking cover, waiting for the sound of a shot, and the sickening impact of a bullet. Merciful oblivion, and not a lingering death up here on this pitiless shoulder of rock.

Then he saw it. An oval-shaped lagoon, no more than half a mile long at a guess. He leaned further forward. The water was still partly in shadow, but he could see the other headland, higher and already catching the first light of morning, like a protective arm. And below it was the entrance, so narrow that only small craft would be able to use it. He could even see some coloured markers, stark and alien, hammered into the rocky walls, guides for boats entering and leaving, the first sign of human occupation. He smiled, tasting salt on his lower lip. The tracer had been real enough. And the exploding landing craft. A matter of a few hours, and yet it was already in the past. Unimportant.

He remembered what the R.N.R. lieutenant had said about this place and other islets like it. Narrow approaches, but depths out of all proportion to them, making useful buoyage almost impossible. Hence the markers; the German commander had done his homework too.

He shifted his body again, the rough ground dragging at his webbing and holster. The other headland was where Despard's party should be, if they had made it. Despard's resolute features came clearly to his mind. It would not be for want of trying.

There was a big overhang of rock there, and the cliff below was almost cave-like. Perhaps the water had been higher in earlier times. He heard the insistent stammer of a boat's engine. Just the one. Probably the same boat as before, which had made Gaillard so impatient.

If Despard's party could get into position and lay their charges, that overhanging cliff would block

378

the channel completely. If not, the boats would try to slip out and head for open water.

Either way, Force *Trident*, or what was left of it, would be trapped. He glanced at his hand. He could feel where the insect had bitten him; he could see it too. Just a few more minutes . . .

He struggled to pull out his binoculars, and, holding his breath, he trained them along the full length of the lagoon. Dark, placid water. No movement. Dead like the rest of the place. He tensed as he steadied the glasses on a flaw in the pattern, a long blue-green stain on the surface. Fuel. The boats must be right there. Deep water, close to the protective cliffs, and invisible from the air, according to the R.A.F.

Even if they blocked the channel, they could never dislodge the troops who were guarding the anchorage. He tried to shut it from his mind. The target would be impotent, for a while. Was it really worth so many lives?

It was pointless even to consider it, to compare costs. They had gone through all that and far more in that other war. *To survive.* Not an objective or a chance of glory, but only to live, even after you had gone over the top with friends falling and dying all around you. *To live.*

He pushed himself away from the edge, his mind clinging to the quiet water, the silence broken only by the stammering engine.

If these explosive motor boats got amongst the next landing fleet, it would be murder. They would not go for the escorts and the faster warships; they would point their deadly cargoes at the troopers and the supply vessels. He thought of the other raids, and of *Husky* itself, and of all those other blurred faces, the Irrawaddy and Rangoon. It would all have been for nothing if the new impetus came to a halt.

Sergeant Paget helped to drag him through the rocks, obviously glad to see him. Fifteen minutes. But it could be a long time when you think you may have been suddenly left in charge.

'I think the boats will try to leave quite soon.' They were all crowded round to listen, faces becoming individuals as the first rays of light touched the razor-sharp rocks.

'What about the Krauts, sir?'

'No sign. But they'll try something once they realise we're here.' He gestured with his hand. 'There's a piece of high ground. A good marksman could pin us down from there.'

Paget nodded, already selecting his men.

'What about Mr Despard, sir?'

That was Marine Pratt, the one they made jokes about. He had done seven years in the Corps before he had volunteered for the Commando. An obvious candidate for promotion on the face of it, but it had so far eluded him. Slow-speaking and lugubrious, he could still come straight to the point. Like now.

Blackwood replied, 'I don't know. If his party can block the entrance, we'll have done what we came for. If not, we'll have to try and stop the buggers ourselves.'

Pratt nodded, his features as mournful as ever. Blackwood remembered someone telling him that he could read a full page of an instruction manual and repeat it word for word, weapons, blockages, the intimate details of everything from a Browning automatic rifle to assembling an entrenching tool.

But if he was asked a question or interrupted in any way he was lost, and had to go right back to the beginning again.

He had also heard Archer telling another marine that if awards were made for gossip, Pratt would be given the star prize.

Paget said, 'One boat at a time then, sir?' He sounded doubtful. But he was also aware that there was no alternative.

Blackwood gazed at the sky. *Despard's party.* Why had he avoided mentioning Steve Blackwood, the man who hoped to marry his sister? Afraid for him? Or afraid of what might already have happened?

'Send a message to the Colonel. Tell him we're going down as far as we can.'

Paget snapped, 'One volunteer!'

Nobody moved.

Blackwood looked at the doleful marine again. 'What about you, Pratt?'

He regarded him uncertainly. 'I'd rather stay, sir.'

Archer smiled. 'Well said, you old sod!'

Blackwood turned to another marine, one who had cut his wrist badly during the landing.

'Get that dressed, Norris.' He smiled. 'And give my message to the Colonel for me, right?' *I'm even beginning to sound like Gaillard.*

The others touched his arm or his shoulder as he made his way back to the slope.

Blackwood turned away, afraid that his emotion might show on his face. They were actually sorry for the youngster he had sent back. *When I've just condemned them all to death.*

Paget was saying, 'Ditch everything you don't

need. Check your ammo, and spare magazines.'

An anonymous voice called, 'What about a prayer, Sarge?'

Blackwood saw Archer watching him, and remembered how he had made the girl laugh that day in Alex.

There was a sudden rattle of machine gun fire. It was almost impossible to fix the bearing; every sound became an echo in this grim place.

Pratt said in his toneless voice, 'Over to the left flank, sir. MG 34. They used them in North Africa.' He nodded approvingly. 'Good piece.'

There was an answering burst of firing, and Blackwood knew it was Craven's Bren. They were watching over the flank. Things were moving.

They crawled across the broken rocks and started to find their way down a deeply cut fissure, like a chimney made by human hands.

Blackwood led the way, the others following in a deluge of loose stones and filth, like some of the exercises they had carried out in Cornwall.

'One of the boats is comin' out, sir!'

They had reached the ground and flung themselves where they could, dwarfed by the rock face, and once again in deep shadow.

The boat was moving slowly, a single occupant squatting on a seat which they now knew was an escape raft, to be used once the boat and its lethal cargo had been set and aimed at the target.

Blackwood levelled his glasses and felt a muscle jump in his wrist from the sheer effort of clambering down the rock chimney.

He caught a brief glimpse of an intent, sun-reddened face, the cap and buttons of a German petty officer. Then he, too, was doused in dark shadow.

Archer said, 'Give the word, sir.' He was lying prone, his rifle already trained across the unmoving water.

The firing device would be at *safe* on the boat, but a bullet might change all that. With the rock wall behind them, nobody would survive the blast. Why waste time? Archer knew. They all did.

The whiplash crack of the rifle was deafening in the deep confines between the two headlands. The boat seemed to swerve aside, then came to rest, bumping gently along the edge of the channel, the helmsman leaning out of his cockpit as if to examine the coloured markers more closely.

Blackwood lowered his glasses. The German petty officer would never see anything again.

There were more engines starting up and revving loudly. But for the noise Blackwood might still have believed that there was only one boat still here. There was firing too, a different bearing. He stared up at the sky, so bright now, so remote.

'Ready, lads!' He groped for his Sten gun, probably useless at this range.

He blinked, imagining for a second that sunlight had caught a levelled rifle somewhere.

But it was moving. Bright green and drifting peacefully in the sunshine. Like the other flares they had seen or fired when they had stormed ashore in Sicily. His eyes smarted. *On my birthday.* But he wanted to cheer.

'Fall back! First section, move!' That was Paget. He had seen it too: Despard and the sapper from New Zealand had made it. They would be watching, waiting to fire the fuses. They would also know what this handful of marines had been about

383

to attempt. Blackwood wiped his mouth with his sleeve. *Suicide.*

The sound of the double explosion was muffled, but seemed to last for ever. It brought with it dust so dense that men fought for breath, gasping and choking, and an avalanche of rock fragments which rained down on their steel helmets and made even thought impossible.

And then, very slowly, the fog moved away, blotting out the entrance as if they had imagined it. At first glance the channel appeared untouched, the placid surface caked with sand and dirt. The painted markers were still in position, and the motor boat with its dead helmsman was still nudging along the edge as if trying to escape on its own.

Blackwood took Paget's arm and said, *'They did it!'*

There was a hump in mid-channel, as if it had always been there, like the great, gaping landslide above it. In years to come nobody would notice any difference, or guess what deeds had been performed here today.

Slowly, limbs feeling like lead, the marines began their climb up the rock chimney, minds and bodies still drained by the explosion, and the sudden change in their own circumstances.

There was still some firing, but it was vague and intermittent. The Germans were probably as surprised as they were, and were having their work cut out to restore communications and order.

But they had done it. Three hours or three thousand, nothing could alter it now.

When they reached the top of the cliff, it was as if nothing had happened. The dust and smoke had

384

gone, and all firing had stopped. The marines were saving ammunition; the Germans were probably regrouping, or awaiting support. Blackwood saw the youngster he had sent to the rear with an officer. He was pointing at him and grinning. Blackwood noticed that he had still not bandaged his hand.

The officer was Lieutenant Fellowes. Something triggered a warning, driving away the strain like an icy shower.

'What the hell are you doing here?' He could not even keep the edge out of his voice, as if a stranger had taken over.

Fellowes looked at the weary marines. He was not experienced enough to recognise their jauntiness and their bottled-up emotion.

He said, 'Your message, sir. The Colonel was watching.' He flinched under Blackwood's eyes. 'It's not enough, sir.' He was repeating it as if he could still not believe it. 'He says the boats will be free to move as soon as the enemy get some engineers here.'

It was possible. It was also madness to pretend they could do anything else.

He snapped, 'Tell the Colonel . . .'

Gaillard walked into the sunlight, and barely glanced at the others.

'Tell him yourself!'

Then he smiled. 'I've sent word to Mr Despard to rejoin the unit as soon as possible. He did quite well.' The smile vanished. 'Not well enough. The attack goes on! Remember, no excuses!' He swung away. 'From anybody!'

Fellowes whispered, 'It's madness, sir.'

Blackwood turned on him. 'I didn't hear that,

385

Mr Fellowes!' Then he touched his arm and forced a smile. 'But you're probably right.'

He saw Archer nod, and as he walked to the edge of the cliff he heard Fellowes say raggedly, 'And I didn't hear *that*, sir!'

Blackwood stared at the sea. But, like the future, it was quite empty.

*　　　*　　　*

Blackwood tilted his helmet to shade his eyes from the glare. Through its camouflage netting the steel rim was already hot, although the sun had barely risen above the nearest island. It was hard to shut out the smaller, more personal vignettes. A marine giving a cigarette to his friend after bandaging his arm for him. And the moment when Despard and his party had come almost at the double from their original landing place beneath the headland, Despard quietly confident. Steve Blackwood had been less restrained and had hugged him, his tanned face creased with pleasure.

Small parts of a pattern. He tried to empty them from his thoughts.

It was like watching from above, a bird's eye view. The separate groups of marines, counting their ammunition, loosening their bayonets. Most of them had emptied their water flasks, and food was unimportant. The enemy would know it was impossible to attempt to clear the channel; the marines would pick them off one by one. They would also know that they were unable to retreat, even though two of the landing craft had used the first daylight to move to safer moorings. Once clear of the island, they would be easy targets for the paratroopers and their array of weapons.

The Germans would not let it rest as a temporary stalemate. They were professional troops, and revenge would play its part.

Paget said flatly, 'The Colonel's coming, sir.'

Gaillard strode to the fallen rocks and stared at the water.

'Are you ready to move?' He faced Blackwood, shoulders quite stiff, as if he were examining a defaulter. 'We've got landing craft. We can keep the enemy hopping, for the whole bloody day if necessary. We'll get air cover. *Then* we can leave.' He stamped his foot. '*Not* retreat! But first, I want those boats destroyed!'

Archer was lying nearby, his rifle butt cuddled against his cheek. He could not hear what the officers were saying, and he thought it was probably just as well. Blackie would think of something to get them off the hook. He listened to the boat's engine. All the rest were silent. He thought of the sapper officer hugging the captain. The joy of it, as if they had been the only blokes there. They were supposed to be cousins, or something. The other one wasn't a Royal, but he was okay.

He lifted his chin and watched a tiny circle on the water below, like a single drop of rain on a pond. He sighed. It would be so easy to fall asleep. To shut it out. To give up.

The thought came like an electric shock. There was no bloody rain, not in this place.

He rolled over, one arm automatically cradling his rifle against any damage. He wanted to shout, to take proper aim, but for those few seconds he felt unable to move.

One silhouette: a man, standing or kneeling, it

was too bright to see. The sun was blinding. But he could recognise the tell-tale blaze of metal. It was already too late.

Seconds, in which his mind and body responded as one. Thumb off the safety catch, blink away the mist, first pressure, then . . . But he knew the sniper had fired first, even though the sound was drowned by his own shot. He was already pulling and thrusting home the bolt for another bullet when he saw the blurred silhouette crumple and disappear, followed what seemed like minutes later by the splash of his body hitting the water.

Blackwood swung round, his hand on his holster as he realised what had happened. Men were kneeling or crouching as if frozen in attitudes of action or self-defence. Someone shouted, 'The bastard's gone under!'

They all looked at Archer, eyes slitted in the sunlight, smoke drifting straight up from his Lee-Enfield.

Archer said, 'He got the jump on me, sir!' He sounded angry. Ashamed.

Despard called, 'The Colonel, sir!'

Gaillard was already struggling to get to his feet again, his eyes flashing wildly as a corporal tried to restrain him. There was blood on his right side, seeping over his belt and down his leg, shining in the strengthening light.

Blackwood dropped on one knee, his mind sharpened by the knowledge that the sniper's bullet had missed him by inches, if that. His back had been turned towards the higher ground, the old rule broken or overlooked in the heat of Gaillard's anger.

Gaillard was controlling himself with a physical

effort, his fingers bloody as he unfastened his belt and waited for Despard and the corporal to wedge a dressing over the wound.

Despard said between his teeth, 'Nothing broken, sir. Nasty, though. Near thing.'

Blackwood said to Archer, 'Thanks.'

Archer shrugged. 'I was slow, sir.' But he did not hide his relief that the sniper had been aiming at an officer with his back turned towards his sights, and had hit someone else.

Gaillard allowed himself to be seated in a patch of shade, his jaw tight enough to reveal the pain he was enduring.

But his voice was as strong as before.

'Get on with it!'

Blackwood said, 'I think you should be taken down to the landing place, sir.'

'Never!' He was beside himself with rage, the wound acting like a spur. 'Nobody retreats! I'll shoot the first man who tries it!'

Blackwood made another attempt. Gaillard was not even armed. The realisation shocked him enough to call, 'Sergeant Paget, take your men down first! Send word to the sergeant-major to bring his Bren over to cover us.' They were all staring at him, like men clinging to driftwood, trying to stay afloat. Fellowes and the athletic Capel, 'Sticks' Welland, and two wounded men who were still carrying their rifles and leaning on one another like dockyard drunks. Faces he had come to know and care about, discovering, when it was almost too late, that they also cared about him.

He said to Marine Pratt, 'Stay with the Colonel.'

Gaillard tried to get up, but Pratt held him almost gently and murmured, 'Easy, sir.'

Gaillard yelled, 'Don't you dare to talk to me like that! Don't you ever . . .' He fell silent. Perhaps he had already lost more blood than they knew.

But Blackwood had to make Pratt understand. He was a man who knew how to obey. To carry out orders without question.

He repeated, 'Stay with the Colonel. If we fall back . .

Pratt said heavily, 'I can manage, sir.' He meant it.

Blackwood turned away. Down to the water's edge again. That would give the enemy a chance to infiltrate their feeble defences. He could find no satisfaction in Gaillard's fate. He was out of it, whether he liked it or not. He was going to be replaced, perhaps dishonoured. It would be far harder to face than this inevitable defeat.

Paget was saying, 'If we can get up closer to the boats, sir?'

He swung round as somebody cried out in pain. He added hoarsely, 'They all want to come with you. You know how it is.'

When they reached a barrier of fallen rocks, just inside the entrance to the lagoon, two more marines were hit by hidden marksmen. Bren fire and rifles responded, more out of fury than with any hope of success.

Blackwood said, 'Bring those men back. We leave no one behind.'

Archer knelt and fired. Blackwood saw the butt plate recoil against his shoulder, heard him swear. 'Missed the sod!'

Someone shouted, 'Here comes a late volunteer!' Another gave a wild laugh. It could not last much longer.

Archer was pressing two more clips into his rifle's magazine, but looked up, surprised. 'You're not supposed to be 'ere, you twit!'

It was Marine Pratt, his features very serious and intent as he dropped on one knee and checked his rifle, as calmly as if he was on the range at Whale Island.

Blackwood heard Despard call, 'Who told you to come here? What are you thinking about, man?' It was rare for him to reveal anxiety.

Pratt looked defiantly across his rifle.

'The Colonel told me, sir. It was an order, he said!'

There were more shots, but nothing seemed able to break the sudden tension.

Blackwood stepped swiftly from one pile of rock to the next. His back tingled, recalling the nearness of the sniper's bullet.

'Tell *me*, Pratt. Why did you leave him? He's wounded, he might not know what he's doing!'

Pratt regarded him impassively. 'It was an order, sir.' He almost smiled, but it made him look even more lugubrious. 'He says to me, good luck, Pratt. We'll show 'em, eh?'

It was exactly what Gaillard would have said. He could hear him saying it.

'An' then . . .' Pratt frowned, the two words dropping like the stone which had betrayed the German sniper.

Despard repeated sharply, *'Then?'*

'He says, give me your grenades before you go.' He frowned again. 'It was an order, sir. From the Colonel himself!'

There was another fusillade of shots, separate weapons, but so close together that it sounded like a machine gun.

'The boat! For Christ's sake, the *boat*!'

Before he had managed to scale the next barrier of rocks Blackwood knew it was Gaillard. He heard the boat's engine coughing and roaring, the sound rising up the steep cliffs to drown out the sharper clatter of small arms.

He did not need his binoculars, just as he knew he would not have used them. It would have been an intrusion.

The motor boat was moving slowly but purposefully in a tight arc, the water boiling from its stern as it idled into the hard light. Feathers of spray spurted all around it, and he knew that the hull must have been hit several times. He could see Gaillard clinging to the controls, the other hand holding his side, blood everywhere. There was no sign of the dead helmsman. Gaillard must have used his dwindling strength to drop him over the side. Alone to the end.

How he had managed to get into the boat and move it away from the sappers' landslide was beyond belief. The engine had been running all this time, since Archer had shot down the helmsman. *All this time.* It was not long; it only felt like it.

The boat's explosive device would be out of action.

He thought suddenly of Pratt's wooden determination to do the right thing. To obey orders, as he had always done.

Give me your grenades before you go.

Just one of those would be enough.

Disregarding stray shots and darting figures, he dragged out his whistle and blew it as hard as he could. Men froze where they stood, as if it were a referee's whistle at a football match. Or an order to abandon ship.

'Get everyone out of it, George! *Fast as you like.*'

Archer was dragging at his arm. 'Come on, sir! Remember what you promised the little lady!' Saying anything that came into his head, to make him move, run with the others.

He had not realised that everyone else had gone. He watched, unable to drag his eyes away. The boat was moving, unhurriedly or so it seemed, towards the inner darkness where sunlight would never reach. No feathers of spray. The Germans had recognised the peril, the solitary boat, packed with high explosive, heading directly towards the hidden moorings.

Blackwood raised his whistle, and hoped Gaillard was still alive and able to hear it before he threw his grenades into the forepart of the boat. Then he turned away, his eyes stinging in the smoke. Except that, with the guns now silent, there was little of it.

Archer was dragging at his arm, but he had to pause. *It had to be now.*

He said quietly, 'Not a retreat, Colonel. Not this time.'

Then, as Archer pulled him around the rock barrier, the world seemed to explode.

The last order had been carried out.

EPILOGUE

Michael Blackwood turned down the collar of his greatcoat and stared out of the train window. He could not recall ever being so cold, or feeling it so much.

He was thankful that the R.T.O. had managed to get him a corner seat by a window. The compartment was full. They always were, but he did not want to speak to any of the occupants. To anybody.

The weather was surprisingly fine and clear, fields moving slowly past as the train reduced speed, probably because of the gradient and the extra carriages. Small houses, one with a flag painted above the doorway. A welcome for someone, perhaps.

November. No wonder it was so cold. He tried again, his mind drifting back over the journey. Flights from unknown airstrips, then on to a larger plane, for England.

Strange to realise that it had been November when he had left here before. A year ago. He had been feeling the cold then, too, after Burma. It seemed much longer in some ways, and yet towards the end, time seemed to have speeded up. And now he was feeling lost, among strangers, even those who were wearing the same uniform.

Force *Trident*, or what was left of it, was returning by a slower route, around the Cape. Jubilant, emotional, pretending to be neither, but at least they were together. Coming back for a brief leave before rejoining a new unit, part of another, bigger Commando. Even Steve and his sappers had returned to their old unit.

Perhaps that had been the worst part. Leaving behind what they had won and created together.

By the time they eventually reached England they would have had time to find themselves again, to discuss and brag about their achievements and their blunders. To talk of the characters, and, after a week or so at sea, even of the dead whom they had tried so hard to forget.

He shifted in his seat again; even the uniform was new. And there was something else. He was Major Blackwood now, albeit brevet. There had been a signal from Vaughan himself. It was settled.

And yet, when he had put on the unfamiliar uniform for the first time he had felt like an imposter, a stranger. That had been in Alex. Maybe that was it.

Looking back, it was difficult, sometimes impossible to measure the significance of what they had done against the greater happenings elsewhere. As promised, the invasion of Italy had taken place, exactly two months after the first troops had landed in Sicily. A lifetime. The invasion had been carried out in the Bay of Salerno, with Naples the first objective. As predicted, the coming of winter had slowed all progress, but the Allies were still advancing, and the Italians had changed sides.

The invasion itself had been stiffly resisted, as everyone on the staff had known beforehand. New weapons, not least the deadly radio-controlled bomb which could be guided by aircraft on to a target, had taken a heavy toll of shipping. Even the gallant old lady, the flagship *Warspite*, had been hit by one, and two American cruisers had also been early victims.

Casualties had been heavy also, and there had been times when the impetus of the attack had been slowed. *Uncertain*, one newspaper correspondent had described it.

But not a single explosive motor boat made an appearance. Only then did that tiny, hostile islet off the coast of Sicily assume its true importance.

All the boats must have been destroyed in a chain reaction of explosions, most of them buried under another avalanche of lava rock. Perhaps nobody would ever know about it. The war might go on for years, although Blackwood had been surprised by the optimism he had encountered in this battle-hardened country. A second front was now being spoken of, an invasion of France, which would lead inevitably to Germany. It was difficult to compare such plans with a remote cross named Angelo on a chart.

Leaving had been the worst part. After the full-scale and heady excitement of the promised air support, the Spitfires diving and rolling above the battered landing craft, and the welcome at Alex, it had been even harder to take.

George Despard had been nicknamed 'the Iron Man' by some of his marines, and it would stick, as was the way with the Corps. He had not remained so calm and steadfast when he had been told of his promotion to captain.

Blackwood had shaken his hand, sharing it, and had said, 'Whether you bloody like it or not!'

And Lieutenant Fellowes, who seemed suddenly a man, no longer playing a part. Sergeant Paget, grinning, and insisting that they would meet again

397

in the next posting. 'Sticks' Welland, much more subdued since the last fight, because he had expected to be killed. He would need somebody to share it, carry the load until he found himself again. Perhaps he had been thinking that when they had shaken hands and said good-bye.

And Percy Archer; he would miss him for all kinds of reasons. For his courage and his ability to make light of almost every problem. For his concern when he had believed his own inattention had all but cost his captain his life.

He had passed it off quite typically. 'You won't need me no more, Cap'n Blackwood. I'll go for me tapes. I can chase some other poor sod about then!' It had been, perhaps, the hardest moment for them both.

And Gaillard; how would he be remembered? A posthumous Victoria Cross? There was no one to cherish either medal or memory. There had never been anything but the Corps for him to believe in.

It was almost impossible to recreate those final moments; they said that the force of the explosion could do that to a man's memory. Blackwood knew in his heart that he wanted to leave it like that. Perhaps, after all, Gaillard's was the only true courage.

The door slid back and a voice said from the corridor, 'Waterloo in ten minutes, gents!'

It was unnerving. It could have been the same man, a year ago.

He thought of the telephone call, his impatience getting the better of him when the R.A.F. type at the airfield had moaned about secrecy and 'the war'.

He had said, 'Where the bloody hell d'you think

398

I've been?' Unfair, unreasonable. Like Gaillard.

But he had got his line, and had been half afraid that she would be away.

She had listened in silence while he had blurted out something about meeting her, and for a moment he had imagined she was upset, or shocked by his unexpected arrival.

She had said, 'I *knew*, Mike. I shall be there.'

He had sensed the irritation of the switchboard operator, had imagined the train leaving before he could reach the station.

And now it was almost time. Not merely a dream, a desperate hope when he had expected to die, like too many others.

There would be a couple of days in London, to make his report, maybe to meet his new boss. But there was somewhere else to go, something else to do.

She might not even like Hawks Hill when she saw it, if she agreed to go with him.

'We must be almost there by now.' A hand touched his cuff. 'I've been looking forward to it for so long. Now I'm thinking it might be a bit dicey!'

He looked round. The other officer had been asleep for the entire journey. In R.A.F. blue, like Joanna's uniform; even 'dicey' brought it all back, like his own uncertainty.

He said, 'Got someone meeting you?'

The young pilot nodded, hand still on Blackwood's cuff. 'Thanks. Yes, I have.'

The train was running into the great station with its bomb scars and boarded-up windows. He was back. But all he could think of was the young airman who had no face. *Dicey.*

She saw him coming before he had found her in the cheerful, anxious, hopeful crowd.

Somebody gave a whistle as he kissed her, and she threw her arms up around his neck. All right for some . . .

She had seen his face when he had looked over towards the disfigured pilot, who had been hugging two women, laughing, crying, it was impossible to know.

But she had *seen his face*, the man she loved, had never stopped loving. The rest would get better.

She said, 'I've found a place. It's private.' She shook her head, remembering. 'Not a bit like Alex!'

She saw a marine turn and throw up a salute. Very young. Brand new, probably.

Blackwood said, 'I love you.'

The marine paused and looked back at them. In some strange way, it seemed to give him confidence.

It's what we do.